PSYCHOLOGY AND THE REFLECTIVE COUNSELLOR

CHARLES LEGG

Department of Psychology, City University, London

BPS BOOKS THE BRITISH
PSYCHOLOGICAL
SOCIETY

UCSM

First published in 1998 by BPS Books (The British Psychological Society), St Andrews House, 48 Princess Road East, Leicester LE1 7DR, UK.

A catalogue record for this book is available from the British Library.

ISBN 1 85433 261 9   361.323 LEG

Typeset by Words & Graphics Ltd., Anstey, Leicester

Printed in Great Britain by Arrowhead Books Ltd., Reading, Berks

Table of Contents

List of Figures   viii

Dedication   ix

1. Introduction   1
The value of research based psychology   2
  Why don't counsellors attend to psychological research?   2
  Why should counsellors attend to psychological research? 5
  Section summary   6
The organization of this book   7
Chapter summary   9

2. Being Social   10
The social context   11
  Language   13
  Roles   14
How can I use this information as a counsellor?   16
  Section summary   18
Thinking about the social world   18
  Understanding other people's minds?   19
  People are creatures of habit   21
  Scripts   21
  Using other people as guides   23
How can I use this information as a counsellor?   25
  Section summary   29
Chapter summary   30

3. Feelings   31
Emotion   33
  What are emotions?   33
  When do emotions occur?   38
How can I use this information as a counsellor?   44
  Section summary   46
Mood   46
How can I use this information as a counsellor?   49
  Section summary   51
Desire   51
How can I use this information as a counsellor?   54
  Section summary   55
Chapter summary   55

4. Thinking and Deciding 57

Establishing goals 58
How can I use this information as a counsellor? 61
   Section summary 64
Deciding what is true 64
How can I use this information as a counsellor? 70
   Section summary 71
Making decisions 72
How can I use this information as a counsellor? 79
   Section summary 81
Chapter summary 82

5. Remembering 84

Recall of past events 85
The passage of time 86
   Short-term memory 86
   Long-term memory 87
How can I use this information as a counsellor? 90
   Section summary 91
Rehearsal 91
How can I use this information as a counsellor? 93
   Section summary 94
Salience 94
   When the event occurs 94
   Surprisingness/novelty 97
How can I use this information as a counsellor? 99
   Section summary 102
How a person thinks about an event 102
How can I use this information as a counsellor? 103
   Section summary 104
How you assess memory 104
How can I use this information as a counsellor? 107
   Section summary 108
Similarity between learning and recall conditions 108
How can I use this information as a counsellor? 110
   Section summary 111
Psychodynamic considerations 111
How can I use this information as a counsellor? 114
   Section summary 114
Neurological considerations 115
   Retrograde amnesia 115
   Anterograde amnesia 115
How can I use this information as a counsellor? 116
   Section summary 117
Chapter summary 117

6. Individual differences   119

How psychologists think about individual differences   120
  Dispositions   120
  Values   124
  Capacity   126
How can I use this information as a counsellor?   127
  Section summary   129
How can we assess individual differences?   129
  Tests   130
How can I use this information as a counsellor?   134
  Section summary   137
Chapter summary   137

7. Growing   139

Major concepts in developmental psychology   141
  Stages   141
  Critical periods   143
  Genetic determination   145
How can I use this information as a counsellor?   146
  Section summary   148
The development of dispositions   148
  Feelings   148
  Desires   150
How can I use this information as a counsellor?   153
  Section summary   155
The development of abilities   155
How can I use this information as a counsellor?   158
  Section summary   159
Identity   159
  Gender identity and sex-typical behaviour   164
  Sexual orientation   165
  Overview of identity   165
How can I use this information as a counsellor?   166
  Section summary   168
Chapter summary   169

8. Epilogue   171

Counselling practice makes psychological sense   171
We know less than we think   174
Be modest about your own accomplishments and
  respectful of others'   179
Summary   180

References   182

Index   191

List of Figures and Tables

Figure 1   An example of the recall of idealized forms   89

Figure 2   The 'serial position effect'   95

Figure 3   Loss of the recency effect   96

Figure 4   The effects of novelty on recall of an item   97

Figure 5   Examples of items from a self-report questionnaire   130

Figure 6   The results of a single case study in counselling   135

Table 1   Values of attributes for each of two styles of travel   75

Table 2   Choices offered by Allais (1953)   76

Table 3   Winnings, offered by Ellsberg (1960)   77

Dedication

I would like to dedicate this book to
Margaret Carey,
my love, support and inspiration.

1

Introduction

'Counselling psychology' has emerged as a distinctive branch of psychology, with unique concepts, research paradigms and practices that set it apart from the rest of the discipline. Introductory texts on psychology for counsellors usually provide you with an outline of the main theories, such as psychodynamic theory, or Rogers' 'client centred' approach, and a description of the practices that they support, such as interpretation of the 'transference relationship', or the importance of offering 'unconditional positive regard'. You are encouraged to recognize the importance of 'theory', to ground your practice in a particular model and to write case studies and process reports that demonstrate your skills in applying your chosen model. At the same time, you are told that it doesn't matter which model you adopt, that critical evaluation of models borders on a breach of professional etiquette, and that mature counsellors develop their own styles that focus far more on the relationship with the client than on the application of a particular model.

We are somehow given the impression that the rest of psychology, with its emphasis on psychological processes like memory or emotion, and its concern for empirical evaluation of ideas, is irrelevant to the practising counsellor. People coming into counselling without having studied psychology are, therefore, often unaware of what it has to offer. Some may even have been encouraged to dismiss it by applying epithets like 'positivist' to its research tradition, and to believe that sitting with clients for hours and hearing their stories gives an insight into human nature and human experience that is deeper and more real than that obtained by studying people within a scientific framework.

While you can learn things about people and practice from experience that you cannot acquire in other ways, there is much that the counsellor can fruitfully learn from psychology. This book is about some of those things, and this chapter is about the reasons why counsellors should pay attention to research based psychology and what this book, in particular, has to offer. In subsequent chapters I will review the main areas of psychology to identify findings that are of relevance to the counsellor, starting with social psychology and then moving on to feelings, thinking, remembering, individual differences and psychological development.

Most books on psychology tell you what we disagree about. They present competing 'theories', and the evidence for and against them, but rarely come down on the side of a single theory. If they do, you will find another book or chapter that draws the diametrically opposite conclusion from the same material. Counsellors, like other practitioners, are right to be bewildered by this and to ask why they should listen to psychologists who can't agree amongst themselves.

The adversarial approach to psychology is great fun for researchers, as they pit their ideas against each other, and most books are written by researchers with others in mind. Even introductory textbooks are written for students who are later expected to grow up and become the next generation of researchers. The problem is that this approach obscures the massive amount on which most psychologists agree; the information that they take for granted when pushing back the frontiers of knowledge. My aim here is to focus on what we can *agree* on, rather than the points of disagreement.

This chapter is about two things; what you can gain from psychology as a counsellor and what, I hope, you will gain from this book. Let us start by looking at what counsellors can gain from research based psychology. Oddly, to do this we have to start with another question, which is, 'Why *don't* counsellors attend to research based psychology?'.

The Value of Research Based Psychology

Why don't counsellors attend to psychological research?

Half a century ago, this would have been a meaningless question because counsellors were part of the research tradition. Carl Rogers, who introduced the term 'counselling' because people objected to him calling himself a 'therapist', believed that he was contributing to mainstream psychological thought and emphasized the empirical underpinnings of his work (see Rogers and Dymond, 1954). He may have disagreed with his colleagues about the most appropriate research methods and theoretical concepts, but he was engaged with them and expected them to change their ideas in the light of his findings.

Rogers' approach reflects the intellectual roots of psychology in 'modernism', the belief that it is possible to have all-encompassing theories of the physical and social world that would permit 'technological' fixes to a wide range of social problems, such as crime, poverty and personal unhappiness. Modernism grew out of the earlier success of the physical sciences in explaining and predicting events in the material world. From the seventeenth century on, people of genius like Newton had been able to propose elegant and simple universal rules for the relationships between matter that could account for everything from the continued stability of the Clifton Suspension Bridge to the rise and fall of tides in the Bristol Channel. At the beginning of the twentieth century people hoped that they would be able to apply the same approach to the social world.

The physical sciences worked by postulating the existence of unobservable universal processes or objects, like 'gravity' or the 'electron', assigning properties to them and then explaining particular events in terms of the operation of these universals. At the turn of the twentieth century, psychologists started to attempt to produce a 'physics' of the mind by proposing the existence of unobserved 'psychic' entities that operated according to specific rules. Thus Pavlov (1927) and Watson (1925) argued that the 'atom' of mental life, the fundamental building block out of which all other mental phenomena arose, was the 'conditioned reflex'. Freud (1943) seems to have been struck more by the principles of thermodynamics and the laws of conservation of energy, putting forward a model of the mind in which 'psychic energy' is channelled into action through the mechanisms of the id, ego and superego. For Rogers (1961), the 'fundamental' component of mental life was the 'self concept', an entity that develops under the influence of conditional and unconditional positive regard.

Counselling's initial concern with comprehensive theories fitted with the intellectual ethos of its day but, since then, mainstream psychology has become more modest while counselling has retained its commitment to theories, thus staying rooted in the psychology of the 1940s and 1950s. By the middle of the twentieth century, academic psychologists had begun to lose faith in universal models as they collapsed under the weight of contradictory evidence and conceptual analysis. For example, the absurdity of the conditioned reflex as a fundamental building block was, unwittingly, demonstrated by Hull (1952) who was forced to violate the principle that all concepts in conditioning theory should be directly linked to

3

observables in order to keep his conditioned reflex model afloat. Critics recognized that, if you need to propose completely unobservable 'fractional antedating goal responses' to account for the fact that animals are sensitive to how much reward they are going to get for doing something, then you might as well say that they have an 'image' or 'expectation' of the reward. Similarly, Skinner's (1957) courageous attempt at demonstrating the power of his 'operant' conditioning approach by applying it to human language enabled critics like Chomsky (1959) to demonstrate the inherent weaknesses and contradictions of the approach.

Faced with the collapse of grand theories under the weight of contradictory evidence, psychology moved in two directions. Academic psychologists largely abandoned large scale theories and settled in to offering small scale accounts of specific psychological phenomena, like our ability to remember some things better than others or our tendency to be seduced by visual illusions. At this point the concept of theory changed its meaning, from a logically coherent account of a range of phenomena in terms of a small set of universal concepts to an *ad hoc* explanation of a single phenomenon, the main purpose of which was to foster further research into the same phenomenon. According to this approach, it doesn't matter whether the theory that generates an experiment is any good as long as the experiment is conducted using an appropriate method.

Counsellors retained their theories but redefined their view of knowledge so that empirical invalidation or qualification ceased to be an obstacle to retaining a theory. Counselling 'theories' no longer claim to be the grand, modernist theories of fifty years ago. Instead, they function in two ways. The first is to provide a structure for counselling and the second is to offer themselves as stories for making sense of your experience when working with clients, allowing you to anticipate and interpret the consequences of your interventions. Each counsellor is encouraged to adopt the model within which they can most fluently work and which makes the best sense of their experience of counselling for them. Since the choice of model is based on personal experience, one can no more argue someone out of a counselling model by advancing empirical evidence than one could argue them out of a religious belief.

Being a counsellor is a bit like being a jazz musician. Your counselling model provides the basic theme around which you are working, just as jazz players usually start off with an established melody and chord sequence. Like the jazz musician, most of what you do is improvised to take account of what is happening in the session, so no two counselling sessions will be the same, any more than any two jazz improvisations could be identical.

Why should counsellors attend to psychological research?

The fact that most of what we do in practice is improvised means that counselling is a craft rather than a technology. Models provide frameworks for improvising interventions, rather than set formulae for working with clients, and most counsellors would have to think quite deeply before coming up with an intellectual justification for every intervention with a client that seemed appropriate and effective at the point at which it was introduced. Good craft depends on a number of factors, including the personal attributes of the practitioner, their practical training and their understanding of the materials with which they are working. Much of the training of counsellors focuses on the first two elements, the personal attributes of the practitioner and their practical skills, hence the importance attached to personal therapy and experiential learning in most models.

Counselling models are supposed to provide the third element, a knowledge of the mental lives of other people, but they are incomplete. Rogers (1961) enjoins us to treat our clients with 'unconditional positive regard' but he doesn't tell us what a particular client is most likely to experience in this way. The point is not whether you have achieved sufficient liberation from your own conditions of worth to experience unconditional positive regard for your client, but whether, in your gestures, posture, tone of voice and content of your speech that regard is effectively communicated. Psychodynamic approaches place great emphasis on interpretation, but they don't tell you how long an interpretation can be before clients will misunderstand you because they have forgotten half of what you have just said. Most counsellors spend a lot of time asking clients how they 'feel' about things but nothing in our models tells us whether people are accurate in remembering and reporting feelings.

These topics are addressed by research based psychology. There is a large literature on social interaction that informs us about how people are likely to interpret verbal and non-verbal cues and attribute psychological characteristics to other people. Similarly, we know a lot about the properties of human memory, the conditions that favour people remembering things and the limits to how much new information a person can take in at any one time. Feelings have been at the centre of psychological research for over a century, research which suggests that people are quite poor at describing their emotions accurately and that we are most likely to recall particular feelings when we are in the same emotional state.

My view of counselling models as frameworks for conducting practice, rather than definitive psychological truths, is endorsed by the view of many bodies that validate counsellor training, such as The British Psychological Society, that trainees should learn to work in a number of models. By analogy, music students are exposed to a number of musical styles so that a skilled improviser can sound like Bach at one moment and the Beatles at another. The problem with having a number of styles on offer is that you have to choose between them. A musician would find it difficult to sound simultaneously like Schoenberg and Schubert, and suddenly swapping between styles can appear ironic or witty, undermining the impact of each of them. Similarly, counsellors cannot simultaneously operate within the psychodynamic and person centred models and swapping between them will create a contrast that alters the meaning of the approaches adopted in isolation.

For some counsellors the choice between models is a once-in-a-lifetime decision as they will operate the same model irrespective of the client or problem. Other counsellors opt to switch between models according to the circumstances, thus becoming 'eclectic' or 'integrative'. The difficulty is that you cannot use the concepts contained within a particular model to decide which model to use, any more than you could use the precepts of Buddhism to decide whether to be a Buddhist or a Catholic. To think about psychological theories and models and to choose between them, you need psychological knowledge that lies outside the particular models concerned. That knowledge is provided by mainstream psychology. Similarly, a musician cannot choose between musical styles without having a general understanding of music that transcends the individual styles.

A further reason for placing your practice in the broader context of psychology is that many counsellors find themselves working in teams, with counsellors of different orientations, or in multidisciplinary settings, with other professionals with an interest in psychological well-being. Jazz musicians may find themselves playing with classically trained orchestras or may have to work with film directors who want music to match the mood of the images they are creating. To be effective in those settings we need to be able to communicate in language that is independent of our particular model. Many behavioural counsellors may not believe in the centrality of 'transference' in counselling but, if they work in a team that includes psychodynamic counsellors, they have to understand what their colleagues mean by this term, so that both groups have a way of thinking and talking about the interpersonal processes that take place during counselling.

Section summary

Although counselling was once part of the tradition of academic psychology, the two have drifted apart in recent years and tend to view each other with mutual incomprehension, rather like a couple who have gone through an acrimonious divorce. Academic psychology places great emphasis on empirical research, the dissemination of ideas through formal publications and the application of quite harsh critical standards to other people's ideas. Counselling places an emphasis on experiential learning, the dissemination of ideas through training and workshops, as well as publications, and great tolerance of diverse ideas.

This split has harmed both parties. Academic psychology has lost contact with practice and often gets obsessed with the minutiae of phenomena that only ever seem to occur in the laboratory. Counselling, for its part, has been cut off from a wealth of information and ideas that can enhance practice, particularly when we view that practice as a craft.

Even if you believe firmly in a single counselling model you can learn from mainstream psychology, because it can inform you about a host of issues not covered in your model. None of the models tell you how much a client will remember from a session, what factors condition clients' expectations of counselling interactions, what rules people apply to interpreting other people's behaviour, or the sorts of errors people are likely to make in reasoning about problems. Mainstream psychology tells you about all of these things.

Many counsellors find themselves dissatisfied with individual models and seek to integrate elements of practice for different approaches. Their problem is that they do not have a framework for thinking about what they are doing, so most attempts at integration end up looking like the translation of the ideas of one model into the terms of another. Mainstream psychology offers a conceptual framework that is not couched in the terms of counselling theories. At its best it offers accounts of how people are likely to think, feel and act in particular situations that will allow us to anticipate the impact of different forms of counselling practice.

The Organization of This Book

In writing this book my challenge was to survey current psychological knowledge and to extract from it a series of points on which most psychologists would be able to agree. In some instances this proved surprisingly straightforward, but in others it was much more difficult than I would have thought possible. When I came to write the chapter on memory, for example, it became clear to me that the theoretical debates of the researchers were superimposed on a broad body of agreement about fundamentals. Discussions between memory researchers read like family discussions about how to decorate the home. Everyone has their own favourite colour scheme, but they can all agree that the place has three bedrooms, one reception room, a bathroom and a kitchen. In contrast, when I came to write the chapter on emotion I realized that most of the discussions were about whether there was a home to decorate and, if there was, how many rooms it might have.

I have tried to be as honest as possible about the state of knowledge in different areas and indicate where I think we are still very unclear about things. Where there are gaps in our knowledge about topics like the development of adult sexual orientation, I have tried to make this clear because I believe that there is more danger in assuming things than in recognizing your ignorance. This is particularly true in helping professions like counselling, where there is the temptation to adopt the position of expert and know better than your client. If you come away from this book with a recognition of what you *don't* know about people, then I will have achieved one of my aims.

Psychologists may be able to agree on things but that doesn't mean that their knowledge is of any use to counsellors. Particle physicists can agree on a tremendous amount about the fundamental nature of matter, but that is not of much use to someone trying to design a house that won't fall down. My next challenge was to think about how psychological knowledge could be applied in counselling. As I started to write I came to realize that this was going to be easier than I had expected because much counselling practice involves implementing the lessons of psychology. For example, research on memory has shown that active listening, involving thinking about what your client is saying and trying to identify themes and links between their ideas, is necessary to overcome the limits of our capacity to remember newly-presented material. Similarly, research on attitude change shows us that people are more likely to adopt new ideas and values if they generate them themselves than if someone tries to argue them into them. The idea that you never argue with clients is fundamental to good practice.

I have tried to link the psychological ideas to practice in two ways. The first is that each of the main chapters begins with a case vignette that reflects the ideas in the chapter and that case is used to provide concrete illustrations of the abstract ideas. For example, the chapter on social psychology begins with a description of a client, George, coming to meet a counsellor for the first time. I use this story to illustrate the expectations we bring to social interactions and the way that those expectations both distort our social lives and, paradoxically, make social life possible in the first place.

The second thing I do is to provide a summary, after each main section of each chapter, of the ideas that you could apply in your practice. In the chapter on individual differences, for example, I discuss the importance of checking how your ideas about people have come about and the ways that you might use well-tested ideas about personality to extend your range of empathic comments to clients. Each of these sections is followed by a set of 'bullet points', summarizing the main conclusions. In offering these suggestions I have been very direct and directive; there are no 'mays', 'coulds' or 'perhaps'. That isn't because I want to force my ideas on you, but because I believe I have a duty to make my ideas clear to you. Feel free to reject them if you want, but I hope that if you do you can explain to yourself why you have done so.

My brief was to be brief, so I cannot pretend to have covered the whole of contemporary psychology in the depth it deserves. For some of my readers this may prove to be as much psychology as they feel they want to know, but I hope that most will build on my brief survey of the field to learn more about it. In most cases, you will find that the more you try to learn about a particular topic, the less you will seem to know about it. At that point you will fit the description of an educated person given to me when I was a student by someone much older and wiser than me; 'An educated person is someone who knows that they do not yet know'.

Chapter Summary

This book is about what counsellors can learn from contemporary psychology. Psychological knowledge is useful because it allows you to address the details of the counselling relationship on which most general models are quite vague and offers a framework for developing integrative practice. Despite the concern of academic psychologists with theoretical disputes, there is a remarkable amount on which psychologists agree that can inform your practice. The later chapters of this book develop these ideas in more detail.

2

Being Social

You are sitting in your consulting room, waiting for a new client, George, to arrive. According to your referral letter, George is a 25-year-old barrister who is having problems with relationships at work. What are your expectations about George? Is George male or female? Is George white or black? Where has George been educated? Does George speak with a regional accent?

Meanwhile, George is sitting on a bus on her way to see you. All she knows is that you are a counsellor, but she too has expectations. You are probably a female, caring, wise beyond your years and eager to make her feel better and help her solve her problems. You probably dress in a neat, casual style and speak with the accent of the region in which you are working. You will ask her about her problem and its history and you will tell her what to do.

George has arrived and you have collected her from the waiting room. What did you say on the way from the waiting room to your consulting room? Did you discuss the weather or whether the bus was the best way to get to see you, or did you avoid conversation until George was safely seated in the 'client's' chair in the consulting room? What did George make of the fact that you didn't say anything to her as you walked up the stairs? Did she think you were professional, unfriendly or just plain awkward? What are you thinking as you take stock of the fact that George is black and female? What is George thinking as she registers that you are a middle-aged white male, speaking in the slightly clipped tones of an ex-army officer and wearing blazer and regimental tie.

As you sit down, George is keen to tell you her story and it all starts to spill out before you can go into your routine for first sessions, in which you explain how you work, the ethical framework and the limits of confidentiality. This leaves you feeling slightly disconcerted, so you listen patiently, wait for a pause and para-phrase what she has said before plunging into your first session script. George listens politely but she looks tense and agitated and, as soon as you pause, she starts her story again, this time ending in tears and imploring you to reassure her that you can do something to help her and that there is nothing really wrong with her, it is the other people in chambers who are all dreadful.

Again you paraphrase, reflecting back her concern for reassurance without actually giving it. What does George think about this? Does she begin to wonder what is going on? Does she feel listened to? Does she feel that you are a warm and genuine person? Does she decide that there is no point in asking for your support because you use all the conversational ploys that she is familiar with from her friends and colleagues when they want to avoid helping her? Perhaps she decides to change the topic at this point and, instead of telling you about herself, she starts to ask you about yourself. How old are you? How did you qualify? Are you married? How much do you earn as a counsellor? Have you ever thought of suicide? When did you last have sex?

By the end of the session, George has given up asking you questions and begging for reassurance and tells you about her life in graphic detail. Up to a year ago, when she obtained her tenancy in chambers, her life had been happy and successful. She had gone from public school to a scholarship at Oxford to law school, followed by a successful pupillage in her present chambers. She had a wide circle of friends whose company she enjoyed and had had a couple of close relationships with men. Problems have arisen in the past year because she has begun to feel inadequate at work and this is making her irritable with colleagues, so irritable in fact, that, a week previously, she had a flaming row with the head of chambers and it was he who recommended that she see you for counselling.

Counselling is first and foremost a social interaction, taking the form of a conversation between two people (possibly more in the case of family or group counselling) and counsellors and clients bring all sorts of beliefs and expectations, based on their experience of other people and the ways in which they think and act, into the consulting room. The problems our clients bring to us are dramas played out on the stages of their social lives, other people provide the context in which our clients' problems develop and their freedom of choice is limited by the actions of other people. Effective counselling means understanding both the social context in which people live, and the mental capacities and limitations that they apply to their social world.

The Social Context

People simultaneously inhabit a physical world and a cultural world. The cultural world gives meaning to objects and events in the physical world and conditions our interactions with them. Skin colour, for example, has immense significance in many cultures that is completely at odds with its biological status. Fair skin is often prized over dark, even though fairness is the result of a genetic abnormality that deprives the individual of a vital protection against the effects of strong sunshine and leaves many millions of people increasingly at risk of skin cancer. Our culture makes it impossible for a counsellor to work with George without the physical fact of her skin colour being an issue.

The significance of culture has been recognized for decades, and there is a long and distinguished history of 'cross-cultural' research in psychology (Frijda and Jahoda, 1966; Smith and Bond, 1993). Early work took for granted the basic psychological categories of Western thought, such as 'memory' and 'emotion', and explored the relationship between them and culture. Segall *et al.* (1963), for example, compared Western and African people to test the role of being raised in a world full of straight lines and right angles in creating susceptibility to some visual illusions. Recent work has been more radical, arguing that our 'basic' psychological categories are, themselves, products of a particular culture. Instead of asking how culture influences our susceptibility to 'anxiety', for example, we now consider how the notion of 'anxiety' itself has sprung from our cultural context (Much, 1995).

Stimulated by philosophers such as Foucault, psychologists like Bruner (1986) and Harre (1995), have begun to explore how the ways in which we think about ourselves and other people reflect cultural expectations and values. For example, our traditions attribute the origins of interpersonal problems to problems in the minds of individuals, ascribing them to 'fixations', 'unresolved Oedipus complexes', 'conditions of worth' or 'neurotransmitter imbalances', seeking to dissolve the interpersonal difficulties by resolving these deficits in the individual. Therapists like Epston and White (1992) have built on these ideas and challenged this position, arguing that this view is a social construction rather than a description of reality, thus allowing for other views that locate the difficulties in the social context. They have incorporated these principles into working with clients, encouraging them to identify and challenge the ways in which 'problems' emerge from the cultural context rather than mental 'pathology'.

George is seeking individual psychological help but her difficulties might reflect the fact that she is black, female, speaks with a regional accent and works in a world that expects people to be white, male and speak with a middle class accent. Her decision to seek counselling could be seen as the triumph of the forces that are marginalizing her experience, because it has converted her colleagues' difficulty in dealing with cultural diversity into her difficulty in dealing with her colleagues (Madigan, 1992).

Language

Language is the vehicle of culture and it is through hearing other people talk about their lives and experiences, and sharing ours with them, that we enter into a culture. Language constrains the way we talk about ourselves and, by implication, the way we think. Individual words acquire complex meanings as a result of being used in different contexts. For example, when I was a child, 'gay' meant being cheerful and happy in a light-hearted way and 'queer' meant odd or ill. Now 'gay' and 'queer' both mean 'homosexual'. However, they have retained some of their old meanings in their new context, so that 'gay' focuses on the positive aspects of the experience of being homosexual while 'queer' focuses on the negative. Hetero- and homosexual males are both allowed to use 'gay' but only homosexual males are allowed to use 'queer'. The term 'homosexual' itself is not as neutral as I am making out, because of its prior use in medico-legal contexts which managed to make it a pejorative term. It is impossible for English speakers to talk about sexual orientation without using one of these terms and, thus, importing the mental baggage associated with the ways in which the words were previously used.

We do not talk in single words but in sentences and paragraphs, which we tend to organize in fairly standard ways, thus limiting how we talk about things. As a number of authors have pointed out (Bruner, 1986; Murray, 1995), when people talk about their lives they tend to tell stories about themselves. Stories are not reality, they are artificial accounts of reality that conform to quite precise rules, such as having beginnings, middles and ends, and having causal links between the elements of the story ('I did something because you did something else') (Bruner, 1996; Murray, 1995; Potter, 1996).

Since it involves talking with people, counselling will reflect the constraints that are built into the way we use language. For example, the tendency to work with stories means that when you ask a client about their problem they either give a bit of history to go with it ('My husband left me and now I feel worthless'; 'My child constantly plays truant from school and I feel inadequate as a parent') or expect you to ask them about the history of the problem ('I have trouble establishing relationships' carries the assumption that you will ask about their relationship history). Language also

13

enforces silence, because it makes it difficult or impossible to say certain things, so events, experiences and feelings that do not fit into the story which a client is telling may simply be dropped. A person who is telling a story from a 'victim' viewpoint will find it difficult to include descriptions of situations in which they exercised choice and power, or may reframe those situations to present them as further examples of victimhood. A story of a life is a story first and a life second. Problem descriptions themselves may reflect the stories clients have heard elsewhere. When a client says 'I am bad at relationships', their notion of what constitutes being 'good' at relationships may tell you more about the culturally sanctioned 'relationship' story than about their individual experience.

Language does more than convey factual information, it also regulates social relationships. Some of this regulation is benign, as speakers work to maintain conversation and heal breaches in relationships that have resulted from an unwise choice of words or misunderstanding (Potter, 1996). If you look at transcripts of real conversations, you will see that a huge amount of relationship maintenance goes on. Some regulation involves attempts at exercising power, such as the counsellor in my example consistently refusing to attend to George's plea for direct advice (Potter, 1996).

Roles

Cultures structure our lives in the form of roles, so we know what to do in most situations because we have learned to play a particular 'part' in a social drama (Goffman, 1959; Harre and Secord, 1972). As a counsellor I am expected to do things that my clients think will help them, such as asking them about their history and their family and offering solutions to their problems. I am also expected to do things that my professional colleagues think will help my clients, such as focusing on their present experiences and refraining from offering solutions. Our clients play out the role of 'client'. They are expected to tell virtual strangers about the most intimate details of their lives, to accept comments and interpretations that, in other contexts, would be deemed offensive, to tolerate prolonged periods of silence and to refrain from interpreting and commenting on the thoughts and actions of the counsellor.

Social roles differ from most theatrical roles in that there is rarely a detailed script to specify what we do. Instead, we find ourselves in the position of an actor called upon to extemporize a part, following a description of what the character is like. Roles simplify social life by giving us guidance about what we should do in particular settings and providing us with expectations about how other people will act. Some of the difficulties experienced by George and her counsellor are the result of George and her counsellor having different ideas about the roles of 'client' and 'counsellor'.

Experimental studies indicate that role may be much more powerful than personality in influencing how people behave. For example, Haney *et al.* (1973) recruited twelve college students to take part in a role play of prison life. All of the participants were volunteers who were screened to rule out individuals at risk for psychological problems. Nine were randomly assigned to the prisoner role and three to the role of guard. No detailed instructions were given as to how to behave, but basic prison rules were laid down. These included the requirements that prisoners were only referred to by number, that they undertook work details and that toilet visits were supervised. Guards were prohibited from using punishment and being physically aggressive. A study that had been scheduled to run for two weeks had to be abandoned after six days as the behaviour of the two groups polarized. 'Guards' increasingly exercised arbitrary power, making 'prisoners' do press-ups or refusing to allow them to go to the lavatory. 'Prisoners' became depressed and showed signs of physical illness.

A less dramatic, but more realistic, assessment of the importance of role comes from a workplace study by Lieberman (1965), who surveyed the attitudes of workers in a factory towards management and union policy. Having established a baseline, he returned to the factory a year later to identify workers who had changed roles to become either foremen or union stewards. People who had become foremen displayed attitudes that were more favourable to management than the average, while people who had become union stewards displayed attitudes more favourable to unions than the average. Eighteen months later, he returned to the factory again, to identify people who had ceased to be foremen or stewards and returned to their previous jobs. Shifting back to the production worker role was associated with a shift in attitude back to the average of the production workers. Changing role is linked to changing attitude.

Role theory tells us that each of us occupies a number of social roles at different points in our lives. Sometimes role shifts are developmental, as we move from the child to the adult role, for example. Sometimes role shifts are linked to institutional context, as we move from being subordinate employee at work to being sole authority at home, for example. Given the power of role, these shifts may create difficulties for the idea that each of us embodies a unique 'self' that is the origin of all of our actions (Harre and Secord, 1972). People who are concerned with self-consistency may find these shifts problematic as they struggle to reconcile their actions in one context with those in another. George has recently changed role from student to autonomous professional. It would be interesting to know what opportunities she has had to learn the new role.

Problems may also arise if roles create 'role conflict' by presenting inconsistent demands (Baron and Byrne, 1997). Someone in George's situation in an organization faces a particular difficulty because her role is mid-way between that of a student and an independent practitioner. As she is young and female she is likely to be expected to behave with the deference of a student but, as a fully qualified member of chambers, she is also expected to act with authority. She may also experience conflicts between different roles. As a success-ful member of a disadvantaged group, she would reasonably expect to be treated with respect and deference but, as a newly qualified member of a reactionary profession, respect and deference are likely to be in short supply.

How Can I Use This Information As a Counsellor?

Good counselling practice tries to be sensitive to cultural issues. The emphasis on listening to clients and developing empathic under-standing is an attempt to ensure that counsellors do not impose their own cultural beliefs and values on clients. However, conven-tional counselling skills may make us too respectful towards our clients' cultural positions and disinclined to explore the stories that structure what our clients are saying. As a consequence we may fail to distinguish between the 'lived experience' of our clients, towards which we should show respect, and their culturally sanctioned ways of talking about their experiences, towards which we may want to adopt a different attitude.

When listening to clients we need constantly to ask ourselves, 'Who is talking, the client or their culture?' For example, if a client describes him or herself as being unhappily married we need to distinguish between their experience of their relationship and their socially sanctioned expectations of what marriage should be like. Culture may also censor our clients, making it difficult for them to talk about aspects of their experience because they don't have language in which to describe it without censuring themselves as they do so. For example, until recently issues of sexual orientation were intimately tied up with concepts of pathology and moral judgements. As a consequence, it was impossible for clients to declare their homosexuality without presenting their sexual choices as deviant and morally objectionable.

Cultural issues are also going to be reflected in counsellors' behaviour. When we ask clients to elaborate on their stories, when we offer reflections or when we offer interpretations, we make cultural assumptions. You cannot avoid this, but you can be sensitive to it. The biggest problems are likely to arise when clients share our own cultural beliefs and values, because culture tends to become invisible at that point. Straight counsellors working with gay clients may well be sensitive to cultural values about sexual orientation, but straight counsellors working with straight clients may not be sensitive to the same values.

Counselling itself exists within a culture. The notion that two people sitting and talking together can be effective in helping one of the participants is relatively new and a product of a particular socio-economic setting. Counselling places the participants in distinct roles. There is a crude classification into 'client' and 'counsellor' and a more refined classification according to the type of counselling involved. The 'client' role in psychodynamic counselling is very different from that in cognitive behavioural counselling, for example. This raises the important question of how clients learn their roles.

Part of learning the client role comes from cultural norms. Clients come to us expecting to do certain things, like tell their life histories, and expecting us to do certain things, like offer solutions to their problems. Both sets of expectations may be disappointed. Apart from cultural expectations, clients have little to go on, so they have to learn their roles 'on the job'. Although we may be unaware of it, much of what we do with clients, especially in initial sessions, will involve teaching them how to become clients. For example, clients who turn to counsellors for guidance or reassurance will find that their requests are consistently frustrated and will learn not to make such requests. Clients who are reluctant to talk about themselves will find that there are prolonged silences and will learn to fill the conversational gaps created by the counsellor. To use the jargon of behaviourists, counsellors will 'shape' the behaviour of their clients.

Being socialized is not a pleasant experience. Clients are likely to experience role conflict as they discover that their view of the client role does not conform with yours, and the techniques you use to shape the client's behaviour may be quite unpleasant for the client. Clients may feel bad at the beginning of counselling, simply as a result of these processes, and then come to feel better as they become more secure in their role. What appears to you as therapeutic gain may simply reflect the waning of counsellor-induced distress!

Section summary

- Try to identify how far what you are hearing reflects the client's culture rather than the 'lived experience' of the client.

- Attend to what the client *isn't* saying and consider how far that reflects cultural constraints.

- Attend to your own cultural assumptions, especially when you share them with clients.

- Remember that counselling involves roles, and that clients have to learn to be clients.

- Review the procedures you use to socialize clients into their roles and consider their likely impact.

Thinking About the Social World

Acting socially means thinking about other people to anticipate what they are likely to do and how they are likely to react to what we do. Culture, and the roles sanctioned by culture, provide us with expectations about how people are likely to act and react but both culture and role leave a lot of room for manoeuvre in specific contexts. George will have learned the role of 'barrister' during her training, and will know that she has a number of options open to her when cross-examining a witness. She can ask direct questions or she can ask indirect ones that encourage the witness to agree to a series of innocuous appearing statements without realizing that they are being worked into a corner. She can treat a witness as honest or she can decide that they are lying and set traps for them. George needs more than her knowledge of her role to decide what to do in court.

Social situations are phenomenally complex. Huge numbers of events takes place in a brief period of time, many of them simultaneously. People talk, vary their facial expressions, use gestures and shift posture. Our task is to handle this stream of information, make sense of what the other person is doing, anticipate what they will do next and decide what we should do. It is little wonder that most research indicates that our social decision-making is crude and subject to a number of biases and distortions. These include:

1) the belief that we can understand other people;
2) using habitual strategies rather than thinking through the demands of a particular situation; and
3) using other people as cues as to how to behave.

Understanding other people's minds?

Humans are seized with the idea that the world makes sense. More remarkably, we act as if the concepts of mental life that we find in our daily language are an adequate way of making sense of people's actions. This belief that our language embodies some sort of privileged account of mental life is very odd, given that the common sense views of the physical world contained in our daily language are recognized to be inadequate. If you ask why somebody did something, you will get an explanation in terms of their 'motivation', their 'personality', their 'rational' thought or some other psychological attribute.

For example, George could interpret her counsellor's failure to talk to her as they mount the stairs to the counselling room in a number of ways. George could offer a motivational explanation – that the counsellor didn't want to talk at that particular time; a personality explanation – that he was unfriendly and didn't like talking to people in general; or a situational explanation – that this was how all counsellors are expected to treat clients.

We make these judgements all the time without realizing that we are doing something very peculiar, namely *attributing* to somebody a characteristic that we cannot directly observe. When we say that a person is 'unfriendly', we think we are describing them in the same way as saying that a rose is red is a description of a rose, but we are not. We do not see 'unfriendliness' directly: we see actions like crossing the road before they meet us, failing to engage in eye-contact, or cutting short social interactions, and these actions all admit other explanations (Baron and Byrne, 1997).

As it depends on attributions rather than descriptions, our language of mental life is different from the language we use to talk about the physical world. Within a given culture and linguistic community, a rose is a rose is a rose, but different people are inclined to make different psychological attributions in relation to the same event. One person might decide that the individual crossing the road in the example I have given was hungry, while a second might decide they are unfriendly, while a third might decide that they were on their way to work. To some degree this can reflect differences in the observers' experiences of the protagonist. The first person might know that the protagonist has a prodigious appetite

19

and that there was a cake shop opposite. The second person might have been snubbed by them on a number of occasions and the third person might be a work colleague who also knows the best route to the office.

'Attribution' is a logical, not a psychological issue, explaining how it is possible for many of the words in our language to have meaning, rather than describing the mental lives of individual people (Wittgenstein, 1968). People usually make attributions in a logically coherent way. For example, Jones and Davis (1965) argue (on logical, rather than psychological grounds) that we will be most accurate in making attributions if we base them on actions that are freely chosen by their protagonist, actions that are not susceptible to multiple explanations (what they call *noncommon* effects) and actions that are low in social desirability.

Whether we attribute events to psychological characteristics, rather than to circumstances, should depend on three factors: whether or not other people behave in the same way in the same situation, whether or not the individual concerned has behaved in the same way in the same setting, and whether the person concerned has behaved in the same way in different situations (Kelley, 1972). If a person repeatedly behaves the same way in the same situation, behaves the same way in different situations and is the only person to behave in that way, then we will attribute their actions to internal, psychological dispositions. If everyone tends to behave in the same way in the situation concerned, the protagonist doesn't usually behave in that way in that setting and does not usually behave in that way in other settings, we will attribute their behaviour to the situation. However, people do not consistently follow these principles and there are biases in the ways in which people make psychological attributions.

If you ask people to explain the actions of others, they are biased towards explanations in terms of abiding personal characteristics, such as unfriendliness or clumsiness, even though short-term, situational factors offer equally valid explanations. This has become known as the *fundamental attribution error*. George's head of chambers may have made this error when he attributed her outburst of temper at work to being due to some abiding psychological problem, rather than to the specific circumstances in the work environment.

When observing our own behaviour, the reverse usually occurs, and we attribute events to circumstances rather than to our abiding characteristics. However, this feature is modified by the value of the outcome. If the outcome is good, we are inclined to attribute it to abiding personal characteristics but if it is bad, we attribute it to short-term situational factors. George may attribute her success as a barrister to her ability and determination but ascribe her outburst in chambers to the provocative words of her boss. This is known as the *self-serving bias*.

People are creatures of habit

Each social interaction is unique, full of possibilities and demanding immense resourcefulness to realize its full potential. However, most of us treat new social interactions as if they are repetitions of interactions we have experienced in the past. In part this is because we act in role, but even within a role, the way that we play it out will be a repetition of the way that we have played that role in the past. Rather than thinking out each situation anew we tend to interact with our social worlds via a series of strategies that reduce the intellectual burdens of our social interactions at the price of making much of our social life 'irrational'. We tend to classify social events, and the people with whom we interact, into categories and apply previously acquired rules for how to deal with those categories. When thinking about other people we tend to apply short-cuts, rather than attending to all of the information available to us.

People classify social situations using well-established frameworks (known as *schemata*) that tell us which behaviours are appropriate and the sequences of events that should occur in particular situations (Baron and Byrne, 1997). Social psychologists refer to schemata for what is appropriate behaviour as *role schemata* and those for sequences of events as *scripts*. We have already looked at roles in an earlier section of this chapter, so let us now look at scripts in more detail.

Scripts

Social interactions develop over time and actions that are appropriate at one stage in an interaction are wholly inappropriate at others. Most social interactions open with some sort of greeting and, where the protagonists do not already know each other, introductions. How they develop depends on the type of interaction so interactions at a party will develop differently from those in a teaching group. The rules for parties tell us to move around the group, take turns in conversation and escalate intimacy with other party-goers, providing they also follow the script for escalating intimacy. Intimacy has to be negotiated progressively and people have additional scripts for doing so (Levin, 1994) . The rules for teaching groups tell us to remain static, direct attention to the teacher and avoid attempts to escalate intimacy. Indeed, in many informal teaching settings, the progression may be away from intimacy as role boundaries are established, so that the teacher may start off very friendly and informal and then reduce intimacy as other role related issues, such as the completion of assignments, are negotiated. Again, teachers and students have additional scripts for reducing intimacy and establishing boundaries. Most of the time we are unaware that we have scripts until something goes wrong and we realize that the person with whom we are interacting is following a different script from us, which seems to have happened to George and her counsellor.

When we first meet a new person we have little information about how they will act. Nevertheless, we have to have some expectations in order to start to negotiate the relationship. One way of dealing with this is to classify people according to *prototypes* and to treat them as if they were examples of one (Baron and Byrne, 1997). Prototypes are classes of people who are considered likely to act and think in particular ways by virtue of being a member of that class. Prototyping is influenced by a variety of cues, such as physical appearance, dress, and statements about occupational role. In Britain, young women are often treated as if they are children or occupy subservient socio-economic positions. Consequently, young women in professions like law or medicine may be treated as secretaries or receptionists by visitors, who ask to see their bosses. Conversely, men who wear soberly tailored, expensively cut suits, and keep their hair short are usually expected to be middle class professional people, and are treated accordingly. If you are told that somebody is a 'lawyer', you will probably expect to see such a soberly dressed male. In Britain, you might also expect a lawyer to have gone to a public school and either Oxford or Cambridge, to speak with a 'public school' accent, to lean to the right politically and probably be very dull at parties.

At their first meeting both George and her counsellor are prototyping. Each has expectations of the other based on their ideas of the 'typical' barrister and the 'typical' counsellor. At their first meeting both have to adjust to the fact that the other does not meet their expectations.

As we acquire more information about other people, we tend to use short-cuts, known as *heuristics*, to interpret it. Our use of prototypes, for example, depends on heuristics which can be quite illogical for assigning people to categories. For example, when we assign people to prototypes, we attend much more to whether they have characteristics that are representative of that prototype than to contextual information, such as the relative number of people in a particular category in a particular setting. For example, if you go to a party where you know that eighty per cent of those present are lawyers you will be most accurate in determining somebody's profession if you assume they are a lawyer, because you will have only a twenty per cent error rate. If, however, you meet a casually dressed woman who speaks with a regional accent you will probably classify her as a non-lawyer, because she is more representative of that group. Someone who does not fit into their prototype, like George, is likely to experience some very odd social interactions as people pigeon-hole her into an inappropriate category. This is the *representativeness* heuristic.

A second heuristic that is widely used assumes that what we can remember most about a person or a situation reflects what was most important or valuable. If you remember a person from a social situation you will tend to think of them as being more significant to the interaction than someone you remember less well. In the academic world, that means that students who get noticed, get better references than students who don't stand out. Is it possible that George has learned to do things that make her stand out but are now inappropriate for someone in her professional position?

A third heuristic is to assume that other people are like ourselves and to attend to events that conform to this expectation. George is clearly not like most of the people with whom she works and if her colleagues treat her as if she is, they will all experience some very unsatisfactory interactions.

A fourth heuristic is to attend selectively to negative information about people. Even if someone has been pleasant to you on ninety-nine occasions, you will tend to remember the hundredth, on which they were rude, and to base your expectations for their future behaviour on that single event. Is our counsellor in danger of doing this with George, remembering her intrusive questions about his competence and forgetting much else that is relevant?

Using other people as guides

People in groups often behave very differently from the way that they would if they were by themselves. The presence of other people can encourage us to make judgements which, left to our own devices, we know are wrong (Asch, 1955), can encourage us into inaction in situations in which our moral values tell us we should act, and can encourage us to take more extreme positions than we would if acting individually (Baron and Byrne, 1997). This tendency to behave differently in groups seems surprising to Western people who are brought up to place a great value on individuality but can be highly adaptive in many social situations.

In Asch's (1955) study, participants were invited to take part in an experiment in which they had to judge which of three lines was the same length as a sample. They carried out the task in a group setting in which the other participants were, unbeknownst to them, accomplices of the experimenter who had been primed to give glaringly wrong answers on some trials. Remarkably, a large proportion of the participants went along with the judgements of the group on these trials and chose lines that clearly did not match the sample. There wasn't anything wrong with their capacity to make the correct judgements, because in a repetition of the study in which the participants had to write down their judgements rather than saying them aloud, their choices were very accurate.

People may end up doing things that they find personally repugnant as a result of social influence. For example, in a series of experiments Milgram (1974) showed that volunteers could be encouraged to administer severe and life-threatening electric shocks to another person as part of an experiment. People were recruited by Milgram to 'assist' him in running an experiment on the effects of punishment on learning. They were taken into a laboratory and asked to help wire up a 'volunteer' to a shock machine, and then give the 'volunteer' increasingly severe electric shocks, each time they gave a wrong answer to the questions asked. In fact, the 'volunteer' was an actor and the 'shock' machine was a dummy that delivered no current at all to the 'volunteer' but this was not revealed to the participants until after the study. During the study, 65 per cent of participants were willing to administer up to 450 volts to the 'volunteer', despite the latter screaming and pleading for mercy.

Sometimes social situations inhibit action. Darley and Latane (1968) were struck by news reports that neighbours ignored pleas for help while a woman was being stabbed to death outside her apartment block. The stabbing lasted 45 minutes and was witnessed by a number of people, but none of them attempted to intervene or even call the police. Darley and Latane set up a laboratory simulation of this situation. Participants were told that they were taking part in a group discussion but were being isolated in separate rooms so that they would not be embarrassed by having to meet the eyes of other participants. In the time-honoured tradition of this type of experiment, there were no other people present except the participant, who listened to tape recordings of students talking about the discussion topic. During the course of one of these recordings, an accomplice mimicked having a fit and choking. The question was: would the participants leave their room to help? If they believed that only one other person was present, the majority of the participants left the room and did so quickly. However, if they thought there were five others present, only 31 per cent went to help and they were slow in reacting.

People in groups often make different decisions from those they would make individually. In some circumstances, people move to much more risky positions but in others they may become much more conservative. In a typical experiment (Kogan and Wallach, 1964), participants are given a list of options varying in risk and asked to indicate how much risk they would accept. For example, the list might consist of a range of probabilities that a new company will prove financially sound, ranging from 1 in 10 to 9 in 10 and the participant has to advise an hypothetical person whether to take a job with the company. Before a group discussion, people tend to make reasonably conservative choices, but afterwards tend to opt for much riskier choices.

There is a danger in assuming that our behaviour is more 'rational' when we act alone, but group situations are much more complex than individual choices and place different demands on people. We receive a lot of information from other people about the nature of the situation in which we find ourselves, which defines the context for rationality. For example, people faced with experiments like Asch's are dealing with two sets of demands, the explicit demands of the instructions given by the experimenter and the implicit demands of the social situation. So long as these coincide, people appear to behave 'rationally'; the problems come when they do not coincide because the accomplices are redefining the interaction as one where you do not choose the matching line. It is no more 'rational' to go along with the explicit demands and do what an experimenter has instructed you to do than it is to work out what the implicit demands of a situation are, by monitoring what those around you are doing, and go along with the group. After all, the participants in Milgram's work were considered interesting precisely because they *did* obey the researcher.

How Can I Use This Information As a Counsellor?

Language forces us and our clients to pigeonhole experiences into a set of linguistically sanctioned categories through which we interpret events. The fact that our psychological language consists of *attributions* rather than descriptions means that we may never get direct access to our clients' 'lived experience' but have to be satisfied with their interpretations.

When clients say 'I am unhappy', they are not describing their psychic landscape, or inspecting a private 'happiness' meter located in their head, they are attending to their bodily state, behavioural dispositions and the way they are being treated by others, and making an attribution based on all of these factors. To misquote James (1884), you know you are unhappy because you cry, you do not cry because you know you are unhappy.

Depending on your model this is either a liberation or a disappointment. It is liberating to cognitive therapists, whose practice is based on helping free clients from cognitive errors that lead them to make self-destructive interpretations and to the new wave of sociologically biased therapists, who work by exposing the inconsistencies in the interpretative frameworks of their clients that reflect conflicts and inconsistencies at the heart of the culture. It is a disappointment to those who wish to work phenomenologically because it casts doubt on the possibility of ever gaining direct access to lived experience (see also Legg, 1997).

Attributional biases and errors can lead to behavioural and emotional difficulties. Alloy *et al.* (1990) have argued that depression is a result of people applying self-defeating, rather than self-serving, attributions. While cheerful people tend to explain positive outcomes in terms of their personal characteristics and negative outcomes in terms of circumstances, depressed people seem to do the opposite, explaining positive outcomes in terms of situational factors and negative outcomes in terms of personal characteristics. Therapy involves encouraging clients to abandon this cognitive bias in favour of self-serving attributions. Self-serving attributions aren't any more rational than self-defeating ones but they do tend to help people live happier lives.

Culturally widespread attributional biases may themselves be the origin of distress. Within couples and families, the fundamental attributional error may lead individuals to interpret the actions of partners, children or parents in terms of abiding personality characteristics, rather than short-term situational factors, leading to blaming rather than problem solving. Coupled with the tendency of individuals to interpret their own actions according to the self-serving bias of attributing good outcomes to their own characteristics and negative outcomes to circumstances, we have a recipe for escalating conflict over trivial events. For example, if a partner consistently comes home late, they may operate the self-serving bias and interpret it in terms of situational factors such as the demands of work and the need to provide for their family by being economically successful. Meanwhile, their partner and children, embodying the fundamental attributional error, may see the same action as a manifestation of selfishness and lack of care for them.

Counsellors make attributions when they talk to and about their clients. This means that we have to inspect our own practice for evidence of attributional biases. When listening to our clients we need to beware of the fundamental attributional error, to avoid attributing problems to the characteristics of the client rather than to the circumstances in which they find themselves. When thinking about our own practices, we need to be wary of the self-serving bias, attributing successful outcomes to our skills as counsellors and failures to the unco-operativeness of our clients.

Scripts and prototypes work for us so long as we share them with other people. Problems can arise when we either lack them for common social situations or they are so idiosyncratic that other people don't know what we are going to do next. When our clients talk about problems in relating to other people, it is worth exploring their habitual ways of conducting particular types of interaction. For example, if a client says that they have low self-esteem because they feel that they are sexually unattractive, it might be worth investigating their scripts for negotiating the escalation of social into sexual interactions. They may lack such scripts altogether or they may operate to scripts that other people read in a different way, so that their attempts to establish sexual relationships are permanently thwarted.

Prototyping may be a source of difficulty in two ways; clients may apply unusual prototypes to strangers or they may dress and act in such ways as to encourage strangers to apply inappropriate prototypes to them. What psychodynamic therapists call 'transference' can be viewed as a form of inappropriate prototyping in which the client views you, and other people, as belonging to the same class as emotionally significant family members and treats you accordingly. A lot of artifice goes into ensuring that strangers put us into prototype categories with which we feel comfortable. If clients get this wrong, they will have frustrating and unpleasant social interactions.

These points apply to you as a counsellor as well. It might be useful to think of your counselling model as a script for conducting counselling sessions. This means two things:

1) consistency may be more important than strict adherence to a theoretical model; and
2) changing models means changing script, which is a form of social anarchy that may be very distressing to clients.

By all means be 'eclectic' in terms of the interventions you use, but you may confuse clients completely if you do not place those interventions within a coherent counselling script.

Prototypes work both ways in counselling. When you first meet a client, you will apply a prototype willy nilly; it's as spontaneous as breathing. Fortunately, all counselling models implement rules to prevent you from acting on prototypes and those rules should be respected. Your client will also have a prototype for counsellors and therapists and you may not fit the frame. While you may not be able to do much about your appearance or speech, you should be aware of the possibility that counselling is not progressing because the client has difficulty treating you as a therapist and you may have to negotiate your status with clients.

Clients use heuristics as the basis for social judgements, which means that many will be illogical. Since social psychology tells us that most social judgements are 'illogical', we should concern ourselves with enabling our clients to be illogical in the same way as everyone else, rather than challenging their illogicality. Sometimes we may have to work to enable clients to trust to judgements which they know are illogical, to let 'intuition' have a free rein. On other occasions we may have to make our clients aware of their biases, in order to help them restructure them. For example, the 'everyone is like me' heuristic is valuable, providing the thoughts and actions of the individual are sufficiently commonplace. If they are not, it is a very dangerous heuristic to apply. Someone who is very aggressive may assume that everyone else is also aggressive, leading to interactions of escalating tension and violence. A teacher who has a ready, fluent grasp of their subject may assume that all their students have a similar facility for the subject, leading to a widening gulf of mutual incomprehension.

Actions vary according to the social context and we tend to take our cues as to how to act from the actions of those around us. This has two implications for counsellors:

1) clients may think and act differently when with the counsellor than when alone;
2) clients may think and act differently in different social settings.

Social situations place demands on people to act in particular ways. If Asch can induce people who are not emotionally vulnerable to say that black is white, what impact might we be having on our emotionally vulnerable clients? It is true that many of us are trained not to lead clients or impose our ideas on them but this only deals with the explicit demands of the situation. Through our ways of interacting with clients we may create implicit demands that influence our clients as much as Asch's accomplices influenced the participants in his experiments. Unless they can suspend all of the mental processes they apply to the rest of their lives, our clients will be looking to us for cues as to what they should say and do next and we will be giving them those cues, however hard we try not to. Indeed, the harder we try not to influence our clients, the more enigmatic the social interaction becomes and the more likely they are to depend on us for signs of how to act.

If our influence carries on outside the counselling setting, it may have therapeutic value. The danger is that our clients construct statements, for consumption by the counsellor, that bear little relation to what is going on in the rest of their lives, because clients believe that they are the sorts of things that the counsellor wants to hear. Abandoning explicit control by adopting 'neutral' or 'non-directive' positions relative to clients does not mean that we have abandoned this implicit influence. We cannot *not* influence our clients, but we can be aware of it happening.

Our clients act out their lives in a number of social contexts and may behave differently in each of them, depending on their implicit and explicit demands. It is unlikely that they will be aware of how far social setting influences their actions. Faced with a verbal description of Asch's or Milgram's experimental settings, few people would say that they would choose the wrong line or administer 450 volts to a volunteer, but this is exactly how most participants behave in these social settings. It is vital for client and counsellor alike to understand the impact of social context on behaviour. Abstracting clients from their normal social contexts distorts our understanding of their actions and may lead us to make internal attributions about their actions, where external attributions may be more appropriate.

Section summary

- **Psychological language involves making attributions about our mental lives rather than describing an inner landscape.**

- **Clients may have problems because they make attributions in unusual ways, such as failing to operate the 'self-serving bias' which preserves self esteem.**

- **Conflict between clients and other people may arise because they operate the same attributional biases in a complementary way, attributing other people's failures to 'personality' while the others attribute them to circumstances.**

- **The goal of therapy may be to help clients swap one set of biases for another.**

- **Clients' difficulties might result from their having inappropriate scripts for many social settings.**

- **Counselling is a social interaction. Counsellors need scripts for the counselling process and clients need those scripts to be consistent.**

- Social judgements are often illogical, but this does not matter providing our clients are making the same errors as everyone else.

- Counsellors need to identify those situations where clients would benefit from trusting their own illogicality and those where the application of common heuristics is leading them into trouble.

- Actions take place in a social context and are likely to be products of social influence. Abstracting clients from that context gives a distorted view of their lives and actions.

- Counselling will create implicit demands on clients to say and do particular things during counselling. These may be divorced from their daily lives.

Chapter Summary

Counselling is a social interaction involving two or more people who inhabit a complex social world. Understanding our clients' problems means understanding the social context in which the dramas of their lives are enacted and the rules for human social interaction. This chapter has looked at what psychologists know about human social interactions, starting with an account of the cultural context in which these interactions take place and then looking at some of the mental processes that people apply to help them deal with the complexities of the social world.

Much of how we think about ourselves is part of our culture and people in different cultures think about themselves in different ways. A number of authors have recently drawn our attention to the importance of culture in defining what constitutes a problem for our clients and in defining the limits of their actions in dealing with it, and have proposed therapeutic interventions that focus on the individual redefining their relationship with the wider culture, rather than adjusting their mental processes.

Within a culture, people apply a number of strategies for successfully negotiating their social interactions. These strategies include making attributions about the causes of their own and other people's behaviour, using short-cuts when thinking about other people and relying on other people as cues as to how to act. These strategies have implications for problem formation and problem resolution. Counselling is complicated by the fact that it, too, is a social interaction, so all of the social processes that can be identified in the world at large will be taking place in counselling itself.

3

Feelings

Alan is 32. He has been married for five years and has come for counselling because his marriage is not working out as he had hoped. The problem, he tells you, is his wife, who persistently does irritating things which make him angry. A few weeks ago he got so angry, after she had put his favourite 'hand-wash only' linen shirt in the washing machine with the rest of the laundry, that he hit her and she left him to go and stay with her parents 'until he got himself sorted out'. Alan maintains that he is quite justified in getting angry when his wife does 'stupid things' but recognizes that he shouldn't hit people when he does. However, when he gets angry he finds that 'something takes him over' and he 'just can't help lashing out'.

As Alan tells you this story you notice that he has become tense, he is breathing deeply, his pupils have narrowed and he is talking loudly. He emphasizes his words by rhythmically banging on the arm of the chair in which he is sitting. As you listen to him, you are conscious of a sick feeling in your stomach and drops of sweat building up in your armpits, even though it is cold November and the heating isn't working very well. You try to think of a way of reflecting Alan's feelings back to him, but you are finding it difficult to think because your mind keeps returning to the question of whether you can get out of the consulting room before Alan hits you, if you say something 'stupid'.

Thanks to your skills, Alan's anger abates and he tells you more about the circumstances in which he has wanted to hit his wife. According to Alan, it all depends on his mood. When he is in a good mood he can laugh off some of the things she does but when he gets low, he finds that she is particularly irritating. He has been feeling low a lot recently.

It hasn't helped that he has gone off sex, while his wife had a strong sexual appetite before she left him. They would often have fights in bed because she wanted to make love and he didn't feel like it. Alan tells you, in confidence, that he hadn't lost his sexual desire completely, he had just lost his desire for his wife. In fact, there was a woman at work whom he found sexually attractive and he had found it difficult to resist the temptation to try to seduce her. Although his wife had no inkling that all this was going on, Alan resented the fact that his wife did not appreciate his struggle to stay faithful to her.

Clients like Alan say a lot about how they 'feel' about things. Sometimes they explain their failure to do things that they intended to do, like talking to a stranger, in terms of feelings that got in the way while, on other occasions, they explain the fact that they have done things that they *didn't* intend to do, like hitting their wives, in terms of other feelings. Failure to talk to strangers is explained in terms of fear or embarrassment, while acts of violence are explained in terms of anger. People usually justify seeking counselling in terms of their feelings, reporting negative feelings, such as sadness or lack of self-worth, as the reason why they have come to see you, and expressing their goals in terms of having other feelings, such as happiness or contentment.

Psychologists divide up how people feel about things into three broad topics; *emotions, moods* and *desires.* Emotion refers to those feelings that occur as a reaction to specific situations and which influence how we react to them. Emotions can be rated in terms of how appropriate they are to situations. For example, Alan's anger would be an appropriate reaction to someone injuring him, but not to the way that his wife does the laundry. Emotions involve changes in our reactions to situations, so Alan's anger involves a desire to hurt his wife when he feels that she has provoked him, a desire that does not arise if he does not feel angry.

Moods are states that persist for some time and are not obviously linked to external events. Alan has commented on the way that he reacts differently according to whether he feels good or feels low, but hasn't indicated any obvious factors that precipitate these states. While he is cheerful, he can shrug off events to which he acts angrily when he feels low.

Desires are feelings associated with particular objects. They take the form of urges to do specific things with those objects, such as eat particular foods, copulate with particular people (or inanimate objects), or ingest particular drugs. Desires tend to be remarkably specific. Alan remarks that he doesn't just want sex, he wants it with the woman at work. Sex with his wife won't do. Hungry people do not want food in the abstract, they want to eat particular foods, like bacon sandwiches or chocolate biscuits. Drug users do not want to be intoxicated, they want to mainline heroin or smoke crack cocaine. In this chapter I will look at what psychologists have learned about emotions, moods and desires, and what this knowledge tells us as counsellors.

Emotion

Psychologists have concerned themselves with two broad issues; the nature of emotions and the conditions under which emotions typically occur. Both are extremely complex. Investigations of the nature of emotions are complicated by the fact that emotions are multifaceted while investigations of the conditions under which they occur are complicated by the fact that they involve cognitive processes that are inaccessible to consciousness.

What are emotions?

From the viewpoint of the person experiencing the emotion, the most obvious feature is a strong feeling that is located in the body. Our stomachs churn, we find tears in our eyes or smiles on our lips, and, in some extreme states, we lose control of sphincter muscles, resulting in wetting or soiling ourselves. If you asked Alan about his anger, he would probably tell you that he felt his stomach churn, his face get hot and his muscles tense. A second subjective feature is a loss of voluntary action; we want to act in one way but find ourselves acting in another. Alan probably doesn't want to hit his wife, but his anger is associated with an overwhelming desire to do so. From the viewpoint of an outsider, emotions are associated with signals about the state of the person experiencing the emotion; they are associated with changes in posture and facial expression, and may be linked to changes in speech pattern and to olfactory cues (since people often sweat a lot when undergoing certain emotions). You know that Alan is getting angry in the session because he looks tense, he is breathing deeply, his pupils have narrowed and he is talking loudly.

Emotion transforms consciousness. Most authors agree that emotion involves evaluation or appraisal of the objects of consciousness while some, such as Sartre (1948; cited in Strongman, 1978), maintain that an emotion becomes the scope of consciousness; during an emotion our consciousness and our emotion are the same thing, hence it is impossible to reflect on a real emotion. When he is not angry, Alan says he loves his wife and wants her to come back but, in his moments of anger, she becomes someone who must be damaged and possibly destroyed. Strongman (1978) suggests that we can view emotion as an altered state of consciousness, akin to the states induced by certain drugs, hypnosis or meditation.

Subjectively, emotions are located in the body and if you ask someone like Alan how they know what they felt at a particular time they would probably refer to bodily feelings. There is a considerable amount of evidence showing that emotions are associated with increased activity in the part of the nervous system that automatically regulates the organs of the body, the *autonomic nervous system*. There are often changes in heart-rate, in the way blood flows to different parts of the body, in the state of the sweat-glands in the skin and in the production of hormones like adrenaline and nor-adrenaline (Strongman, 1996). There are also involuntary changes in facial expression and posture and involuntary movements, such as smiling when happy, lowering one's head and averting one's gaze when embarrassed, and jumping when frightened or startled.

Although autonomic reactions typically accompany emotions, it is unclear whether people are capable of sensing the small changes in heart rate, the activity of the sweat glands, or the temperature of the skin that have been described in laboratory studies. Indeed, there is evidence that people's reports of bodily changes during emotions are much more dependent on what they *expect* to happen than on what is happening in their bodies. For example, Pennebaker (1982; cited in Parkinson, 1988) describes a study in which people were shown slides that depicted sexually arousing or neutral scenes. Sexual arousal is believed to be associated with an increase in skin temperature. While they watched the slides participants were asked to press one button if their skin temperature had risen and another if they experienced stomach contractions. Skin temperature was monitored continuously. The researchers found that participants pressed the button to indicate increased skin temperature when the erotic slides were presented. However, actual skin temperature was unrelated to both whether they had pressed the button and the nature of the slides. It is as if people are largely insensitive to small changes in bodily state but infer that they must be taking place from the fact that they are experiencing an emotion (Parkinson, 1988).

Other studies indicate that people can use this common sense view of emotion to reason in the opposite direction, from bodily state to emotion. For example, Valins (1966; cited in Strongman, 1996) showed erotic pictures to college students and gave them feedback about how their heart rates changed in response to the pictures. Following this, the students were asked to rate how much they liked the pictures. Unbeknownst to the students, the information they were given about their heart rates was false; the experimenters told them their heart rates had risen in response to some pictures but not others, irrespective of what actually happened. However, ratings of liking were linked to the feedback given, rather than actual heart rate.

We also know that people who are incapable of generating or sensing autonomic reactions, because their spinal cords have been damaged, still experience emotions. For example, Bermond *et al.* (1991) interviewed people who had suffered spinal injuries that had paralysed them and cut them off from bodily sensation. They were asked to recall incidents of fear and of anger from before their accidents and from after. Surprisingly, participants reported much stronger emotions following the accident than preceding it.

Autonomic reactions alone do not lead to the experience of emotion (Strongman, 1996). We can evoke autonomic activity by giving people injections of adrenaline, which provoke palpitations, tremors, flushing and increased rate of breathing. Maranon (1924) showed that, when people were given adrenaline injections, they reported experiences that were *like* emotions but were not the same as them. They felt 'as if' they were afraid, but they did not feel fear.

Schachter and Singer (1962) suggested that the flaw in these studies was that people could discount the effects of the drug because they knew that they were the result of the injection. In a very complex experiment they attempted to disguise the effects of the drug, by misinforming participants about what would happen after the injection, and giving them a plausible alternative explanation in terms of an emotional state. They achieved the latter by putting the participants with a confederate of the experimenter who either behaved in a very playful or a very angry way and encouraged the participant to join in. Participants who did not know what effect the drug would have reported themselves as being more euphoric or more angry than those who knew what the drug would do and could, therefore, discount its effect.

In addition to autonomic reactions, to which we may be insensitive, there are changes in facial expression in emotion and a number of authors have suggested that feedback from our expressions plays a significant role in our *experience* of emotion. Indeed, there is some evidence that some of the autonomic changes I have just discussed are actually produced by changes in expression (Levenson *et al.*, 1990; Manstead, 1988; Zajonc *et al.*, 1989).

A number of studies have been carried out in which people have either been coached into adopting facial expressions characteristic of particular emotions, or exposed to emotion provoking events and asked to modify their facial expressions by either exaggerating or minimizing them. According to Manstead (1988) these studies have produced very inconsistent results, with some showing changes in emotional state according to the expression adopted and others showing contrary results. The only reliable finding is that variations in facial expression can modify the strength of emotional reactions elicited by other events. In other words, if something has made you happy, increasing your smile will increase your feeling of happiness while frowning will diminish it. However, smiling by itself will not reliably make you feel happy.

Subjectively, emotions are linked to dispositions to behave in particular ways but psychologists and philosophers are unable to agree about whether these dispositions constitute goal-directed actions in their own right or whether they constitute disruptions of ongoing action (Frijda, 1994). For example, Alan's disposition to behave violently when angry could be considered adaptive, goal-directed behaviour, but, given its effect on his relationship with his wife, it could also be seen as a disruption of ongoing behaviour.

I suspect that the main reason for the disagreement is that most authors are not taking account of the social context in which emotions take place, and of the communicative aspects of emotion. In the context of dealing with the physical world, emotions are associated with behaviours that interfere with attaining our goals. Screaming in anger at a car that won't start doesn't get the car to start; freezing with terror when the car you are driving goes into a skid doesn't prevent the ensuing crash. In the social context, these emotional behaviours may be more adaptive. Screaming in anger about a recalcitrant machine can be highly effective in coercing other people into helping you, especially when you have some sort of power over them. Freezing with terror is a strong signal to other people that they need to take control of a situation. Admittedly, in the case of a skidding car there isn't much they can do apart from bracing themselves for the crash, but there are other situations in which other people can take over. For example, a trainee pilot who freezes at the controls of an aircraft will be relieved of control by the instructor. Emotional behaviour is a statement of what we want of other people and of what they can expect of us if they do or do not comply with our wishes.

Alan's anger has damaged his relationship with his wife but it has changed his situation. He no longer has to deal with his wife's behaviour and he is being left alone to sort out his mood. Had his wife been unable to leave him, her fear of being hit may have led her to change her behaviour in other ways. Alan need not have intended any of these things when he hit his wife for his anger to serve a function.

Divorced from their social context, many aspects of emotion are puzzling but there is now a lot of evidence to indicate that emotion is a social phenomenon. Unless we make intense effort to dissimulate we find that emotions are associated with changes in expression and posture that are highly visible to others. More subtle clues, such as blinking and shifts of gaze also communicate emotion. People tend to be very good at identifying other people's emotional states and can even do it from still pictures of actors imitating emotions (Strongman, 1996).

Not only can we make intellectual judgements about what other people are feeling from their expressions, we also react emotionally ourselves to the expression of emotion in others. Dimburg (1988) reports that showing people pictures of happy or angry faces produces changes in heart rate and the activity of sweat glands. More surprisingly, the pictures also influenced the expressions of the viewers. To investigate this, Dimburg measured the electrical activity in two of the muscles in the face, the corrugator muscle, which is linked to frowning, and the zygomatic muscle, which is linked to smiling. When people viewed happy faces, their zygomatic muscle activity increased but when they viewed angry faces, it was corrugator muscle activity that went up. In the words of the song, when you're smiling, the whole world smiles with you!

Although dramatic, studies like Dimburg's are very artificial. Their value lies in encouraging researchers to investigate the same phenomena in more natural, but much more complex, settings. Wagner and Calam (1988) have studied the linkage between the emotional behaviour of mothers and their children while they were having conversations about three topics: the events of the day, tidying the bedroom (presumably the child's) and spending money. The researchers monitored emotional behaviour, such as facial expression, sweat gland activity and heart rate during these conversations. They found that all three aspects of emotion in one participant could be predicted from the immediately preceding state of the other. In the case of emotional expression, the relationship between the mother's and child's expressions was very simple; the expression adopted by one of the pair at one moment tended to be adopted by the other within a few seconds. In the case of the autonomic reactions, the changes were much more complex. In some cases, increases in the autonomic measure on one of the pair were associated with increases in the other but in other pairs, increases in one member were associated with decreases in the other. Emotional communication takes place rapidly but the patterns of influence in couples are complex. As you sat with Alan, you were picking up his anger and reacting to it.

People often resist displaying emotions and can be quite successful at hiding their feelings. According to Levenson (1994) this does not block the emotional reaction but it may modify it. If people are exposed to a disgusting scene they can reduce their facial expressions (although they find it very difficult to eliminate them entirely) but they cannot reduce their subjective experience of disgust. Furthermore, although blocking the expression of disgust reduces heart-rate, it leads to increased blood pressure. In relationships, one member of a couple may engage in 'stonewalling', in which they block the expression of emotional reactions to their partners. Although this may hide the reaction it is typically associated with negative feeling and increased autonomic activity. Alan cannot deal with his anger by blocking it; he needs strategies for dealing with situations so that he does not become angry.

Emotion is not just a complex pattern of behaviour, it is also an altered state of consciousness. When we are in an emotional state, our experience of the whole world is coloured by the emotion and, for that brief moment, we *are* that emotion because there is no room left in consciousness for anything else. The idea that emotion is a discontinuity in our experience is supported by phenomenological accounts, and fits with our common sense distinction between rational thinking and emotional thinking. When he is not angry, Alan knows that hitting his wife damages his marriage and that he shouldn't do it. In his anger these thoughts get squeezed out or other thoughts dominate them.

The way you feel depends on how you think about things, and the way that you think depends on how you feel. This is not as paradoxical as it first appears, providing we recognize that emotions are complex sequences of thoughts and feelings (Clore, 1994a,b; Ellsworth, 1994) in which a thought provokes a feeling that modifies thinking so as to provoke a new feeling, and so on. A good example of the way that feeling can modify thinking is the fact that feeling happy can make people less inclined to attend to detailed information when making decisions (Clore, 1994a,b). Someone who is not attending to detailed information is less likely to notice things that can provoke other emotions, so their opportunities for new feelings are reduced until something dramatic happens to grab their attention.

When do emotions occur?

Why should Alan get angry when his wife washes a shirt in a way that he doesn't like? Psychologists have tried to develop universal models that account for all occurrences of emotional experience. All agree that emotion depends on the meaning an individual gives to a situation but they differ in how that meaning is acquired. Behavioural models focus on acquiring meaning though association, psychodynamic models on acquiring meaning through symbolism and cognitive models on acquiring meaning through logical reasoning. No single model alone is completely satisfactory, as it is invariably possible to identify circumstances in which a particular model fails but for which one of the other models can readily account.

Behavioural models

Humans, and other animals, are born with an innate repertoire of reactions to certain environmental stimuli. For example, pain may lead to anger or fear, food placed into the mouth of a hungry animal may lead to happiness, while the smell of excrement may provoke disgust. These innate reactions are termed 'unconditioned reflexes' (UCR) and the stimuli that evoke them, 'unconditioned stimuli' (UCS). Emotional reactions to other stimuli are created by pairing previously neutral stimuli, known as 'conditioned stimuli' (CS), with these biologically significant stimuli, in a process known as 'classical' or 'Pavlovian' conditioning. Such pairing leads to the CS evoking a reaction, known as the 'conditioned reflex' (CR), that is usually similar to the UCR (Pavlov, 1927).

The most widely cited example of the application of these ideas to the emergence of human emotion is a study by Watson and Rayner (1920), who carried out what would now be considered a rather cruel study on a young boy called Albert. Albert was shown a white rat and, while Albert was looking at it, the experimenter made a very loud noise behind him. After a number of pairings of the white rat and the loud noise, Albert became very frightened and began to cry every time he was shown the rat.

Its simplicity makes this an exceptionally attractive account of emotion. However, while classical conditioning is a very reliable laboratory phenomenon, it is difficult to obtain evidence for it in our daily lives. The problems are:

1) we use the model to explain our present feelings in terms of events that occurred some time in the past and it is difficult to obtain evidence for those experiences. Without that evidence, classical conditioning accounts of emotion are circular; we explain emotions in terms of conditioning but the only evidence we have for conditioning is the emotional reaction;
2) it is very difficult to identify discrete stimuli in the natural environment, so we are forced to infer the presence of conditioned stimuli from the occurrence of the emotional reaction;
3) classical conditioning is a very fragile phenomenon, even in the laboratory. It takes a number of pairings of CS and UCS to establish it, the interval between the onset of the CS and the

UCS is often critical and the reaction extinguishes unless virtually every CS is followed by a UCS;

4) the model suggests that people should be afraid of all sorts of things, as a result of individual conditioning histories, but most people are afraid of a relatively limited set of objects or situations.

It is rare for people to be frightened of dangerous objects like cars or electricity sockets, yet they are often frightened of safe ones like spiders and non-poisonous snakes. And many people go to the dentist without learning to experience the fear that one would expect from the reliable pairing of dentists with pain. A final problem is that the model mainly deals with the development of fear. It has little to say about other emotions like joy or envy. A number of authors have attempted to deal with the specificity of emotional reactions. Seligman (1971) argued that we are innately prepared to associate particular emotions with particular types of stimuli. We may not be born with an innate fear of snakes, but we are, Seligman argued, born with an innate capacity to *learn* to fear snakes. This argument doesn't get us very far, because our main evidence for an innate capacity to learn to fear snakes is that people are often afraid of them and it doesn't specify how we distinguish an innate capacity to learn from an innate but weak tendency to fear these objects.

A more sophisticated solution relies on the observation that extensive prior exposure to potential conditioned stimuli reduces the ease with which we can acquire conditioned reflexes to them. We are unlikely to form reactions to very familiar stimuli, which might explain why people learn to be afraid of objects of which they have little experience, like snakes, but not of objects with which they have a lot, such as cars. According to Davey (1989) it explains why only some people are afraid of the dentist. Davey surveyed students who had recently been to the dentist and asked them when they first visited the dentist, when they first experienced real pain at the dentist and how much they feared dentistry. He found that people who feared the dentist the most had the shortest interval between starting to visit the dentist and having a painful experience. Those who feared dentists the least had the longest interval between starting visits and experiencing pain.

Undoubtedly, there is good evidence that classical conditioning can contribute to extending the range of conditions in which we experience emotions and where there are clearly identifiable conditioned and unconditioned stimuli, such as lightning flashes reliably preceding loud thunder claps, it may well constitute an adequate account of emotion. However, in most other situations, such as

Alan's anger towards his wife, there is little independent evidence for conditioning processes.

Psychodynamic models

Desire is the root of emotion in psychoanalytic theories (Brown, 1964; Freud, 1943; Klein, 1986; Strongman, 1996). Developing children experience unconscious desires to experience specific forms of bodily stimulation, or to possess specific objects. The unfettered satisfaction of these desires leads to happiness while their frustration occasions a range of negative emotions. The other significant feature of this approach is that one's relationship with the world is symbolic rather than physical, so that objects can stand in for each other in relation to desires.

For example, Freud (1943; see also Brown, 1964) argued that children pass through a series of developmental stages in which their desire is focused on stimulation of particular parts of the body surface, starting with the mouth, moving to the anus and finally to the genitals. Satisfaction of these desires may be frustrated by a number of factors, including the child's lack of grasp of reality, the behaviour of the child's parents, and the discovery that the satisfaction of one desire might jeopardize the satisfaction of others.

Desire itself is unconscious and has no knowledge of the outside world. Freud referred to this unconscious desire as the *id*. Satisfaction of desire is, therefore, initially a very hit or miss affair. As the child ages, it develops a sense of reality and of its own existence in a real world. This gives rise to a component of the mind known as the *ego*. Finally, the ego's attempts at reconciling the desires of the id with the constraints of the external world leads to internalization of socially sanctioned rules and prohibitions, creating the *superego*. Early in life, desires are frustrated because of the child's inability to act effectively or because of the actions of parents. Later, satisfaction of desire is limited because of internally imposed restraints, as the ego and superego limit its expression.

Frustration of desire leads to the energy associated with that desire being channelled into other objects that are symbolically related to the original. For example, someone frustrated at the oral stage may get pleasure and happiness by engaging in oral activities that are not related to eating, such as speaking sarcastically. Defence mechanisms constitute more complex symbolic transformations of the original desire that disguise its 'true' origin and allow it expression while limiting anxiety, which arises when desire from the id starts to overwhelm the ego.

According to the Freudian view, fear and anxiety are products of desire, rather than being direct reactions to external events. For example, paranoid fear is seen as having its origins in homosexual desire which males are unable to express directly, so they transform desire into hatred. Hatred of others is also difficult to express directly, so it is projected onto other males and is seen as coming from the outside world rather than from the individual.

In Freud's model there is no distinction in the young child's mind between the internal and external world. In contrast, 'object-relations' theorists like Klein (1986) argue that, from the earliest stage, the child can relate to objects in the outside world. Early in development the primary object is the mother's breast which can be both a focus of satisfaction and happiness, and frustration, anger and hatred. Satisfaction and happiness are manifestations of a life instinct while frustration and anger are manifestations of a death instinct.

Initially the child does not realize that these reactions are being addressed to the same object. When that realization dawns, the child experiences a strong emotional reaction as it contemplates the fact that it has been willing the destruction of the very same object that has been nurturing it. This leads the child into the 'depressive position'. A number of strategies are available to resolve the depressive position and emotional reactions later in life reflect how the child has dealt with this initial challenge. Like Freud, Klein maintains that these strategies include a series of defence mechanisms that involve symbolic transformations of desire and the objects of desire.

According to most psychodynamic models, as a child develops its desires become invested in particular objects or situations and those investments persist into adulthood so the foundations for adult emotional patterns are laid in childhood. In social interactions, emotional reactions to other people may reflect 'transference' of emotional reactions to people who were significant in childhood. This is considered to be a particularly important process in therapy, with clients transferring feelings from their parents (for example) onto the therapist and therapists transferring their feelings from other relationships onto the client (in 'counter-transference).

Psychodynamic models are particularly powerful in accounting for emotions that occur without obvious external eliciting stimuli and for the fact that fears are often directed to objects or situations that are, in fact, safe. For example, one may be fearful of non-poisonous snakes because they symbolically represent the penis, and desire for the penis may be a source of anxiety. The power of psychodynamic models stems from the fact that our emotions are mediated by unconscious symbolic transformations but this is also their weakness, because it is difficult to obtain independent evidence for these transformations.

Both Freud and Klein recognized a fundamental desire to destroy and explained much of human unhappiness in terms of our attempts to deal with it. Alan's anger towards his wife could be viewed as the result of this innate desire being channelled onto an inappropriate object, his wife, possibly because he reacts to his wife as the symbolic representation of somebody whom he wished to destroy earlier in his life.

Cognitive models

There are as many cognitive theories as there are authorities writing about the cognitive bases of emotion but there are a number of common themes that run through them. The over-riding principle is that emotional reactions are determined by the meaning of situations, rather than their physical properties (Strongman, 1996). Meanings, in turn, are related to beliefs which are capable of being stated verbally and which can be related logically to other beliefs held by the individual. For example, when faced with an examination one individual might think: all examinations are easy; this is an examination, hence I will succeed; success is good hence I will be good; being good leads to praise, hence I will be praised. A second person facing the same examination might think: I fail all examinations; this is an examination, hence I will fail in this situation; failure is bad; being bad leads to punishment hence I will be punished. Their emotional reactions will derive from the conclusions they draw, one expecting praise and the other punishment.

The problem raised by cognitive models is why certain meanings give rise to feelings. A number of factors seem to be important:

1) the importance of the situation to the person; something must be at stake for someone to experience an emotion (Lazarus, 1994; Oatley, 1992; Scherer, 1994a,b; Strongman, 1996);
2) comparison; emotions may arise from a contrast between what is currently happening and what was expected to happen (Ellsworth, 1994; Frijda, 1986; Oatley, 1992; Scherer, 1994);
3) ability to cope with a situation.

For example, in Oatley's formulation, emotion arises when an event occurs that was not foreseen by the current plan of action and with which the current plan cannot deal. The same authors have attempted to tell us what types of emotion belong in particular settings. Oatley (1992), for example, tells us that 'happiness' occurs when goals are being reached while 'sadness' occurs when we fail to achieve a goal or the possibility of achieving a goal is lost. However, most of their accounts are common sense. It is notable that Alan's anger occurs when things have not worked out as he has expected them to and he is having difficulty coping with the situation because he is feeling low.

The main advantage of cognitive models is that they link emotional experience to what the person is currently thinking. They do not, therefore, force us to propose unverifiable histories for clients to explain why they feel as they do. They also suggest we can intervene with emotions by helping people change what they believe. Nevertheless, cognitive models have their problems. None can cope with the degree of emotional involvement generated by artistic productions like drama and music (Ellsworth, 1994). In contrast, psychodynamic models account for these experiences very well.

Cognitive models also exhibit a degree of circularity, in that our emotional reactions often tell us what is important to us in the first place and it may be an emotion itself that interferes with a current plan. Although they do not require us to attribute histories to people, they still require us to attribute beliefs to them. So long as we can check these beliefs out against what people tell us, this isn't a problem, but as Izard (1994) suggests, emotion may be the result of relating to the environment in ways that cannot be captured verbally and which are beyond the competence of cognitive psychologists. If this is the case, then attributing beliefs to explain emotions may be as inappropriate as attributing conditioning histories or desires and defence mechanisms. In the moment of his anger, Alan may have moved out of the world of rational cognition into a world in which meanings make no logical sense.

How Can I Use This Information As a Counsellor?

Psychologists have catalogued some of the important features of emotion but are some way off providing a comprehensive account. There are many things we have yet to learn about emotion, and counselling practice should respect that ignorance. That does not mean that we cannot deal in emotional issues – that would be absurd – but it does mean that we should be modest in our claims of expertise and respectful of our clients' accounts of their experiences. We simply do not know enough to be able to tell our clients what they 'really' feel or why they 'really' feel those things. In the absence of a convincing and comprehensive theory of emotion we should be particularly careful about viewing all emotion through a single theoretical lens, as that will lead to distortion.

On the positive side, we have learned a lot about the factors that influence emotional experience. Although research on people with spinal injuries indicates that visceral reactions are not necessary for emotion, people tend to interpret bodily reactions as having emotional significance unless they are given alternative explanations. This suggests that one way of altering emotional experiences is to provide clients with alternative explanations for their bodily reactions, which is what cognitive behaviour therapists do when working with people experiencing panic attacks.

One of the most surprising findings is that the relationship between reported emotion and reported bodily reactions is a two way street; people attribute emotion to themselves on the basis of their bodily reactions (or, more correctly, what they believe their bodily reactions to be) and attribute bodily reactions on the basis of how they describe their emotional states. This may thwart attempts at behavioural analysis, in which we try to get clients to talk about their bodily reactions independently of the label they have just used to describe their feelings. If you ask someone who says they are fearful to describe their bodily state, what they tell you may simply reflect the bodily reactions they believe belong with fear.

When working with clients who experience strong emotions the focus should be on identifying and modifying the conditions under which the emotions occur, rather than trying to enable clients to deal with feelings once they have arisen. Emotional expression can vary the intensity of emotional experience but it cannot transform it. If you smile when you are happy, you are likely to feel happier than when you frown, but if you smile when you are angry you will not feel happy, simply less angry. Moreover, studies of 'stonewalling', in which people block the expression of negative emotions suggest that the strategy backfires, leaving the individual feeling worse than they would otherwise have felt.

A further reason for believing that it is more effective to modify the circumstances that lead to emotion, rather than the emotion itself, is that all of the evidence suggests that emotions are such all-encompassing states of consciousness that it is impossible to intervene in them once they have started.

Emotion is a social phenomenon; the emotional state of one individual can influence the state of another. Difficulties experienced by clients may be exacerbated because people around them are echoing back their emotional states, unhappy people might perpetuate their own unhappiness by inducing the same state in people they meet. Our clients do not exist in isolation; their emotions may be echoes of the feelings of other people, rather than reflecting their own belief systems. Clients and counsellors can induce emotions in each other that may have little to do with the verbal content of the session. An unhappy counsellor may produce an unhappy client, and *vice versa*.

Changing the meaning of situations changes their emotional impact. However, rather than restricting ourselves to a single account of how meaning is acquired or changed, it makes more sense to recognize that meaning can be acquired in a number of ways and may need to be modified in different ways. Placing meaning, rather than the processes whereby meaning is acquired, at the heart of emotion favours *technical* eclecticism in dealing with emotional issues, rather than adherence to a single theory. It also suggests that we should look more widely than conventional theories of personality for our ideas, and that a study of the literary and dramatic devices whereby meaning is communicated and changed would repay the counsellor.

Section summary

- We know very little about emotion. Listen to your clients rather than relying on theory.

- People use a variety of cues, including their bodily state, to *attribute* emotions to themselves. We can help people change their feelings by helping them reinterpret these cues.

- When carrying out behavioural analyses, remember that people can attribute bodily states to themselves on the basis of the emotion they believe they are experiencing.

- It is difficult to modify emotions once they have started. It is best to focus on helping people avoid damaging emotional states.

- Emotion is a social phenomenon. A client's low mood might reflect the low mood of someone important to them, including you, the counsellor.

- Changing the meaning of situations changes our emotional reactions to them. Many interventions help achieve this.

Mood

Alan says that his anger is influenced by his mood, so that it only occurs when he feels low. Mood is very much the poor relation in the study of feelings, being overshadowed by its much more glamorous sibling, emotion. Emotions are much more dramatic, both to those experiencing them and those interacting with the emotional individual, and it is easy to equate drama with importance. Moods are also much more difficult to study in the laboratory. Psychologists have developed all sorts of ways of inducing emotion (usually fear) under quite precise experimental control but they haven't achieved the same control over mood (Strongman, 1996; Westermann *et al.*, 1996). This is a pity, because mood is much more pervasive and probably has a greater impact on our actions than individual emotions.

Structurally, moods are like emotions in that they embody feelings, thoughts and behavioural dispositions. They differ in their eliciting conditions. Indeed, in many instances, the hallmark of mood is the *absence* of eliciting conditions and the lack of obvious relationship to what is happening outside of the individual. In normal social interaction, we attribute moods to other people precisely because they persistently act in ways that either bear no relationship to what is happening to them or are contrary to the way that we would expect someone to act in a particular situation. Someone who is short-tempered with everyone they meet, irrespective of the content of the interaction, is said to be in a bad mood. Someone who is nice to everyone they meet and conciliatory when people do things that are offensive, is said to be in a good mood.

Mood can be changed both physically and psychologically. Giving people drugs that alter the chemistry of the brain reliably alters mood and many people use drugs like alcohol recreationally for this effect (Green and Suls, 1996; Johnson *et al.*, 1996; Westermann *et al.*, 1996). It has recently been shown that drugs that increase the amount of a substance called serotonin in the brain are effective in making people less irritable (Coccaro *et al.*, 1992; Kavoussi *et al.*, 1994; Kyes *et al.*, 1995).

Drugs not only affect mood when people take them, they can affect it when people *stop* taking them. When people stop long-term use of sedative drugs like alcohol or tranquillizers they often experience quite intense anxiety and depressed mood (Michelini *et al.*, 1996). Since these are often the reason why they have used the drugs in the first place, the temptation is to suppress these experiences by resuming drug use. Another physical way of influencing mood is through diet. According to Lloyd *et al.* (1996), people have better moods following low-fat/high-carbohydrate breakfasts than after breakfasts that have a higher ratio of fat to carbohydrate.

Psychological factors are also important and psychologists have explored a range of interventions to alter mood. Westermann *et al.* (1996) have reviewed all of the techniques used to induce mood in the laboratory and have found that presenting people with films or stories is the best way of changing their moods.

It is reasonable to suppose that some spontaneous variations in mood are the result of physical changes in the individual (Manki *et al.*, 1996) while others are the result of their experiences. This idea is supported by Wefelmeyer *et al.* (1996), who studied mood variations in melancholic patients and compared them with non-melancholic controls. Both groups experienced the same degree of mood change during the course of a day but the melancholic patients were unable to attribute the changes to any external cause while the controls could link their moods to specific incidents. Does Alan get to feel low because of things that are happening to him, such as having to resist the attractions of his colleague, or do they arise spontaneously?

Even if moods are triggered by specific events, they outlast them so that the mood ceases to be congruent with the immediate circumstances of the individual. Why are moods so durable? Explaining the durability of moods is not a particular problem if they are the result of changes in the functional state of the nervous system but it is a problem if mood is a result of psychological factors alone. Why should some situations lead to short-term experiences that we call 'emotions' while others lead to long-term changes that we call 'moods'?

One possibility is that the individual gets locked into a vicious or virtuous circle of self-reinforcing emotion. The idea, which forms the basis of 'cognitive behaviourism', is that emotions lead to thoughts that generate more of the same type of emotion, thus prolonging the experience and making it largely independent of what is happening around the person concerned. For example, as will be discussed in the section on memory, negative emotions lead to the recall of negative events that precipitate further negative feelings.

There is a considerable amount of evidence that shows that your mood affects the way that you think about things. However, the relationship between mood and thought is complex and it would be wrong to think that negative moods are associated with irrational thinking while positive moods are associated with rational thought. For example, Oaksford *et al.* (1996) studied the effects of induced mood on performance on reasoning tasks. On one task, both positive and negative mood made participants *less* logical than controls while on a second task it was the people with positive moods who performed less well. Being in a good mood often makes people less sensitive to relevant information, unless the importance of the information is pointed out to them (Queller *et al.*, 1996). Perhaps Alan gets angry when his mood is low because it is only then that he really attends to his wife's behaviour! Mood seems to interfere with logical thinking for two separate reasons. One is that it occupies mental capacity, so that the person has less to devote to other demands (Oaksford *et al.*, 1996), the other is that moods encourage mood-specific ways of thinking (Bless *et al.*, 1996). According to Bless *et al.*, happy people make use of general knowledge of situations while sad people tend to attend to specific information. If you are told a story while you are happy and asked to repeat it to someone, you are likely to base your answer on your general knowledge of the type of situation involved, even if it means making mistakes. If you are sad, you are likely to recall the specific story.

How Can I Use This Information As a Counsellor?

Although mood can change without any apparent cause it is possible for clients to do things to influence their moods. Mood is affected both by the physical state of the individual, particularly the levels of certain chemicals in their brains, and by their thoughts and it may be addressed at both levels by the counsellor. The fact that mood can be influenced by physical factors means that the counsellor should bear these in mind when working with mood problems. For example, a depressed or anxious client may be self-medicating with a legally sanctioned drug like alcohol and unwittingly inducing changes in the nervous system that are associated with lowered mood during withdrawal. The possibility that a client is using illegal drugs to alter mood, and that lowered mood is an unintended side-effect, should also be considered.

In some cases counsellors may want to take advantage of the mood altering effects of drugs to assist clients through particularly serious episodes of depression or anxiety. In the United Kingdom this would require enlisting the support of a medical practitioner. Please note that, in advocating the use of prescribed drugs, I am not suggesting that drugs alone are sufficient to help the client, nor am I claiming that the causes of lowered mood are necessarily physical. All I am suggesting is that we act pragmatically and take advantage, where appropriate, of the mood enhancing effects of drugs to assist us in therapy. A client whose mood is so depressed that they cannot see any hope for the future is unlikely to be motivated to engage in therapy anyway.

Psychological factors also influence mood, so mood problems experienced by our clients may be linked to events and their interpretations of them. Given the power of stories to create mood, the stories that our clients tell about their lives are likely to have a significant impact on their moods. This is why it is important to attend to clients' stories about their lives rather than trying to establish an accurate historical record of events. Most counselling practice recognizes that events that are incorporated into autobiographical stories are likely to influence mood long after they have taken place and changes in mood may take place that are unrelated to the immediate circumstances of the client. The focus on clients' interpretations and stories makes good psychological sense.

Mood can be changed by exposing clients to experiences like listening to stories, watching movies and listening to music. This means that counsellors have an armoury of non-physical means of helping clients change their moods. Movies and music are likely to have fairly short-term effects but may be useful in helping clients achieve a frame of mind that facilitates therapy. Stories are likely to have a much more enduring impact because the client can retell them. Stories are most likely to engage the client if they are about them or relate to them. Most forms of counselling incorporate story telling, although different models give the stories different names, such as 'interpretations' or 'reframes'. Recently, therapists like White and his collaborators (Epston and White, 1992) have taken this process further and based their approach on explicitly providing clients with new stories for old experiences.

The mood-inducing effects of stories can work in two directions and there is no reason to expect counsellors to be free from the depressing impact of some of their clients' narratives. This is a problem for both counsellor and client. It is a problem for the counsellor as the mood changes may be unpleasant. It is a problem for the client because:

1) the cognitive consequences of the mood changes may interfere with the performance of the counsellor; and
2) the counsellor may communicate their mood back to the client, thus inducing a vicious circle.

Some of these effects can be mitigated by good training and by recognizing what is happening when listening to clients, but supervision is also important in helping counsellors deal with the emotional impact of what their clients tell them.

Mood affects how people think about things and most of the evidence suggests that both positive and negative moods interfere with rational thinking. Part of the irrationality is a result of the way mood reduces mental capacity and part the fact that happy people are often inattentive to detail and rely on general schemes for their understanding of situations. Interventions that require clients to think rationally are unlikely to work particularly well when clients are either elated or depressed and should either be avoided altogether under these conditions or introduced very carefully to ensure understanding.

Depressed people are not less logical than others. What they either lack, or fail to use, are what I referred to in an earlier chapter as 'heuristics' that substitute for logical thinking. An heuristic is a rule of thumb for dealing with a situation that may not be particularly logical but has worked in the past for people. For example, someone might apply the rule of being pleasant to everyone and continuing to be pleasant until the other person behaves unpleasantly. Another person might apply the rule of 'get your retaliation in first'. Clients with depressed moods may be trying too hard to think logically and the goal of therapy may be to enable them to loosen the bonds of reason and rely more on socially productive heuristics.

Section summary

- Mood can be rapidly changed by the use of drugs. Clients may be self-medicating to alleviate mood, and counsellors should consider the ethical implications of whether to recommend that clients obtain prescription mood enhancing drugs.

- Clients may modify their moods by the stories they tell themselves about their lives. Mood may reflect rehearsal of stories about the past more than current experience.

- Mood can be altered by telling people stories. Some effective modern practice centres on getting clients to develop new stories about their own lives that they can tell themselves.

- Counsellors are unlikely to be exempt from the mood inducing effects of their clients' stories. A depressing story may well produce a depressed counsellor.

- People do not think rationally in extreme mood states. Cognitive interventions may not be very effective in very depressed or very happy clients.

- Lowered mood is often associated with thinking too much. Challenging the rationality of depressed clients may not always be effective.

Desire

'Desire' is a delightfully old-fashioned word that used to be banished from psychology altogether but is now making a comeback (Booth *et al.*, 1994; Legg, 1994). It refers to the urge to engage in particular actions with particular objects, such as eating a particular type of food, having sexual relations with a particular person or injecting a particular drug. Like emotion, desire narrows our field of attention so that we focus on the object of our desire and our thoughts and actions become recruited into pursuing that object. Like emotion, desire is involuntary; we cannot make ourselves want things nor can we make ourselves not want them. Alan reports that he has lost sexual desire for his wife but has retained it for a colleague. He is aware that this has damaged his marriage but he says that he is unable to do anything about it.

Psychologists used to object to the notion of 'desire' because they didn't like the idea of current actions being caused by something that is going to occur in the future, but they have abandoned that objection now that they recognize that it is the *idea* of the object that energizes our action, not our future contact with it. The problem is to explain how the ideas of certain objects become suffused with the impetus to possess or ingest them.

Some desires may have a fairly simple explanation. In normal circumstances our desires are for objects that have significance for our survival or reproductive effectiveness. However, it looks as if these mechanisms can be hijacked by activities like drug-taking, so that we form desires for objects that damage us and researchers have suggested that we can use our knowledge of how we form desires for unnatural substances, like heroin, to explain how we can form desires for natural substances like foods.

One of the most remarkable discoveries of recent years is that addictive drugs like heroin and cocaine all activate a common system in the brain. Even more remarkable is the discovery that giving food to a hungry animal will activate the same pathway. This suggests that the desire to use drugs may be the result of the drugs 'fooling' the brain into reacting as if a biologically significant event, such as eating nutritious food or having sex, has just taken place. Direct stimulation of these systems in humans often leads to reports of experiencing pleasure or excitement (Wise, 1994). Desire for particular objects results from learning about the association between contact with the object and the activation of this brain system.

Whether or not contact with an object will activate this system and lead to desire often depends on the current bodily state of the individual. For example, Booth and his colleagues (Booth *et al.*, 1994) have shown that people develop the desire for distinctively flavoured food if the person is deprived of food at the time they eat. In males, the desire for sexual contact is significantly reduced following ejaculation (Levin, 1994). Bodily state sets the scene for the development of desire but it is not always enough. Desire for food, for example, not only requires you to be hungry but also requires the food you have eaten to satisfy significantly your need for food. Giving hungry people a high calorie food like chocolate will generate a desire for it but giving them low calorie foods like lettuce will not create a desire for salad.

Desire does not always depend on bodily state, however. In some instances people form the desire for activities like gambling which are not linked to the state of the body but which can yield a strong thrill linked to a particular activity or setting (Carroll and Huxley, 1994). Much of the research has focused on desire for the presence of biologically significant objects but we can also form desires for the absence of objects that cause us pain or distress. According to Gray (1975), cues that are associated with the termination of unpleasant events like electric shocks become as highly desired as those associated with the occurrence of pleasant events.

This approach can explain how we form desires for things that we have experienced, but it doesn't explain how we desire things that we have not yet 'consumed'. The best example is sexual desire. Our client, Alan, has reported a very common experience, that he has developed a strong sexual desire for a person with whom he has not yet had sex and, at the same time, lost his desire for someone with whom he has had sex, his wife.

Over the course of our lives we develop the potential to desire a huge range of objects. Why, then, do we not desire them all at the same time? Desire is evoked by cues associated with prior satisfaction of the desire. Some of the cues will be found in the environment, such as the sight of food, but others, such as the amount of food in the gut, are located in the body.

Since humans can replace their physical environment with thoughts about it, thoughts can also act as cues that generate desire. If you tend to drink in pubs/bars, the desire to drink will be generated by entering them. If you think about entering a pub/bar, you may also develop the desire to drink. Alan's colleague might offer the cues that generate sexual desire in males, and these might be augmented by Alan's thoughts and his hormonal state.

If desire comes about through learning the link between objects and their impact on your nervous system, then desires can be lost as a result of the same processes. If someone is repeatedly exposed to the object of their desire but not allowed to satisfy it, the desire for that object should diminish. We know from Pavlov's work that if exposure to the sight of food is followed shortly by the opportunity to eat it, a set of reflexes (known as the 'cephalic phase reflexes') that enhance the palatability of the food become linked to the sight of it. One of the components of the cephalic phase reflex is the release of the hormone insulin and the reduction in blood sugar evoked by insulin release reliably induces hunger (Campfield *et al.*,

1990). Consequently, repeated exposure to the sight of food before eating it confers appetite generating properties on the food. If the same organism is subsequently exposed to the sight of food alone, these reflexes diminish (Pavlov, 1927), so the appetite generating properties of the sight of food are lost.

How Can I Use This Information As a Counsellor?

Talking about desire may be of some benefit, by altering the symbolic significance of objects so that they are no longer linked, in the clients' minds, with other objects of desire. Talking might also influence the motivation of the client to experiment with changes in their relationships with the objects that they desire. However, the desire for objects builds up through experience with them and it will be very difficult to help clients change their desires without direct experience.

The desire for objects is best reduced by repeated exposure to them without allowing the client to experience their normal consequences. For example, the model suggests that the most effective way to deal with drug addiction would be to permit the addict to experience every aspect of their normal drug-taking situation while blocking the impact of the drug on the nervous system. The desire for specific foods will be best dealt with by exposing people to their sight, smell and taste while preventing the usual nutritional consequences. In some cases this might be very easily arranged. For example, if someone has a craving for crisps but only ever eats crisps when they are very hungry, the desire for crisps may be diminished by encouraging the client to eat them after meals, when their stomachs are full and blood glucose levels high.

Straightforward avoidance strategies are likely to be ineffective, as the desire will return as soon as the individual re-establishes contact with the cues that usually precipitate the desire. Institution based withdrawal procedures, be they 'detox' clinics for drug addicts or 'health farms' for the overweight, are likely to be extremely effective in reducing desire so long as the person remains within that setting but there will be major problems with generalization to the normal environment.

When working with anorexic patients counsellors should be aware of the possibility that the cephalic phase reflexes that ensure the palatability of food have been lost in these clients, hence many foods will be unpalatable to them. This is because in anorexia, unlike in conditions of famine, individuals are constantly exposed to food and food cues but do not eat. Consequently, when anorexic clients say that they do not like food, they may be telling the truth. Part of the task of working with this group of clients will be restore the palatability of food, which will be a slow and difficult process.

Section summary

- Talking about desire can change the meaning of situations and encourage clients to experiment with change.

- Desires are most likely to change when clients can experience new ways of relating to their objects of desire.

- Desire is most likely to be reduced if the client can experience the object of desire without experiencing the usual outcomes.

- Avoidance strategies are unhelpful because they do not prepare people for subsequent encounters with their objects of desire.

- Treatment of anorexia nervosa may be complicated by the fact that patients have 'extinguished' their desire for food and they may have to learn to eat to recover fully.

Chapter Summary

Feelings hold powerful sway over our actions, so they are central to what we do in counselling. Much of what we do is dictated by how we currently feel and our other actions are guided by how we anticipate we will feel in the future. Many of the issues that clients bring to counselling stem from their feelings and some of the things that we find ourselves doing as counsellors are likely to be influenced by how we feel about ourselves and our clients.

We know less about feelings than we think and we should, therefore, be cautious about how we interpret our clients' descriptions of their feelings. For example, some approaches encourage us to distinguish between the thinking, feeling and doing aspects of emotion but recent research has cast doubt on this simple separation. For example, if you think you are experiencing a particular emotion, you will attribute bodily reactions even if they are not taking place. Although we use the term 'feelings', bodily reactions play a relatively minor role in emotions and moods. Much more important are our dispositions to interpret events and act in particular ways.

Emotions and moods make sense, but only in a social context, and you need to take account of their role in the social relationships of the client when trying to understand them. Much emotional behaviour seems to be directed at manipulating other people and emotional reactions usually convey messages about what is wanted and what the consequences of compliance or non-compliance will be. Problems arise when there is a conflict between the short-term and long-term consequences of emotional displays.

Feelings are directed at particular objects and situations, so we have to learn to experience and display them. There is no single convincing explanation of how we learn to display feelings and I see no need to force a single explanation onto the diversity of feelings that we experience. The fact that 'traumatic conditioning' may make a good explanation for fear of thunderstorms, or of dentists, does not mean that it has to be a good explanation of fear of snakes.

Desire is influenced by experiencing the consequences of consummatory behaviour like eating, sexual behaviour or ingesting drugs. This suggests that the most powerful way of helping people change their objects of desire is to alter those consequences by encouraging consumption in other contexts in which those consequences do not occur. Abs(tin)ence makes the heart grow fonder and familiarity breeds contempt!

4

Thinking and Deciding

Peter is a 21-year-old student in the final year of his degree course. He has been referred to you because he is finding it difficult to make himself work. He tells you that it is because he doesn't know what he wants to do after he graduates. How does Peter decide what he wants to do? How do you decide how to help Peter decide?

Clients and counsellors face choices like these all the time. Many clients are prompted to come to counselling because their plans and decisions have not worked out as they intended, or their lives have stalled because they are unable to make crucial decisions. Clients often know that they have been helped because they find that they are making more appropriate decisions that lead to the outcomes they expect.

Making good decisions is difficult. It often requires us to handle very large amounts of information very quickly, to act when we lack some of the information necessary for a 'logical' decision, and to use decision-making rules that are sometimes counter-intuitive. Humans have to, and are able to, make good decisions in circumstances in which the world's best computers would fail at the same task, and it is a marvel that so many people manage to make satisfactory decisions every day.

One way to simplify the process is to break it down into three stages and work on each stage separately. Most of us make decisions too quickly to go through separate stages every time we make a decision, but this approach is useful when people, like Peter, are having difficulties with making decisions. The three stages are:

1) establishing the goals of your decisions;
2) deciding on the facts on which you can rely when making the decision;
3) deciding what is the best thing to do, given the goals and the facts you have decided are true.

In practice it is difficult to maintain a watertight division between these stages because the conclusions we draw at a later stage may lead us to alter or elaborate those we draw at an earlier one. Deciding what is true may influence conclusions about what you value and deciding what to do may affect your conclusions about goals and what you consider true. A good decision maker will take advantage of those insights and re-enter the loop, armed with the new knowledge, and may go through the loop a number of times before making a final decision.

Establishing Goals

Probably the hardest part of making good decisions is working out what the goals involved are. The simplest strategy appears to be asking people what they 'really' want in life. This would be excellent if we carried around in our heads a filing cabinet full of entries labelled 'goals,' so that all we needed to do was to open the cabinet and inspect the files. However, most of us are like Peter and find it difficult to say what we 'really' want in life, so either the entries in the filing cabinet are very disorganized or the filing cabinet does not exist. If we don't have neat files listing our goals in life, how do we then decide what we want?

In many instances we may focus on making the small, manageable, decisions, letting the big ones take care of themselves. As we saw in *Chapter 2*, statements we make about psychological characteristics tend to be *attributions* rather than *descriptions* and we make attributions on the basis of currently available evidence, rather than looking deeply into our souls or the souls of others (Baron and Byrne, 1997; Baron, 1994). This means reviewing the decisions we have made in the past to see whether there are any consistent trends in either the way we resolve issues or the ways that we have reacted to the outcomes of earlier decisions, to identify what our long-term goals are. For example, if someone is very successful at work but their private life is chaotic or barren, they may decide that their principal goal is success because that is the only goal that makes sense of what has happened to them so far. Establishing personal goals can be achieved through a 'bootstrapping' procedure in which you make a series of decisions, review those decisions for common themes, and identify those themes as personal goals. Perhaps you could start by reviewing Peter's past decisions, to see which have been successful and which have led to outcomes he has enjoyed.

Focusing on short-term issues rather than working towards large-scale, long-term goals can be a good strategy under certain conditions. It makes sense when the future is uncertain and when you have no direct experience of that for which you are aiming. The world is an uncertain place and it would be unwise to strive for goals which may be inappropriate when we get in position to attain them. There is little point in 16-year-olds preparing themselves for occupations that are not going to be around when they are old enough to be eligible for them, or if something better may come along. Saving money for the future makes good sense so long as the money is going to retain its value and you are going to be there to spend it. However, the money you save might lose its value, either through inflation or your sudden acquisition of immense wealth, or you might die before you get to spend it (Baron, 1994).

Long-term goals are rarely things we have experienced, so we are taking a gamble on them turning out to be as desirable as we think they will be. On the other hand, when we look at the near future, we are usually dealing with things that are similar to things we have already experienced. When he chose his university courses Peter could base his decision on experiences at school, but he has no experience of the sort of work he could do upon graduating on which to base subsequent career choices.

Making decisions based on short-term goals and allowing long-term goals to take care of themselves is a useful rule of thumb (known technically as a 'heuristic') for decision-making, but it can lead to problems as people discover that their present circumstances are dictated by decisions that they made in the past. To take an extreme example, the decision to use heroin when you are 18 and unemployed may be rational if your primary goals are to have a good time, be like your mates and forget the future (Alexander and Hadaway, 1982). However, when such people get older they often regret the decisions made by their younger selves as they discover that they are committed to a criminal life-style to provide the money to maintain their habit, that they have destroyed the circulatory system in the arm in which they habitually inject, and that they have contracted a life-threatening disease through using infected kit. Other people seem to find themselves in what they consider dead-end jobs or marriages through a similar process of focusing on short-term goals, a state summed up musically by the singer Marianne Faithful in her 1979 recording, 'The Ballad of Lucy Jordan' who, 'At the age of thirty-seven . . . realized she'd never ride through Paris in a sports-car with the warm wind in her hair'.

Goal setting is improved if you distinguish between final goals and sub-goals, which are the targets we have to attain before we can attain our main goal (Baron, 1994). Peter can see that getting his degree is a sub-goal, rather than an end in itself, that can enable him to reach his final goal but, since he doesn't know what that final goal is, he cannot see whether his degree is relevant. What he wants to be when he graduates could be a final goal or it could, itself, be a sub-goal. Some people just want to be painters or doctors and believe that all of life's satisfactions will stem from achieving that goal. For others, being a painter or a doctor is a vehicle for achieving other goals, such as the acclaim of an audience, or a sense of doing something that few other people can do. Peter needs to clarify whether what he does on graduating is going to define him for the rest of his life, or whether it is a stepping stone on the way to other goals. His overall goal in life might be nebulous and hard to define and he might only find out what it is by experimenting with different occupations and life-styles.

After a few sessions, Peter may have concluded that it is his overall values that are important, not what he does on graduating and that he should concentrate on identifying the sub-goals he needs to attain to ensure that he lives a life that conforms to those values. Identifying sub-goals is a problem-solving activity that involves breaking down complex tasks into simpler, manageable components and working out the sequence in which those components need to be executed.

Thanks to your skill, Peter may have recognized that he doesn't actually want to work at all, he wants to travel and meet people. This, however, requires money, so his first challenge is to work out how he can acquire enough money to travel. 'Enough money to travel' itself has to be broken down, because 'enough' depends on the style in which he wishes to live and what he is prepared to do when he gets somewhere. If Peter's idea of travel is first-class seats, five-star hotels and a life of indolence wherever he goes, then he is going to need a lot more money than if he is prepared to travel tourist class, live in hostels and work to earn his keep on arrival. Working out how Peter wishes to live and travel influences what he does now. If he wants to travel in luxury, he needs a way of earning very large amounts of money very quickly so that he can work for brief periods and then take off. If he is prepared to work his passage, his most urgent need is to acquire skills that he can sell wherever he finds himself in the world. In the first case, doing exceptionally well at university to enter a well-paid profession like banking or accountancy would be a good idea. In the second case, he might be better off dropping out of university and going on a vocational training course to become a carpenter or a hairdresser. Peter still needs to think about what he does on leaving university, but this has become a sub-goal rather than the focus of his life.

Some people seem to be better at working out appropriate sub-goals than others. Baron (1994) suggests that there are two secrets to this. The first is to generate the widest range of possibilities for different sub-goals or sequences of sub-goals. The second is to focus on the final goal, and work back from it, rather than focusing on the present situation and work forward from it. In other words, Peter will be more successful at working out appropriate sub-goals if he says, 'This is where I want to be, how do I get there?' than if he says, 'Here I am, where can I get to from here?'.

How Can I Use This Information As a Counsellor?

Different counselling models approach goal-setting in different ways. Some, such as the *skilled helper* approach (Culley, 1991; Egan, 1994) explicitly involve a stage in which clients explore their values and set their long-term goals. *Existential counselling* (Van Deurzen-Smith, 1988) also focuses on clients' values and allows them to identify their goals. Other models, like *psychodynamic approaches* or *person-centred work*, implicitly treat problems of goal-setting as indicative of a more fundamental psychological problem and, despite what clients say, counselling focuses on these issues. Which model is appropriate depends on why the client is having difficulties with goals.

Since most people find it difficult to articulate long-term goals, we should not be surprised if clients lack them. What is significant is that they have *noticed* that they lack them. This could mean one of five things:

1) they have suddenly been faced with a challenge that can only be met by working out what their long-term goals are;
2) they have inappropriate expectations for long term goals;
3) they have decided to abandon their goals because they cannot see how they can achieve them;
4) they are having difficulty applying the inferential rules the rest of us use to work out what our goals are; or
5) they are inferring a lack of goals from a lack of motivation.

Clients are often faced with transitions that force them to reconsider the assumptions on which they have so far lived their lives and have to go back to first principles to work out what really matters to them (Hoffman, 1989). In graduating from university Peter is at such a transition point, as he has to move from the world of education and family to the world of work, which means moving into an environment in which he is suddenly responsible for his decisions. Under these circumstances it would be inappropriate, in the first instance, to presuppose a fundamental psychological problem.

Culture (see *Chapter 1*) tells us what long-term goals should look like and which are most socially acceptable. In capitalist countries, long-term goals are usually equated with occupational roles, particularly in the young. Clients, like Peter, may be confused because this is not how they experience things and they may not be able to identify with any particular occupation. Good counsellors will free clients of these culturally-determined bonds and help them see their goals in other, possibly more 'selfish' ways. Again, clarification is what is required.

There is little point in having goals that you cannot attain. When clients say that they don't know what they want, they may mean that they do not see how they can get to their goals and are looking for new goals that are attainable from their present circumstances. Peter may have entered university with a long cherished aim in life but, as he comes closer to graduation, he is less able to see how he can achieve that goal. The problem is most likely to arise when people try to establish sub-goals by working forwards from their present position and clients, like Peter, might be helped by being encouraged to centre on their long-term goal and work backwards.

Difficulty in applying the inferential rules might be the result of cognitive impairment, but it is more likely to result from a lack of relevant information. Either clients are not attending to relevant areas of their experience or they simply do not have sufficient information on which to base a decision. Peter may not be thinking about the pastimes he enjoyed before he came to university, the pleasure he got from doing voluntary work during the vacation, or how awful he found the time he spent working in a local business, while he tries to work out his goals. Alternatively, he might not have any experience of work at all and have no information on which to base a career choice. You might also consider the possibility that clients' past experiences have been so chaotic that they do not provide meaningful information. In this instance it would be useful to know whether this reflected the clients' choices or was due to circumstances beyond their control. In the former case, the issue of lack of goals becomes of subsidiary importance and you have to address other psychological issues in counselling.

One of the best pieces of evidence for identifying our goals is our degree of motivation to achieve things. Consequently, someone who lacks motivation, perhaps because they are depressed, may experience this as a lack of goals rather than a lack of desire and might say, 'I don't know what I want to be', when they actually mean, 'I don't care what I do'. Clients like Peter might be more prepared to talk about their goals than their feelings but sensitive counsellors will be prepared for the fact that talk about goals may conceal an agenda about feelings. In this case, it would be appropriate to work with a model that focused on such emotional issues.

Counselling is a goal-directed activity and is most likely to proceed smoothly if its goals are clearly stated and shared by client and counsellor. It is unlikely that the goals of client and counsellor will coincide at the start of counselling, because clients tend to have problem-focused goals while the goals of counsellors are usually set by their models, which specify end-points for counselling. Peter may have come to counselling in the hope that you will suggest a career which he hadn't previously thought of or that you will describe a career in such alluring terms that he will instantly fall in love with it. It is unlikely that you will do either.

Whichever model you work with, your primary goal as a counsellor is to ensure that you and your clients are working towards the same goals. If you are going to concentrate on the psychological issues that have caused Peter to feel uncertain and concerned about his future, your goal might be to resolve the complex or fixation or free him from his 'conditions of worth', rather than help him make a decision. If the therapeutic goals are not negotiated, you and your client may find yourselves pulling in different directions.

Not setting goals with the client may slow down counselling because the client will find it difficult to make sense of the experience and may not be motivated to co-operate with the process. As we have seen in other chapters, people are not passive in social situations but strive to make sense of them. Particularly in the early sessions, clients working without having negotiated specific goals are likely to invest considerable intellectual energy in working out the implicit goals of the therapist, in much the same way that participants in psychological experiments invest effort in trying to work out what the experiment is about and what they are expected to do to be 'good' participants (Rosenthal, 1966). Once clients have worked out where they think counselling is heading there is no guarantee that they will co-operate, as they may use their inferences about being a good participant to subvert the process, in much the same way that people exposed to attitude changing messages use a range of techniques to resist attitude change.

It is best to treat the goals of therapeutic models as sub-goals of the overall aim of therapy, which is to help the client. This attitude favours flexibility of approach and a willingness to abandon specific therapeutic techniques if they prove unhelpful with a particular client.

Section summary

- Do not expect clients to have clear long-term goals. One of your tasks may be to help them work out appropriate goals.

- Long-term goals are not usually an issue for most of us.

- Ask why an absence of goals has become an issue for this client at this point in their life.

- Goals can become an issue when people face major challenges, such as the transition from education to work.

- Clients may abandon long-term goals because they do not see how they can attain them. Working backwards from the goal is a better strategy than working forwards from the present position.

- Be cautious about attributing difficulties clients have in establishing goals to psychological factors.

- Counselling involves decision-making, so you have to establish your own goals and sub-goals as a counsellor.

- Learn about your client's goals.

- Counselling will proceed most smoothly if the goals are negotiated with the client.

- Keep your eye on the prize and distinguish between the overall goal of counselling and the sub-goals you have set to achieve it. Sub-goals are negotiable and can be abandoned if they don't work out.

Deciding What Is True

Peter has assumed that if he knows what he wants to do, then he will feel motivated to work. As a counsellor working with Peter, you will assume that if you do certain things with him, like give him unconditional positive regard, interpret the transference relationship or get him to do homework exercises, then his problem will be resolved. How did you and Peter arrive at these conclusions and what further conclusions are you entitled to draw from them? How do we decide what to accept as true and what to reject as false? There are three ways of thinking about this question – the *descriptive*, the *prescriptive* and the *normative* (Baron, 1994). Descriptive accounts of thinking are attempts to represent what people tend to do when asked to evaluate assumptions; prescriptive accounts are statements about how people might arrive at better conclusions; and normative accounts are statements about how an 'ideal' thinker, who has an infinite amount of time and access to all of the relevant information, might draw conclusions.

Take a statement like 'all psychologists have blue eyes'. A descriptive approach might involve asking people whether it was true and the reasons for their answer. In a descriptive study, someone might tell you that it is untrue because they know a lot of blue-eyed people and not all of them are psychologists. A prescriptive approach might instruct people to focus on exceptions to the rule so that they would bring up mental images of all the psychologists they knew to see whether any of them had brown eyes. If they can identify an exception, then the rule must be wrong. A normative approach would deal with the laws of logic, showing how the pursuit of exceptions was logical but recalling the professions of blue-eyed people was not. A lot of the literature on thinking compares the descriptive with the normative approaches and it shows that humans are not very good at thinking in idealized ways.

'Logic' lies at the heart of most normative models of thinking. I have put the word in inverted commas to indicate that I am using the word in its technical sense, to refer to a set of inference rules that allow you to reach valid conclusions from assumptions that transcend the content of individual assertions. There are two main valid forms of inference which are called *affirming the antecedent* and *infirming the consequent*. An example of affirming the antecedent would be 'If I know what I want to do, then I will be motivated to work; I know what I want to do, therefore I am motivated to work'. An example of infirming the consequent would be 'If I know what I want to do, then I will be motivated to work; I am not motivated to work, therefore I do not know what I want to do'. All other conclusions from the initial assertion are logically invalid. Neither infirming the antecedent nor affirming the consequent allows us to draw any valid conclusions. If I do not know what I want to do (infirming the antecedent), we cannot say whether or not I will be motivated to work, and if I am motivated to work (confirming the consequent), we cannot say whether I know what I want to do. In the second case, something else, such as the promise of a very large sum of money, might motivate me to work even though I do not know what I want to do, and in the first I might not be motivated to work because what I want to do does not need a degree.

I have put in these examples to illustrate two points. The first is that valid logical inference, especially infirming the consequent, is counter-intuitive and most people do not recognize it as a valid form of inference while invalid inference, such as affirming the consequent, is widely endorsed. The second is that logic is of fairly limited use as a tool for inference, because it only allows us to draw valid inferences in restricted conditions. Formal logic deals with the validity of the link between two assertions, such as 'I know what I want to do' and 'I will be motivated to work'. Peter can apply it to the syllogism 'If I know what I want to do then I will be motivated to work' and legitimately conclude that since he is not motivated to work, then he does not know what he wants to do. He can also use formal logic to work out how to test the validity of the link between knowing what he wants to do and being motivated to work. If the syllogism is valid he should never be able to identify a situation in which he has known what he wanted to do but not been motivated to work. He could do this either by reviewing all the situations in which he has known what he wanted to do to confirm that he was always motivated to work or by reviewing all of the situations in which he was unmotivated to work to confirm that, in all instances, he didn't know what he wanted to do.

People find this sort of reasoning remarkably difficult to apply. This is illustrated in a series of studies conducted by Wason (1968). Wason presented people with four cards. One card had a vowel printed on it, one a consonant, one an even number and one an odd number, giving sequences like E, K, 4 and 7. Participants were told that their task was to indicate which cards they should turn over to test out the truth of a statement like: if a card has a vowel on one side, then there is an even number on the other side. Most people (for 'people' read highly-educated undergraduates at one of Britain's most respected universities) say that you should turn over the E and the 4. Turning over the E allows you to draw a logically valid inference, based on affirming the antecedent, because the statement is only true if there is an even number on the other side. An odd number would immediately invalidate the rule. Turning over the 4 tells you nothing because the rule tells you nothing about what will be true if a card has an even number on it. This is an example of affirming the consequent. What they should do, according to this normative rule, is to turn over the 7 as this will allow them to infirm the consequent. If a card has an odd number on one side and a vowel on the other, then the rule cannot be valid.

We are rarely faced with clear rules, such as 'If it has a vowel on one side it will have an even number on the other', but with simple assertions like 'John has curly hair', 'Petra has a PhD', 'Sunil is good looking' or 'I don't feel like working today', we have to apply our knowledge of the world to decide what is likely to follow from them. When we try to work out what follows from assertions we usually have statements that begin 'most' or 'usually' to guide us, rather than True or False statements.

Baron (1994, building on Toulmin, 1958) suggests that, if you cannot have watertight normative rules in this situation, you can follow a prescriptive rule that optimizes the chances of coming to an appropriate conclusion. His approach, which he describes as the *search-inference framework*, involves three elements: generating possibilities, establishing goals and applying evidence. A number of things could be true if the statement 'I don't feel like working' is true; Peter could conclude that his course is boring, that his social life is so much fun that he doesn't have the energy for work, that he doesn't see the point of working hard because he doesn't know what he wants to do, or that he is depressed.

The possibilities Peter will evaluate and how he interprets the evidence will depend on what his possibilities for action are. If Peter has the possibility of changing his course, he might evaluate whether his course is boring, but if he is thinking of seeking counselling, he may well review the possibilities that he doesn't have a clear goal, or that he is depressed.

The evidence comprises sets of assertions that strengthen or weaken your confidence in the link between the initial assertion and the conclusion you are drawing. 'I am not working because the course is boring' would be supported by observations like 'Everyone else says the course is boring', 'None of my friends are working hard at it', and 'The lecturers have monotonous voices' but would be contradicted by observations like 'All of my friends are engrossed in their work', 'Dr Smith is an excellent communicator', and 'Everyone says that the course is at the cutting edge of knowledge'. 'I am not working because I don't know what I want to do' would be supported by observations like 'I had a period like this before coming to university but my motivation came back when I worked out what course I wanted to do' and 'People need goals to feel motivated to work'. None of the pieces of evidence alone needs be conclusive but, together, they favour a particular conclusion.

This prescriptive account of day-to-day thinking approximates very well to what people actually seem to do when trying to work out what follows from assertions. People do not seem to have any difficulties in offering assertions to support or deny conclusions that they, or others, are seeking to draw. Where people do find difficulty is in generating the possibilities before applying the decision rules. Indeed, Johnson-Laird and his colleagues (in Baron, 1994) have suggested that our failure to use formal logic properly stems from not generating the possibilities properly. For example, in the experiment by Wason that I described earlier, we can view the tendency to ignore the 7 as a failure to generate the possibility that it could have a vowel on its back, rather than as a failure of logic.

Johnson-Laird *et al.* (1972) repeated Wason's experiment but used different materials. Instead of cards, participants were shown four envelopes, one back view of a sealed envelope, one back view of an unsealed envelope, one front view of an envelope with a five pence stamp on the front and one front view of an envelope with a four pence stamp on the front. They were asked to indicate which envelopes they would inspect to test the rule that, if a letter is sealed, then it has a five pence stamp on it. Most of the people in this study were able to work out that they had to inspect the sealed envelope and the one with the four pence stamp on it. Letters and stamps are real to us and making mistakes about the amount of postage you put on a letter can be quite costly to the recipient, so participants could more easily imagine checking that a letter onto which they were about to stick a four pence stamp wasn't sealed. Results like these indicate the importance of 'active open-mindedness' when thinking (Baron, 1994).

Drawing conclusions from evidence would be simple if all assertions were either true or false, but they are not. Most assertions with which we are dealing have some probability of being true that is greater than zero but less than one. At the end of the search-inference process, Peter may have concluded that it is probable that he doesn't have any clear goals but he cannot be certain because none of the evidence is conclusive. Probability creates a lot of problems for us. We turn out to be quite bad at both estimating the probabilities of events and drawing appropriate conclusions once we have reasonable estimates of them. If people were better at working with probabilities, they might spend less money on risky ventures like gambling.

Part of the problem in dealing with probabilities is a reluctance to accept that probabilistic rules apply in our world so that, even when the world is probabilistic, people seek out interpretations that make it deterministic and entirely predictable. This is demonstrated in the laboratory in experiments in which people are given packs of cards with coloured shapes printed on them to sort according to a rule thought up by the researcher. In a classic study by Bruner and his colleagues (Bruner *et al.*, 1956) the cards varied in terms of the number of shapes (1, 2 or 3), the number of borders (1, 2 or 3), shape (circle, square or cross), and colour (green, red or black). The researcher would point to a card and the participant would have to guess whether it conformed with the rule of which the researcher had been thinking. Participants were given feedback about whether they were correct. For example, the researcher might have the rule: 'all cards with black shapes, irrespective of form, number or number of borders'. If the participant is shown a card with two black circles with one border and says 'Yes', they are told that they are right. If they say 'No', they are told that they are wrong. If they are shown green circles and say 'Yes', they are told that they are wrong. This is the limit to the information they are given. So long as the rule is 'all-or-none' (all black objects, all circles and so on), participants usually arrive at the right rule and stick with it. If the rule is probabilistic, such as black objects being 'right' on 80 per cent of trials and red objects on 20 per cent, then participants rarely arrive at the correct solution, which is to say 'Yes' every time they are shown a black figure and 'No' every other trial. Instead they shift from strategy to strategy, in a forlorn hope of identifying the non-existent deterministic rule (Coombs *et al.*, 1970; cited in Baron, 1994).

After a few sessions Peter might reveal that he has lost interest in his course because he secretly fears that he isn't any good at it. When you ask him why, he tells you that he sometimes gets disappointing marks and he has drawn the all-or-none conclusion that he is not very good. When you remind him of the work on which he has got good marks, he tells you that there are a few lecturers that always give him high marks to encourage him but he knows that, really, the work is not that good. Peter has ignored the possibility of a probabilistic interpretation, 'I must be good because I get it right on 80 per cent of occasions' in favour of two, inappropriate all-or-none interpretations, 'I'm not very good' and 'Dr X gives out marks to encourage people'.

Even when people know that events are probabilistic, they are poor at estimating probabilities accurately. What they tend to do is to underestimate the probability of very likely events and overestimate the probability of very infrequent events. For example, Lichtenstein *et al.* (1978; in Baron, 1994), asked people to estimate the probability of dying from various causes, such as cancer and smallpox. Their estimates of the number of deaths per year from cancer tended to be much lower than the actual figures, while their estimates of the number of deaths from smallpox was much higher.

Reasoning from probabilities is not much better. For example, Tversky and Kahneman (1982) gave people the following information:

A taxi was involved in an accident at night.

- There are two taxi companies in town, the Green and the Blue.
- 85 per cent of the taxis are green and 15 per cent blue.
- A witness identified the taxi as blue.
- In an experiment conducted under the same lighting conditions as the accident, the witness could correctly distinguish green and blue on 80 per cent of occasions.

69

Participants have to estimate the probability of the taxi involved in the accident actually being blue. Most people give estimates of over 50 per cent but probability theory tells us that the actual probability of the taxi being blue is 41 per cent. Why is there such a difference? It looks as if people, faced with these complex tasks, narrow down their field of attention to what they believe to be the most important information, the accuracy of distinguishing blue from green, while ignoring the other information, the prior probability of a taxi being either blue or green. Studies involving a range of tasks like these have shown that people tend to ignore prior probabilities when drawing conclusions from probability information.

How Can I Use This Information As a Counsellor?

Following Baron (1994) you can distinguish between being rational and being logical. Rationality is about arriving at the most appropriate conclusions, given the information available and the opportunities to apply sound principles to your reasoning. Logic is a formal system of rules which, under some circumstances, can form the appropriate principles by which to reason. Peter may be logical in concluding that he doesn't have any goals from the fact that he is not motivated to work, but he may not be being rational.

Failing to draw rational conclusions from information is often the result of failing to consider all of the possibilities. In most studies of thinking, people make much more rational inferences when important information is made salient to them or they are encouraged to imagine all of the conclusions that could be drawn from a set of assumptions before they use evidence to narrow them down. This suggests that, if clients like Peter appear to be irrational, the problem may not lie in their ability to think properly but in their capacity to generate the possibilities from which to select, so counsellors will benefit from developing strategies to free up the imaginations of their client and from encouraging clients to separate the phase of generating ideas from the phase of selecting between them.

Most of us find it difficult to evaluate rules critically. Either we accept statements like 'if I know what I want to do then I will be motivated to work' at face value and do not question them at all, or, if challenged, we test them by trying to confirm them rather than disprove them. So long as our assumptions allow us to live contented lives, these errors do not cause problems. When assumptions lead people to live unhappy or conflictful lives, they need guidance in how to test out their assumptions, which is the rationale of cognitive therapies (Scott and Dryden, 1996).

It is much harder for people to think rationally when they are dealing with probabilities than when they are dealing with all-or-none events. We seem to prefer simple generalizations, like 'All of my plans go wrong' than more accurate generalizations like '50 per cent of my plans go wrong', and when faced with probabilistic events we seek to identify all-or-none rules, even if the latter are inappropriate and fail to respect the evidence available. It is quite possible that many of our clients who appear to have developed irrational cognitions have done so because they are attempting to deal with probabilistic rules, like 'My father hits me on 80 per cent of the occasions on which I see him'. Instead of arriving at a probabilistic rule like this, they may have done what the rest of us tend to do, and devised alternative, deterministic, hypotheses about how the world works, such as 'My father only hits me when I am bad', even if this hypothesis fits the evidence less well or forces them to define 'bad' as anything they do.

Beware of assuming that people leading unhappy lives are less rational than those who are happy since the evidence indicates that we are all bad at rationally testing rules. Since cognitive errors are widespread we should be careful about attributing our clients' problems to their particular propensity for making them. Instead, it may be more helpful to enquire about the factors that have seduced clients into making these common errors in areas of their lives where they have damaging consequences.

Counsellors are unlikely to be exempt from the bias against probabilistic laws when it comes to evaluating their practice. We know, from many decades of well-conducted outcome studies that, irrespective of the model someone uses, counselling rarely exceeds 70 per cent effectiveness. This means that if you are reflecting on your own practice to work out what strategies are effective with clients, you are going to have to form probabilistic rules like 'Leaving clients to cry when they are upset rather than interpreting their feelings enhances the quality of the therapeutic relationship in 70 per cent of cases', rather than seeking rules that make the outcome 100 per cent predictable. Counsellors who do not recognize the significance of probabilistic rules may well have a completely false impression of what is happening in their practice. If they have an academic bent, they may well communicate those impressions to others.

Section summary

- **Being rational and being logical are different. One often has to abandon logic to be rational when one has imperfect information.**

- People reason best when they have considered all the possibilities.

- All of us have difficulty testing the validity of rules. Cognitive therapies enable clients to reason in a way that is alien to most people.

- We have immense difficulty thinking about probabilities and try to arrive at all-or-none rules even when they are not appropriate.

- Guard against misinterpreting probabilistic events when evaluating your own practice.

Making Decisions

After a number of sessions, Peter has worked out that he wants to travel and that he needs a way of earning money to pay for it. He can either opt for a career that will enable him to earn large amounts of money in short periods of time, so that he can save up quickly for trips, or he can acquire skills that he can practise anywhere in the world, so that he can earn as he travels. Which should he do?

The normative theory of decision-making tells us that Peter should opt for the choice that maximizes 'utility', which is related to the chances of a choice enabling Peter to reach his goal, and the value he attaches to it (Baron, 1994). Utility is defined as the result of multiplying the value of the outcome of a decision by the probability of the decision yielding that outcome. Since each decision can give rise to a number of outcomes, it is necessary to calculate the utility of each outcome and then arrive at a net value of the utility of the decision by adding together all of the separate utilities.

Calculating utility is simplest if we can measure value properly. One way of doing this is to equate value with money, so that the value of £10 is ten times the value of £1, and the value of £100 is ten times the value of £10. Suppose I were to present you with a pack of cards and strike a deal with you so that I paid you £13 every time you drew an ace from the pack and you paid me £1 every time you drew any other card. Would it be worth your while playing this game with me? The utility to you of getting an ace is £13 multiplied by the probability of getting an ace, which is 1/13, giving us a utility of 1. The utility of drawing any other card is –£1 (minus because you give it to me) multiplied by the probability of drawing any card other than an ace, which is 12/13, giving a utility of

−12/13. If your goal is to make money you should take me up on this offer because the net utility is 1−12/13, which is 1/13.

Peter could apply utility theory to his decision. Being able to travel could be assigned 100 units on his value scale while not being able to travel could be assigned some other value, such as 0. The probability of being able to obtain a job that will earn him enough to travel regularly and allow him the time to do it might be 0.05, while the probability of being able to acquire and use skills that will enable him to earn as he travels might be 0.5. The utility of looking for a lucrative career is 0.05×100 plus 0.95×0, giving you 0.05. The utility of acquiring 'portable' skills is 0.5×100 plus 0.5×0, giving 0.5.

You can see the problem immediately. In these conditions the rational choice is whatever gives you the highest probability of success, but that is usually what you don't know. We can calculate probabilities very exactly when working out the value of gambles on cards or lotteries but we cannot do so when dealing with the rest of life's decisions. The best that Peter can do here is to apply the search-inference approach to trying to estimate the probabilities. Relevant information would be the number of people who have very highly paid jobs, the degree to which Peter possesses the characteristics that make people economically successful, the number of highly paid occupations where you can disappear for months of the year and resume your career on return, the market for particular skills in the places to which he would like to travel, the legal framework that might restrict his right to work in particular countries and his aptitude for the skills that he might have to acquire.

I have simplified Peter's choice by giving the outcome, being able to travel, the same value in both cases but, in real decisions, different outcomes have different values. Peter might have developed a taste for luxury living that leads him to value staying in five star hotels much more than earning his keep as he goes and living in hostels. Clearly, the values he attached to the two forms of travel would affect which choice he should make. If he values luxury sufficiently, he should go for the riskier choice simply because its utility is higher.

How can we scale values? It is even difficult to scale the value of money because the value people attach to cash diminishes as they acquire more of it. If you only have £100 in the world, another £100 constitutes a huge amount of money. If you have £1,000,000 then an extra £100 has negligible value. If we cannot scale money in simple cash terms, how can we scale the values of attaining non-financial goals like going on holiday, having a baby or having a job in which you only work from 9.00 a.m. to 5.00 p.m.? It is impossible to put an absolute value on an outcome, but there are procedures that you can apply to determine their relative values. One is to get people to rate the values of different outcomes, one is to get them to estimate the *differences* between outcomes and the third is to offer them the opportunity to gamble on different outcomes and see what odds they will accept before taking up the gamble. No single method is going to give you an unequivocal estimate of value, but together the methods should converge if people have consistent values.

The simplest method is to ask people to rate outcomes on a numerical scale, having given them an anchor point for the scale. You could tell Peter that travelling frugally has a value of ten and ask him to indicate the number he would attach to being able to travel in luxury, to which he might reply 100. We could check on this by using the method of difference. Peter could be asked to imagine a situation in which he could not afford to travel in luxury all of the time, but he could do so for part of the time. What proportion of luxury would Peter place mid-way between no luxury and 100 per cent luxury? If he is being consistent you would expect him to say 50 per cent. If he says anything other than 50 per cent, it means that the value of luxury is not a simple multiple of the amount available. He might put the mid-point at 80 per cent luxury, which would suggest that he attached little value to small amounts of luxury. If Peter values travelling in luxury ten times more than travelling frugally then he should be prepared to take commensurately larger risks to achieve this goal. If you present him with a choice between the certainty of being able to travel frugally and some probability of being able to travel in luxury, Peter should be prepared to accept odds slightly better than ten to one.

Peter's choice is not as simple as I am making out because, as is true of most decisions, he has to compare options that vary along a number of different dimensions at the same time. He has to take account of comfort, excitement, 'authenticity' (how much he gets a sense of what life is like for the people who live in the country he is visiting), and opportunities to make friends. Travelling in luxury will be better than travelling frugally on some of these dimensions but not others. How does Peter make a decision when neither choice wins on *all* of the criteria he is taking into consideration? Providing the criteria are independent of each other it is possible to apply the normative rules of *Multiattribute Utility Theory* (Baron, 1994), which helps you break down the complex decision into a series of much simpler decisions.

According to Multiattribute Utility Theory, what you should do is to use the strategies I have outlined to work out the scale of utilities for each of the separate dimensions and then scale the dimensions relative to each other. To make life easier, it is a good idea to put all

Table 1: Values of attributes for each of two styles of travel (utilities in parentheses)

Style	Comfort	Excitement	Authenticity	Friends
Frugal	Low (0)	High (100)	High (100)	High (100)
Luxurious	High (100)	Moderate (50)	Low (0)	Moderate (50)

of the attributes onto the same utility scale. This might give Peter a table of differences between styles of travel, and the utilities he attaches to those differences, as illustrated in *Table 1*.

Luxurious travel wins on comfort but frugal travel wins on all of the other dimensions. In order to decide whether the increased levels of excitement, authenticity and opportunities for making friends associated with frugal travel offset the cost in terms of comfort, Peter has to be able to put all of these attributes onto the same utility scale. You could do this by asking him how much of a change in comfort he is prepared to exchange for changes in excitement, authenticity or opportunities for friendship. He might decide that 50 units change in excitement are worth 50 units of comfort but that 50 units of authenticity are only worth ten units of comfort, while 50 units of change in opportunities for making friends are worth 100 units of change in comfort. This gives weightings of 1.0 for comfort, 1.0 for excitement, 0.2 for authenticity and 2.0 for opportunities to make friends.

To work out the overall utility of each option, you multiply the utility assigned to each of the attributes for that option by the weighting given to each attribute. Frugal travel gets an overall utility of 1×0 plus 1×100 plus 0.2×100 plus 2×100, giving a total of 220 units. Luxury travel gets an overall utility of 1×100 plus 1×50 plus 0.2×0 plus 2×50, giving a total of 250 units. Although luxury travel only wins on one of the attributes, the weightings given to them mean that it is the preferred option.

These are some of the principles telling us how people *should* make decisions, but they are not always applied in practice. A very clear example of this is the Allais paradox (Allais, 1953). In this

Table 2: Choices offered by Allais (1953)

Situation A

	Outcome	Probability
Choice 1	£1,000	1.00
Choice 2	£1,000	0.89
	£5,000	0.10
	£ 0	0.01

Situation B

Choice 1	£1,000	0.11
	£ 0	0.89
Choice 2	£5,000	0.10
	£ 0	0.90

work, people are given the choices between bets laid out in *Table 2*.

In situation A, people tend to opt for Choice 1, the certainty of winning £1,000 over the possibility of winning £5,000. In situation B, people tend to opt for the chances of winning £5,000 over the chances of winning £1,000. However, utility theory tells us that people should go for choice 2 in both cases. In Situation A, the utility of choice 1 is the probability of winning (1.00) times the value of the winnings (£1,000), giving a utility of 1,000. The utility of choice 2 is the probability of winning £1,000 times its value (0.89 × 1,000) plus the probability of winning £5,000 times its value (0.10 × 5,000) plus the probability of winning nothing times its value (0.01 × 0), giving a utility of 1,390. In Situation B, the utility of Choice 1 is 0.11 × 1,000 plus 0.89 × 0, giving a total of 110. The utility of Choice 2 is 0.10 × 5,000 plus 0.90 × 0, giving a total of 500. Which choice you prefer will depend on the values you attach to the outcomes, but the direction of preference should be the same in both instances; you should either prefer choice 2 in both cases or choice 1. In situation A, people are faced with a choice between risk and certainty and opt for certainty, irrespective of what utility theory says but in Situation B, people work more appropriately with the probabilities and can apply utility theory appropriately.

Our preference for certainty over uncertainty is also apparent when people are faced with situations in which the probabilities of

Table 3: The winnings, offered by Ellsberg (1960), available if a particular colour of ball is taken from the bag

	30 balls known to be red	60 balls may be black	may be yellow
Situation A			
Choice 1	£100	£ 0	£ 0
Choice 2	£ 0	£100	£ 0
Situation B			
Choice 1	£100	£ 0	£100
Choice 2	£ 0	£100	£100

events are simply unknown. Ellsberg (1961) presented people with the following problem. They were told that the researcher had a bag containing 90 balls, of which 30 were known to be red and the remaining 60 could be either black or yellow but they had no way of knowing in advance how many black or yellow balls were present. They were invited to choose between gambles on different coloured balls being drawn from the bag, with the choices laid out in *Table 3*.

According to utility theory, people should not be able to decide between either choice because, although the net utility of Situation B is higher than Situation A, the net utilities of choices 1 and 2 are the same in both situations. However, most people opt for choice 1, the choice in which winning is linked to the colour for which the probability is known.

What motivates people to over-rate certainty relative to uncertainty? One factor that seems to be important is the contemplation of regret. If you opt for a risky choice you expose yourself to the possibility of the gamble not paying off, of ending up with nothing rather than £1,000 or £5,000 and, if you get nothing, you will regret the choice because you would have been guaranteed to get something if you had gone for the safe choice. Another way of putting it is, when faced with certainty versus a risky choice, people compare the utility of the certain outcome with the utility of the poorer outcome of the gamble, rather than taking into account the better outcome. Risk aversion may complicate Peter's decision, as he finds himself faced with an easy, sure-fire option that guarantees a modest outcome and a more difficult, riskier outcome, that offers a better return. As long as he concentrates on the decision rule, he will go for the riskier option but as soon as he thinks about implementing the decision, he will switch to the safer choice.

Most decision making models assume that all of the options are immediately available and all you are doing is choosing between one and the other. In many cases this is not true and the problem is deciding between one option that is immediately available and another that is available at some time in the future. Peter might have to choose between dropping out of university and going onto a vocational course that will allow him to travel immediately, but in a frugal style, and staying on at university, going through a professional training and travelling in luxury at a later date. He may well choose immediate but frugal travel, even though it has lower utility than luxury travel. This is an example of a well established phenomenon known as *discounting the future*.

Discounting the future is not necessarily irrational, although it can get us into trouble. Utility is the product of value and probability and events in the future are much less certain than those in the present. If Peter chooses to defer his travel, he might have an accident that makes travel impossible or there might be political changes that make it too dangerous to visit the places he wants to visit. In any event, the future may not pan out as Peter expects it to and he would be unwise to invest too much in it. In other instances, the value of something can accumulate, so something obtained today will end up worth more than the same thing obtained at some point in the future. The simplest example is money. If I give you £100 today you can invest it and make money on it so that, at the end of the year, it may be worth £105. Under these circumstances, it would be perfectly rational to prefer £100 today to any sum under £105 in a year's time.

Discounting the future becomes a problem when the utility ascribed to one outcome, usually the more distant, is influenced by the utility attached to the other, usually the more immediate. If Peter can ascribe utility to travelling in luxury when he is 35, independently of the utility he ascribes to travelling frugally when he is 22, then he can apply utility theory to make the decision. However, if the utility he ascribes to later, luxurious travel, is in any way influenced by the utility he ascribes to travelling immediately, so that the more strongly he desires to travel immediately, the less he values travelling when he is older, then he cannot apply utility theory.

Just as we discount the future, we also tend to overvalue the past (Baron, 1994). If we have invested in something in the past, be it a business or a relationship, we will continue to invest in it in the future, even though the later investment brings us no gain or even makes a loss. This is known as the *sunk-cost effect*. Suppose you have invested £1,000 in a business which is presently about to become insolvent and you are given £1,000 to spend any way you like. You can either put the money into the business, in which case you will get a rate of return of two per cent a year, or you can put the money into a deposit account and make five per cent per year but the business will fail. What do you do? Most people will put the money into the business, even though it produces a poorer rate of return on the money than putting it on deposit. If, however, the same people are given the choice between putting the money on deposit at five per cent and putting it into a *new* business at two per cent, most of them will put it on deposit. In terms of what will happen in the future, the two decisions are identical but the first decision is influenced by the amount already invested in the business. Similarly, Peter may be reluctant to abandon his degree course simply because he has already invested two years of his life in it, even though he knows that he will never use his degree and there is something else he wishes to do with his time.

How Can I Use This Information As a Counsellor?

Be respectful of the difficulties clients have in making decisions. Decision theory is extremely complex, hard work and often counter-intuitive and very few of us are particularly good at applying it. To enhance your respect for the difficulties of your clients, you could look back over some of the decisions you have made in your own life to see how far you followed the principle of good decision-making.

Acknowledging the difficulties in making good decisions reduces the pressure for you to start making them for your clients and it also normalizes the experiences of clients who are having difficulty with important choices. How you would use this knowledge depends on the model you are using. As a cognitive therapist you might use direct instruction to inform your client or use the information to challenge negative beliefs held by your client, such as rephrasing statements like, 'I am incompetent because I cannot make my mind up' as 'I am as competent as the next person but I am dealing with a very difficult task'. You could even go further and suggest that failure to make a decision reflected the client's greater understanding of the difficulties of making a decision. If you work in a client-centred way you could use the knowledge to guide your empathic reflections by including comments about the processes involved in good decision-making. For example, instead of just saying 'You seem to be having trouble making your mind up', you could use your knowledge of decision-making to say 'Faced with the difficulties of working out what the options are open to you and what those options mean to you, the difficulty of comparing choices that vary in so many different ways and the difficulty of making sense of all of that information, you are having trouble making your mind up'.

The only realistic way of helping someone make a decision is to help them break it down into small, independent and manageable units. If someone cannot decide whether to change jobs it is better to break down the work situation into its different components such as pay, work-load, colleagues, and talk about those separately than to try to arrive at a global evaluation of the jobs on offer. This will probably highlight the fact that the client has not thought about particular aspects of the choice properly and may need more information before they can do so. For example, a client may indicate that they put a great value on the location of their job but discussion with you may lead them to realize that location is too crude an issue and that they need to think about aspects of the location, such as transport links, local amenities (such as shops and restaurants) and physical appearance (open countryside versus inner-city tower blocks).

Use the models of decision-making as a framework for helping clients explore the factors that are important in their decision-making but remember that the final arbiter of whether your client has come to the right decision is their willingness to go along with the conclusion, not the application of the appropriate method. If, for example, the application of Multiattribute Utility Theory suggests that the client should take Job A but they feel reluctant to do so, this should be treated as an opportunity to explore the factors that have not yet been taken into account when making the decision, not a moment to reflect on the client's irrationality

Discounting the future can be a major source of problems, particularly when desire for the more immediate goal distorts someone's estimate of the utility of a more distant goal. The distorting effect tends to be particularly strong when the more immediate goal is very close at hand (Baron, 1994). One solution to this problem is for people to make binding decisions when both goals are relatively distant. For example, if someone is on a diet the immediate prospect of ice-cream may outweigh the distant prospect of weight loss but if they bind themselves to not eating ice-cream by not buying any when they go to the shops, when the desire for ice-cream is lower, then they will find it easier to resist the urge to consume it later.

Overvaluing past investment may create resistance to change in clients. For example, someone in an abusive relationship may want to persist with it simply because they have put so much effort and suffering into maintaining the relationship. Paradoxically, the more someone has suffered at the hands of a partner in the past, the greater their investment in the relationship and, if the sunk-cost effect is working, the more strongly they will value the relationship in the present and the more they will invest in the future of it. Understanding the sunk-cost effect can be of use to you here in two ways. The first is that you can direct interventions towards weakening the effect, perhaps by giving the client less emotionally charged examples to think about so that they can explore their own reasoning and see its weakness. The second is that it reduces the temptation to view the client's thoughts and actions in pathological terms.

The difficulties associated with decision-making affect counsellors as well as clients. Huge numbers of decisions are made with each client, ranging from strategic decisions such as whether to take on someone as a client at all to fine-grain decisions such as whether to ask an open-ended question or paraphrase what the client has just said. It is unlikely that all of these decisions will be good ones and quite likely that some of them will be really bad. You cannot stop yourself making bad decisions altogether but you can reduce them by constantly reviewing the decisions you have made in practice. The temptation is to review them in the light of their consequences and convince yourself that one decision was a good one, because the client benefited, and another was a bad one, because the client didn't. What you should actually do is review your decisions in the light of the information you might reasonably be expected to have had available at the time you made them. This will encourage you to identify biases in your own reasoning and also to evaluate the knowledge on which you are basing your practice. Those of you involved in training and supervision should bring these principles to bear on these activities as well, getting trainees and supervisees to consider how well their decisions are grounded in the knowledge they are expected to have.

Section summary

- Making good decisions is very difficult.

- Do not assume that you are better at making decisions than your clients. You may just be luckier!

- Help clients with the process of making decisions, do not make them for them.

- Decision-making is improved by breaking the process down into small, manageable units.

- Decision-making rules are aids, not cages. If clients don't like the decisions that result from applying rational principles, it probably means that the principles have not been applied properly.

- People tend to undervalue the future and overvalue the past. One of the goals of counselling is to reverse this and encourage clients to re-value the future and de-value the negative parts of the past.

- Be honest about your own decision-making as a counsellor.

Chapter Summary

Nobody can make perfect decisions, because there is too much uncertainty in the world, but there is a lot we can do to help clients like Peter make *better* decisions. We can help them by encouraging them to break problems down into manageable chunks which they can think about without being overwhelmed. We can also help them by alerting them to the biases of reasoning to which we are all prey, that encourage us to ignore essential information when making decisions. It helps to distinguish between logic and rationality. Logic is an artificial aid to reasoning that helps us draw valid conclusions when we have complete information while rationality is an approach to reasoning that makes best use of the available information.

Good decision-making is very difficult. We rarely have enough information and the rules for interpreting that information effectively are often counter-intuitive, leading us to reject valid conclusions because we are not comfortable with some of the stages in making a decision. Counsellors should be modest about their own decision-making abilities and, I believe, avoid using pejorative terms like 'irrational' when describing their clients' thinking. We all tend to be irrational but our clients may favour forms of irrationality that the rest of us reject. The difficulties of some clients may stem from their desire to be rational in circumstances that do not permit rational decision-making, such as 'deciding' whether they love somebody, rather than an inability to think rationally and we may find ourselves helping clients escape the bonds of rationality!

As counsellors we have to make decisions about our own practice, and we owe it to our clients to ensure that these decisions are rational. What are the goals of your practice? What sub-goals do you need to set to meet those goals? What can you accept as being true? Why do you believe these things? What conclusions can you reasonably draw from the things you believe to be true? If you can answer all of these questions, you are on the way to having a rationally justified practice.

5
Remembering

Jennifer is 21 and has problems with eating, particularly bingeing while trying to keep to the very strict diet she feels she needs to adhere to in order to keep her figure as a dancer. She has seen her counsellor for three sessions. Nothing much happened during the first two, but, as her counsellor starts to write up her notes on the third session she feels that she has got to the core of Jennifer's problems as a result of her disclosures about her relationship with her father. She recalls Jennifer telling her that she remembers being abused by her father, that he used to touch her in ways that she didn't like and that he used to play with her very roughly and make her cry. She has asked about Jennifer's father on a number of occasions in previous sessions, but this is the first time she has talked about him, which she feels is significant. Her notes for the session focus on this clear example of sexual abuse and she makes a mental note to read more about working with survivors of sexual abuse before the next session.

At the end of the week she goes to her supervisor, who always asks to hear tape recordings of her sessions so that she can get a sense of the counselling process. She proudly produce the tape of the session with Jennifer and waits to be patted on the back for her skill in enabling Jennifer to disclose her sexual abuse. She is horrified when she finds that the first reference to anything like abuse appears halfway through the tape and that she can recall nothing of what went before. She is even more horrified when she hears Jennifer saying:

'Yes, my father used to abuse me regularly. He would shout at me, and tell me off for quite trivial things so I didn't like him much as a kid.'

She hears herself saying:

'Did he ever touch *you?'*

To which Jennifer replies:

> *'Oh yes, he touched me when he played with me. He used to do things like pick me up by the arms and swing me around, which I didn't like because he used to grip me too tightly and bruise me. When I yelled at him to stop he would often carry on because he thought I wasn't serious. He didn't mean any harm, but he was a very big man who found it difficult to be gentle with people.'*

At the end of supervision the counsellor resolves never to jump to conclusions without checking back on what the client has actually said and realizes that her memory can play tricks on her. She can forget much of what has happened in a session, recalling only the information that stands out in some way, and the way she recalls it is biased by what she expects the client to say. She also recognizes that, if she can forget what a client has said 30 minutes previously, clients might have difficulty recalling conversations with their fathers that took place 20 years ago.

Recall of Past Events

Whatever your counselling model, sessions always consist of conversations about what your clients recall about past events. Your model influences how you react to these recollections and the sorts of prompts you may give your client to aid recollection, but without these memories, counselling is impossible. The fact that clients like Jennifer are willing to offer up their memories in this way, and often seem to do so with great facility, obscures the marvel of our being able to reconstruct the past in the present, and may lure us into accepting these reports as *accurate* representations of the past.

Memory is also important in the process of counselling. As anyone who has ever transcribed a session for a process report will confirm, counsellors and clients say an awful lot in a session yet when we come to write up notes at the end of a session we find ourselves struggling sometimes to recall the details of what has just happened. If we, as calm, practised professionals can recall so little of the details of a session, how much is our client likely to remember a few hours later?

Clearly, we and our clients do not remember everything that has happened to us. Do we just lose bits of information at random so that our memories develop holes, like an old pair of curtains that is being eaten by moths, or are we inclined to recall some things better than others? Psychological research indicates that our ability to recall things is influenced by a number of factors, including the passage of time, the amount of rehearsal, the nature of the material and the circumstances under which the experience occurred. Research also tells us that the experience of memory is not always the same as recall of events, so you can feel as if you are remembering something accurately, even though your account of events bears little relation to other records of those events, such as tape recordings of conversations or films of historic events. It is also possible to be quite accurate in recalling information, even though you don't feel like you are remembering it.

Memory research tells us that what clients recall during sessions, and what we and our clients recall after sessions, is going to consist of selected highlights of the events that actually took place. Furthermore, although we may be confident that we are recalling the past, the reconstructive nature of memory means that we can be *creating* a past when we think we are remembering it.

This chapter is about what we currently know of the properties of human memory. It is organized around the main factors that limit our capacity for accurate recall, starting with the quantitative ones, the passage of time and the amount of rehearsal, and moving on to qualitative factors like the type of material remembered.

The Passage of Time

All other things being equal, our ability to remember events declines with the passage of time. Sometimes the decline is alarmingly rapid, such as when we are told people's names at social events and can't remember them five minutes later, and sometimes the decline is so slow that we don't realize it has happened until we try to recall something that we have previously learned. Psychologists distinguish between the rapid forgetting of new experiences and information and the much slower forgetting of things we have previously learned. They use the term 'short-term memory' to describe what happens with those rapidly lost bits of information like names at parties and telephone numbers, and the term 'long-term memory' to describe what happens with those more slowly forgotten bits of information, like the material you have revised for an examination or the details of current news stories.

Short-term memory

Information in short-term memory has a vividness and immediacy that makes it hard to believe that we will ever forget it but forget it we do, unless we do something to build up a long-term memory of the event or information. One way of thinking about short-term memory is to see it as a mental note-pad, on which we jot down information while deciding what to do with it. Only if you act on that information in some way will it become available to you on a longer term basis. Just as the pages of a note-pad will allow you to jot down a few words or phrases, but won't allow you to write a book chapter, so short-term memory has a limited capacity. During this crucial third session, Jennifer's counsellor will have put material into her short-term memory for the purposes of paraphrasing and reflection. At the time, it will have seemed vivid and unforgettable but it will have been lost rapidly as new information displaced it from memory.

According to Miller (1956), the capacity of short-term memory is about seven units, or 'chunks', of information. If you try to cram anything more into your short-term memory you will find that you have forgotten something that was previously in your memory. Some people like to think of this in terms of bits of information being pushed out of memory, a useful metaphor providing you don't take it too literally.

You will have noticed that I have been very vague about the capacity of short-term memory, referring to 'units' or 'chunks' without defining them. This is because it is impossible to define them objectively without reference to the knowledge of the listener. What might be one chunk of information to one reader or listener might be ten chunks to another. Consider the number sequence 10661492177617891939. If you approach it as a string of individual digits, it exceeds the capacity of your short-term memory. However, if you know a bit about history you can break it up into four digit chunks, making it much easier to handle: 1066, 1492, 1776, 1789 and 1939, the dates of the Battle of Hastings, Columbus's voyage to the Americas, the start of the American War of Independence, the French Revolution and the start of World War II. A knowledge of history can turn twenty chunks into five! Our ability to remember things, even over short periods of time, is dependent of what we know. We are never passive recipients of impressions. Our counsellor will have relied on her knowledge to 'chunk' what Jennifer has told her, so that she can be empathic by reflecting or paraphrasing. Her capacity for this is constrained by the knowledge she applies to what Jennifer is telling her.

Long-term memory

Most of what we think of as memory, such as recalling the name of a friend, the date of your birthday, or the meaning of a word, involves long-term memory. In a later section we will look at the factors that influence which bits of information become available in long-term memory, but, for the moment, we will focus on the impact of the ravages of time on our memory. Owing to the slowness of loss of long-term memories, it is often difficult to demonstrate that information is actually being lost. People often describe very accurate memories of events taking place many years ago, filling their accounts with vibrant, convincing detail that encourages the listener to believe that they are listening to a description of an event that is unfolding before the eyes of the narrator. Sometimes these accounts turn out to be very accurate, but they are frequently unreliable.

In most instances it is difficult to determine the reliability of the recall because only the client's account is available to you. Psychologists have approached this problem in two ways. One has been to look at recall of events in the public domain, such as news items and media events, and the other has been to expose people to contrived situations, such as films of staged crimes, the content of which is known to the researcher, and compare what the person subsequently says was happening with what did actually did happen in the situation. In both instances, accurate recall gets worse as the interval between the events and the recall opportunity increases. All things being equal, we would expect Jennifer to remember little from her childhood.

Where there are clearly right and wrong answers, such as on questions of historical fact, recall failures may be experienced as gaps in memory but when people are asked to narrate events that they have experienced themselves the failures are more subtle, often taking the form of distortion of, or filling in of, detail to make the story more coherent. Under these circumstances the individual may be unaware of the unreliability of their memory.

A good example is the testimony given by John Dean, one of ex-President Nixon's aides, to the Senate committee investigating the Watergate break-in during the 1970s. Dean gave highly detailed, persuasive testimony to the committee, but when tapes of his conversations with Nixon were finally obtained, it was discovered that his testimony bore little relation to what had been said. Not only did he not remember the exact words but he failed to recall the gist or meaning of what had been said. Moreover, as Edwards and Potter (1995) point out, what Dean recalled varied with who was asking the questions, so he was not only failing accurately to recall the initial events, he was also failing to recall his own previous testimony of those events. Jennifer's recall of her childhood may vary with the questions she has been asked, so different counsellors might elicit different stories.

A number of factors contribute to the development of these distortions. One of them is, paradoxically, the *rehearsal* of material. Each time we recall an event we create it anew in our memory and provide ourselves with something new to remember. Minor variations in the way in which we recall something can lead to a series of copying errors which, over time, lead to the formation of an inaccurate memory. Baddeley (1983) provides a analogy of this process in the copying of pictures. If you give someone a picture to copy and then give their copy to a second person to copy and so on down a chain of copiers, eventually you end up with something that looks nothing like the original. Is Jennifer recalling her childhood or is she recalling the results of her previous attempts at recalling her childhood?

These random errors are superimposed on a tendency for our thoughts and ideas to become structured around idealized forms. For example, if you give people distorted shapes to copy from memory, they tend to reproduce much more regular shapes (see *Figure 1*). As Bartlett (1932) showed, if you give people stories to learn, their memories for the details tend to reflect their cultural expectations as much as their content. For example, participants in his experiment were given a long story, called *The War of the Ghosts*, to read. At one point in the story, the narrator says:

> *When the sun rose he fell down. Something black came out of his mouth. His face became contorted. The people jumped up and cried. Now he was dead.*

When asked to recall the story, European participants tended to

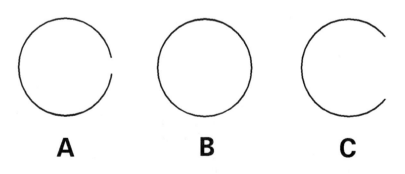

Figure 1: An example of the recall of idealized forms. If someone is shown a circle with a gap in it (A) they will either remember it as a complete circle (B) or the letter C (C).

leave out the supernatural details and to subtly alter the phrasing to fit in with their own way of talking about things, for example, by saying 'foamed at the mouth' where the original said 'something black came out of his mouth'. Has our counsellor done something similar, in recalling Jennifer's story of abuse as *sexual* abuse?

Recently, psychologists have recognized that one of the major sources of regularity in thinking is our preference for linking our descriptions of the past into stories that have a defined narrative structure. A good story has a beginning, a middle and an end, the events within the story are linked to each other so that nothing is incidental, and stories are told for a purpose, such as amusing, edifying or persuading people, depending on the context. In turning events into stories, things get left out and other things get put in (Mancuso, 1986). How far do our counsellor's notes reflect Jennifer's story and how far do they follow the counsellor's model for sexual abuse stories?

How Can I Use This Information As a Counsellor?

You already apply your knowledge about short-term memory. To be effective listeners we have to be *active* listeners, trying to make sense of what our clients are saying to us, so that we can break the stream of information up into manageable chunks, and make an effort to build up a long-term memory of what the client has said so that we can bring our other counselling skills, such as empathic reflection, reframing or interpretation, to bear on what we have just been told.

No matter how hard we try to attend to what the client is saying and put aside our own prejudices and assumptions, we will not succeed. Our prior knowledge will influence how readily we recall specific things that a client tells us and may lead us to 'chunk' information differently from the way that they intended. This is also recognized in the way counsellors are encouraged to check their understanding of what a client has said, rather than assuming that their interpretation matches the client's intent.

Counsellors talk a lot about the 'lived experience' of their clients. Research on long-term memory tells us that we have to be very careful in how we think about this, because a client's experience of remembering something in the present may bear little or no relation to what happened in the past. As counsellors we have to respect their experience of remembering something as they report it in the session, but we should not assume that the event of recall is the recall of an event, especially when dealing with the distant past.

One way of keeping this in mind is to change the language we use when talking about the mental lives of our clients. Conventional psychology tends to talk about mental events as things. We talk about 'memory' as if it is something that exists independently of the person who is doing the remembering, which implies that we can somehow pull the memory out of the person and inspect it. In talking in this way, we tend to treat 'memories' as immutable entities, lying within the person, waiting for the person to access them.

Edwards and Potter (1995) argue eloquently that it makes more sense to talk about the act of 'remembering', a constructive process that takes place in a social context and serves a purpose within the relationship. If we talk about our clients 'remembering', rather than about their 'memories', we remind ourselves that what they are saying may be true for the moment at which they say it but need not accurately describe events in the past.

Section summary

- Without active listening all that we hear is lost from our memories in seconds.

- Thinking about what you are hearing helps break it down into more easily remembered chunks.

- 'Chunking' what you are hearing makes assumptions. Check your interpretations with your client.

- People forget huge amounts about what happened to them in the past.

- The more distant the events, the less they are likely to remember.

- When asked to recall the past, people fill in any gaps.

- Remembering the past involves reconstruction, not recall.

- Reconstructing the past is a social process to which you, the counsellor, will contribute.

- The experience of memory is not the same as the memory of an experience.

Rehearsal

Rehearsal is a double-edged sword in memory. In conditions of guided learning, where the material to be remembered is continuously available to the person, rehearsal strongly facilitates recall, but, as I have already pointed out, in conditions in which the person rehearses a unique event, the act of rehearsal can lead to significant distortions.

In laboratory studies, psychologists give participants lists of words or nonsense items to learn and invariably find that the more times the person sees the list and tries to learn it, the more items they remember. The same is true for skills. The more times you practise a skill, the better you become at it and the easier it becomes to reproduce the skilled performance at a later date, providing the practice is guided and feedback is given.

A lot of people object to the artificiality of laboratory studies. Linton (1978) did a fascinating study on the impact of rehearsal under more natural conditions. She kept a diary for five years and each day noted down two events that had happened. At predetermined intervals she tested her memory for those events, so that each memory test also became an opportunity to rehearse the material, with feedback because she had to check the diary to determine whether she was right. As a result, some bits of information were only tested once, but others were tested up to four times. By doing the study over six years she was able to study her memory over a long period of time. She found that she forgot more after six years than after one but that she forgot much less if she had rehearsed the material four times than if she had only rehearsed it once.

As Parkin (1987) points out, rehearsal is very easy to produce and manipulate under laboratory conditions and has a major effect on the amount we recall, but, and this is very important, in the real world rehearsal is the exception rather than the norm. In the real world we do not always know what is important and what is worth rehearsing, nor do we always have opportunities for guided rehearsal. I do not, however, agree with Parkin that the relative infrequency of rehearsal in the real world makes it 'of little broader significance'. Given how little we seem to remember without rehearsal we must expect our clients and ourselves to have relatively poor memories for remote events. More importantly, given the immense impact that rehearsal has on memory, any factors that predispose people to rehearse information are likely to predispose them to recall that information at a later point. Look at the way our counsellor has rehearsed a brief interlude in a session, the rest of which she has largely forgotten.

At a practical level, the goal of therapy is to enable our clients to relate to familiar situations in unfamiliar ways. However, because they are well-rehearsed, familiar but inappropriate ways of reacting to situations tend to predominate and people operating on the cusp of the old and the new tend to display significant degrees of absent-mindedness, lapsing into inappropriate but well-established habits of thought and action when intending to act in other ways (Cohen, 1989). As Reason and others (in Cohen, 1989) have catalogued, in some circumstances absent-mindedness can be fatal while in others its effects are simply irritating. Typical examples in daily life are forgetting to take a letter to post, or making a cup of tea without putting any tea into the pot, but in safety-critical environments it may lead to major accidents.

How Can I Use This Information As a Counsellor?

We need to distinguish between remembering the past and remembering plans for the future. Some readers, such as psychodynamic and person-centred counsellors, will be working with models that focus on recalling the past; some, such as cognitive behavioural solution focused counsellors, will be working with models that require remembering the past and planning for the future.

All other things being equal, events in the past tend to be forgotten unless they are rehearsed. When listening to clients' accounts of earlier events you should constantly be wondering why they have remembered this particular event, out of all of the possible things they *could* have remembered. Have they been rehearsing the information? If they have been, have they been doing so with feedback (which is very unlikely) and why did the client choose to rehearse this particular information? What I am suggesting is that counsellors might benefit from standing the logic of the psychodynamic concept of repression on its head and move from wondering why things have been forgotten to wondering why things have been remembered. In doing so, they should think about the context of rehearsal. Has the client rehearsed this material by pondering silently on the past or does the material form part of a family story that is rehearsed by frequent public retelling?

Modern therapies often require clients to take ideas away from the therapy session and apply them in their daily lives. Cognitive behaviour therapy requires clients to implement instructions for monitoring types of thoughts and practising new thought patterns and behaviours. Solution-oriented brief therapies require clients to break habits by implementing non-preferred but more productive solutions that they have employed intermittently in the past. In both instances it is important that the client implement the programme accurately.

Many cognitive behaviour therapists acknowledge the memory problems involved by sending clients away with work-sheets that detail what they should do, but this is the exception rather than the rule in therapy, and even in this situation there is no guarantee that they will remember to carry out the tasks as scheduled. Evidence on rehearsal indicates that if you want clients to carry out plans in the future you need to incorporate specific, guided rehearsal in the session to ensure that the information is remembered properly. In the absence of opportunities for rehearsal, clients may simply forget what they were supposed to do or they may behave absent-mindedly, applying an inappropriate solution to a problem and then remembering the more appropriate one afterwards.

Section summary

- **Good memory is often a sign of regular rehearsal. Ask yourself why your client has rehearsed this material.**

- **Rehearsal without feedback can distort memory. Ask yourself how your client's story might have changed with repeated telling.**

- **If you want clients to remember new ideas, build rehearsal into the session.**

- **Feedback should be provided during rehearsal.**

Salience

At a number of points in the previous sections I have qualified my statement by saying 'all other things being equal' but, of course, in the world in which we live, all other things are *not* equal. One factor that biases us towards remembering things is the degree to which events stand out from their backgrounds, their salience. Salience is a woolly concept and very hard to define in a rigorous way, so it is easier to talk about the factors that seem to make events stand out. Of these the most important are when the event occurs, and the surprisingness or novelty of the event.

When the event occurs

When people are presented with a series of events they tend to remember the ones that occurred first (known as the *primacy effect*) and those that occurred last (known as the *recency effect*). Together

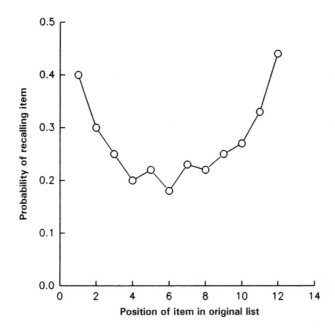

Figure 2: The 'serial position effect'. This graph shows how the probability of someone remembering a word after being shown it only once in a longer list of words varies with its position in the original list. Providing the interval between presentation and recall is short and the person is not distracted, they will tend to remember words that appeared at the beginning of the list, the 'primacy effect', and those that appeared at the end, the 'recency effect'.

these are known as the *serial position effect*. Recency effects tend to be quite fragile and easily disrupted, but primacy effects are strong.

Primacy effects are easily demonstrated using word lists in an experimental procedure called *free recall*. In a free recall experiment, the participant is given a list of words, one after the other, and then invited to recall them in any order they like. Typically they recall the most recent items first and then the initial ones, and if you draw a graph of the likelihood of a person getting the word right in relation to where it was in the list, it is the items at the beginning and end of the list that are most memorable (see *Figure 2*).

However, if you distract the participant at the end of the list, they will forget most of the items at the end of the list but still do particularly well with those at the beginning (see *Figure 3*).

Most of the information we receive is not presented in serially

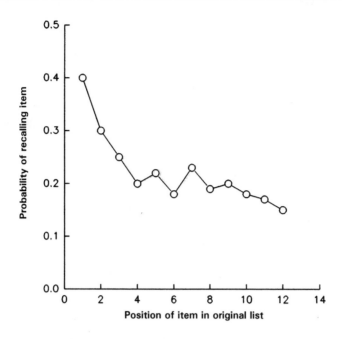

Figure 3:   Loss of the recency effect. This graph shows how the 'recency effect', shown in the previous figure, is lost if the person is distracted between being shown the list and being asked to recall it. Short-term memory is very vulnerable to distraction.

ordered lists like this, but a surprising amount of it is. One context in which it happens is in broadcasting, where factual information like news and weather forecasts is broken up into chunks and presented in sequence (Cohen, 1989). Another important context is in medical consultations, where the patient is typically first told the diagnosis, then the type of treatment and then the details of how to implement the treatment (Ley, 1978). I wonder how many times my readers have come out of a consulting room remembering all of the details of the diagnosis, but being unable to remember whether they were supposed to take one pill three times a day or three pills once a day.

Jennifer's counsellor seems to have forgotten the beginning of the third session, which seems to contradict what I have said. However, if you reflect on how most sessions open, they tend to be very similar so that one session runs into another. As a consequence, the counsellor will have been trying to recall the opening of this session out of a series of session openings with this and other clients.

Furthermore, the start of a session may be so prosaic that counsellors simply do not bother to record the events in their notes.

Surprisingness/novelty

Irrespective of where they occur in a sequence of events, surprising events tend to be well remembered. It is possible to demonstrate this in laboratory studies using the free recall method, by, for example, giving the participants printed words to read and presenting one of the items in a different coloured ink. A word presented in the middle of the list will be remembered quite poorly if it is written in the same colour as the other words but the same word will be remembered well if it is presented in a different colour (see *Figure 4*).

Similar factors seem to have been at work in Sheingold and Tenney's (1982) study of memory for the birth of siblings. They

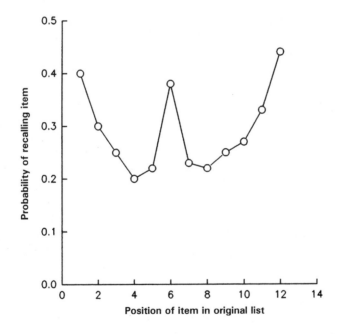

Figure 4: The effects of novelty on recall of an item. This graph shows the results of a study on the 'serial position effect', like the one illustrated in *Figure 2*. The difference is that one of the items, item 6, has been printed in a different colour to make it stand out. Note how making something distinctive improves someone's ability to remember it.

asked college students twenty detailed questions about the birth of a sibling, such as, 'Who told you that your mother was leaving to go to the hospital?' and, 'Did you get any presents at that time?', and found that college students whose younger siblings had been born when they were about four could still answer about ten out of the list of 20 questions. Contrast this with Linton's (1978) study on memory for ordinary events, who found that she had forgotten nearly everything about most day-to-day events after about five or six years. Jennifer might recall the events with her father because they stand out from the rest of her childhood, either for their unpleasantness or because she saw her father only rarely.

Surprising events don't just imprint themselves in our memories, they also seem to imprint the circumstances that surround them. This is the phenomenon that has come to be known as 'flashbulb' memory. It is a curious form of memory, because it is memory for what was happening to you at the time that something important or significant was happening, rather than memory of the event itself. The standard way of demonstrating this phenomenon for a number of years was to ask people, especially Americans, about what was happening to them when they heard the news that President Kennedy had been assassinated in 1963. Most people who were three or older at the time can remember some of the details of their setting at the time they heard the news. I can remember being at home, and there being a special edition of a television programme I enjoyed watching being put on to mark the event and honour the man. Other people have even more vivid and detailed memories (Cohen, 1989).

You might think that the impact of surprisingness on memory would make us excellent witnesses of events like crime, but it turns out that eye-witness testimony of events is quite poor. People do not remember critical details and they may be persuaded to 'recall' things that didn't happen by being asked leading questions. In laboratory studies people are shown films of staged events like car accidents and then asked questions afterwards. Loftus and Palmer (1974) showed that if you show people a film of a car accident and then ask them, 'About how fast were the cars going when they smashed into each other?' they provide a higher estimate for the speed and are more likely to agree to seeing broken glass at the scene (even though none was shown in the film) than if they are asked, 'About how fast were the cars going when they bumped into each other?'. Our counsellor has to be careful about how she asks Jennifer about her father, in case the way she phrases her questions suggests particular answers to Jennifer.

The problem with surprise is that it usually comes at the end of the sequence of events the witness is being asked to remember, rather than at the beginning. For example, if you witness a car accident in the street it is likely to be the collision itself to which you attend, rather than the events leading up to it. In many instances the surprise comes as a sound, such as the bang that happens in a collision, and sound takes time to travel so the event is likely to be over by the time you attend to it.

Our attempts to recall sequences of events may tell us more about how a person thinks about *classes* of event, rather than any specific situation. According to Cohen (1989) people carry around with them models for how particular classes of event normally unfold. These models are referred to as *scripts*, which is a bit misleading because it makes them sound very rigid. What the researchers really mean is something like the set of instructions given to a performer who is improvising a part in a play. The performer is given an outline of the sort of thing their character is likely to do or say in a particular situation, but the actual words and gestures are left to them. Researchers typically find that the details of events that fit in with the script are poorly remembered while the details of events that do not fit with the script can be quite vividly recalled. For example, Nakamura *et al.* (1985) staged a lecture in which the lecturer was primed to engage in a series of actions that fit with the typical lecture script, such as pointing to information on a board, and a series of actions that did not fit with the script, such as bending a coffee stirrer. After the lecture the participants were given a list of events, some of which had happened in the lecture and some of which hadn't, and asked to judge which had actually taken place. They were very good at correctly identifying which script-irrelevant actions had taken place, but poor at identifying script-relevant actions, being predisposed to 'recognize' events that hadn't actually taken place. In other words, when we ask people about sequences of events they, not surprisingly, will make use of their general knowledge of how the world works to fill in gaps in their memory, but seem prone to rely on this so that they don't particularly attend to script-relevant events. Scripts can make the surprising commonplace.

As issues of childhood sexual abuse enter public consciousness, people are more likely to develop scripts for abuse stories, and both Jennifer and her counsellor may be using a script to fill in details of Jennifer's childhood.

How Can I Use This Information As a Counsellor?

Counselling, unlike life, occurs in discrete episodes. Our clients typically have one session a week (sometimes fewer) and each session lasts for about 50 minutes. We therefore have many opportunities for primacy effects. We would expect clients to remember more details from initial sessions than from later ones and we would expect them to remember more from the opening part of a session than from the later parts.

Initial sessions may be routine for you as a counsellor because they unfold before you have come to know the client. You may well conduct them in a fairly stereotyped way so that the initial session with one client may be very similar to the initial session with another. You can check this out by putting this book to one side for a moment and writing out a summary of the first session with your most recent client. How much did you remember?

From the client's point of view, the experience will be completely different. Unless clients have a serious therapy addiction, this will probably be their first encounter with a therapist and it will be a completely novel experience. They will remember all sorts of details that were insignificant to you. Counsellors have to be very careful about what they do and say in the first session.

Primacy effects within sessions dictate that all advice and instruction be given at the start of a session, rather than at the end. This may seem contrary to common sense and may disrupt your own flow of thought, but it is vital if your clients are to remember the advice and instruction. When counsellors are using structured therapies like cognitive behaviour therapy it may be appropriate to start sessions with an outline of the exercises to be carried out in the subsequent week, encouraging them to practise them in the therapy setting before moving on to review progress from the previous week.

Primacy and recency effects may influence your recall of sessions. If your practice is to write up notes immediately after a session has ended, both effects may influence your recall of the session. If you write up notes some time later we would expect the primacy effect to predominate. You can investigate whether this happens by tape-recording a session (with the client's agreement), writing up your notes in the normal way and then comparing what you have written with what actually appears in the recording. If you find that a serial position effect is operating and your notes over-represent events occurring at the beginning or the end of the session, what strategy are you going to adopt to improve note writing? If you find that you do not have a serial position effect, what aspects of your therapeutic style are facilitating recall?

People remember events that surprise them. This has three implications for us. The first is that emotionally significant events occurring after a certain age are likely to be remembered when everything else has been forgotten. The second is that they remember events that surprise *them*, rather than you. The third is that people remember the surprising events themselves, and the circumstances surrounding them, but may not be able to give an explanation for them, in terms of the events that led up to them.

Considerable publicity has been given recently to the idea of recovered memories, dramatic reports of people being enabled to recall traumatic abusive events that took place many years before which they had since forgotten (Bekerian and Goodrich, 1995; Destun and Kuiper, 1996; Haaken, 1995; McElroy and Keck, 1995). Research on memory suggests that the opposite should happen, namely that traumatic events should be particularly well-remembered and should not require therapy to reveal them. This is, after all, what happens with what is now known as *Post-Traumatic Stress Disorder* (PTSD) in which people recall vividly the circumstances surrounding a traumatic event such as an accident, a bomb blast, or being the victim of a crime.

Surprise is in the mind of the beholder. What may seem surprising to you as a counsellor may seem commonplace to your client while an innocuous remark you make in the middle of a session may stay with your client for years. For example, in pursuing an empathic rephrasing of what a client has said you may accidentally hit on a form of words that is particularly poignant for the client and which they then remember long after everything else of that session has been forgotten. If the rephrasing was consonant with what the client was trying to say, this may be a good thing, but if you had got the wrong end of the stick, the consequences might be unfortunate. Clearly you cannot watch every word you utter, but if you find yourself getting stuck with a client it might be worthwhile checking over their recollection of previous sessions to see whether something infelicitous has stuck with them.

As we have seen with the account of eye-witness testimony, people are not very good at remembering what led up to a significant event. They may, for example, be able to remember vividly the fight with their partner that led them to seek counselling, but may not be able to remember the circumstances that led up to it. Since people who are not undertaking counselling show a similar pattern of memory loss for events, we should not be too ready to attribute negative characteristics, like resistance or repression, to our clients. They may genuinely be unable to remember.

When people claim to be remembering events they may be relying on scripts, rather than memory for particular situations. A client with a history of domestic violence may have a fight script which represents an idealized version of how fights take place. Part of this script may reflect the lived experience of the individual but part of it may be culturally influenced (Bruner, 1986). When you ask the client to tell you about a recent fight, what they may be telling you is a story that embodies what our culture says about fights. For example, it is culturally unacceptable to hit somebody without provocation but culturally acceptable to respond to provocation with violence. An abusive client's fight script may include provocations, even if none occurred during the original event. The same may be true for victims, who may recall having provoked their aggressor because people in our society do not get assaulted unless they have provoked somebody.

Section summary

- Attend to what you do in initial sessions. Your clients will remember them better than you will.

- Advice and instructions will be remembered best if they are given at the start of sessions.

- Check your own recall of sessions for primacy and recency effects.

- Expect your clients to remember surprising or unusual events.

- Do not be surprised by what surprises your clients. Expect them to remember parts of sessions that you have forgotten.

- Do not expect clients to be good at remembering what leads up to surprising events.

- Expect clients to be poor at remembering the details of routine events.

- Expect clients to fill in gaps in accounts of routine events by relying on 'scripts' for those events.

How a Person Thinks About an Event

A number of lines of evidence indicate that we remember things best when we have tried to make sense of them and elaborate their meaning. Material we have learned by rote tends to be forgotten fairly rapidly, unless it is regularly rehearsed, but material and events we have sought to understand often remain with us for years. These points are illustrated by two types of research study, those on *levels of processing* and those on the *generation effect*.

A typical 'level of processing' experiment involves giving two groups of people a list of words to read. One group is asked to judge whether the words are in upper or lower case print while the other is asked to provide a synonym for each of the words. Neither group is explicitly told to learn the list but, after an interval, both groups are asked to recall as many of the words as they can. People asked to generate meaning remember more words than people asked to focus on their physical features. This work is significant because it shows that even if we don't make a specific effort to remember things, we will be able to recall things when we have thought about their meaning. Our counsellor has thought a lot about Jennifer's abuse story and elaborated its meaning by linking it into her ideas about the relationship between abuse and eating disorders.

Anybody who has been exposed to recent advertising campaigns will have been exposed to the 'generation effect'. If you pay attention you will notice that many advertisements refrain from naming the product being advertised, which may seem perverse given that the aim of advertising is product recognition. The wily advertisers are relying on the fact that, faced with an enigmatic advert, most people will generate the product name for themselves from the clues provided in the advertisement. Surprisingly, they have found that you will remember the name much better if you supply it yourself than if they repeat it during the advertisement. This effect can also be demonstrated under laboratory conditions. If you give one group of participants a list of words to learn using rote learning techniques and give a second group a task in which they have to generate the same words using cues like anagrams or rhymes, the second group remembers them much better than the first. Has she remembered Jennifer talking about *sexual* abuse because our counsellor generated the word 'sexual' while listening to the story?

How Can I Use This Information As a Counsellor?

Once again, you already do. No matter what model you work with, counselling is about encouraging the client to think about new ideas and to generate their own answers to questions, rather than passively accepting the advice of an outsider. The use of open-ended questions, such as 'What was good about that event?', is much more likely to encourage later memory for the answer than closed questions like 'What was best about that event, A or B?'.

Similarly, encouraging insight is encouraging the *generation* of an answer, thus tapping into the generation effect.

Section summary

- **Current good counselling practice encourages good memory.**

- **If you want clients to remember ideas, get them to think about them in as many different ways as possible.**

- **If you want clients to remember solutions to problems, get them to generate them.**

How You Assess Memory

Most psychologists have tended to equate memory with conscious retrieval of information. We assess memory in terms of the number of words a person gets right from a list they saw a few minutes previously or the number of events surrounding the birth of a sibling that they can narrate. One of the implications of this sort of testing is that if a person cannot recall something on demand, they must have forgotten it.

More subtle investigations of memory confirm what we all know from our daily experience, which is that things we know can become temporarily unavailable in memory, so we have the strange experience of knowing that we know something but cannot recall it and we find that things that we cannot recall on one occasion are readily recalled on another. In addition to material varying in its availability from moment to moment, it has recently been recognized that we can have information available in memory without having the experience of remembering it. One context in which this happens is in general knowledge. People have a huge amount of knowledge stored but are usually unable to describe the conditions under which they acquired it and are unlikely to recall it unless prompted. Consequently, the experience of *knowing* something can be distinguished from the experience of *remembering* something. There is also evidence that memory can operate indirectly, affecting our thoughts and actions even when we are unable to recall the material to consciousness, leading to a distinction between 'explicit' and 'implicit' memory tests (Schacter *et al.*, 1993).

The fact that someone doesn't recall something at a particular time does not mean that they are incapable of recalling it completely. Most of us have experienced tip-of-the-tongue incidents, in which we are convinced that we should be able to remember something but we cannot do so at the point at which we have been asked. Brown and McNeill (1966) studied this by asking people a number of factual questions and then asking them to describe their experiences when they were unable to recall the correct answer. For example, participants were asked to give the name of 'a small boat used in the river and harbour traffic of China and Japan'. Many of them were unable to answer the question but when they were told the answer ('sampan') they recognized that it was the correct answer. Moreover, they were good at supplying partial information, such as the word having two syllables or beginning with an 's', or other words that were like the correct word but wrong. When they came up with wrong answers they were able to judge how wrong they were. People seem to know what they know!

According to Lachman *et al.* (1979), people are also good at judging how well they know something that they cannot immediately recall. Participants were given a series of general knowledge questions. Each time someone said that they didn't know the answer to a question, such as 'What is the capital of Cambodia?', they were asked to rate the degree to which they didn't know it, ranging from 'definitely do not know' to 'could recall the answer if given hints and more time'. They were then given a multiple choice test of four items, such as Angkor Wat, Phnom Penh, Vientiane and Lo Minh, one of which was the correct answer (Phnom Penh) and asked to pick one. The more strongly a participant indicated that they didn't know an answer, the less accurate they were in picking it out on the multiple choice test.

Work on the tip-of-the-tongue effect reveals two further aspects of memory, the importance of cues and the difference between recalling and recognizing material. Many studies have shown that giving people cues about the material they have to remember, such as category names or first letters, greatly facilitates recall. Other studies, such as Lachman *et al.*'s, show that people can recognize the correct answers to questions even when they cannot recall them. Jennifer may have been able to recall her father's behaviour because, in the third session, the counsellor provided her with suitable cues.

People 'know' things that they cannot 'remember' and can distinguish between the experiences associated with 'remembering' and 'knowing' (Gardiner, 1996). Researchers define 'remembering' as occurring when a participant in a study not only has access to an item being used in a memory test but can also report on the circumstances in which they experienced it. 'Knowing' occurs when the participant makes correct judgements or decisions about items but cannot report on the circumstances under which they were encountered. In a typical experiment, participants are presented with word lists and then given a recognition test in which they are presented with a longer list of words, including words from the original list. During the recognition test the participants are invited to judge whether a particular word occurred in the original list and also to indicate whether they remember it or know it.

Not only are people willing to make judgements on remembering and knowing, suggesting that the distinction makes sense to them, but the two types of judgement are affected differently by experimental manipulations. For example, getting people to think about the meaning of items in the original list enhances the likelihood of them saying that they remember something but doesn't increase the likelihood of their saying that they 'know' something. Conversely, getting people to repeat items without thinking about their meaning, increases the likelihood of someone saying that they know something but doesn't increase their chances of saying that they remember things. Jennifer may have had difficulty remembering her childhood because the events didn't have any meaning for her. When given hints by her counsellor she may have recognized that she knew that something had happened to her but she may have been unable to recall the events directly.

Turning to the explicit/implicit distinction, explicit memory tests are like the ones I have described in previous sections, where people are required to provide a verbal account of the material with which they have been previously presented. We judge the quality of memory in terms of whether or not the person gets the item 'right'. In studies of implicit memory, performance is judged in terms of how exposure to material influences the performance of new tasks, in the absence of specific recall instructions.

Typical studies of implicit memory involve priming tasks. If you give people a list of words to read, without instructing them to learn the list, and then give them a test involving the same items, such as completing word stems, the prior exposure influences the performance of the new task. For example, if the list of words includes 'forest' and one of the stems consists of 'for', people who have seen the list are much more likely to complete the stem as 'forest' than those who have not seen the list, who are just as likely to offer 'forget' as 'forest' as the answer. Priming occurs even when the participants are unaware that the answers they have given involve words on a list they have seen recently. If, for example, participants are asked to recall the list they have seen, they will fail to mention words that they subsequently give as responses to the stems. If, after they have completed the stems, you ask the participants whether the answers that they gave had appeared on the list they had seen previously they will say 'No'.

If implicit memory were restricted to priming effects like these, it would be of little practical interest. However, other work has demonstrated implicit memory effects using more naturalistic tasks (Gardiner, 1996). For example, Blaxton (1989) gave people word lists to inspect under various conditions and subsequently gave them a general knowledge test and found that the answers people gave tended to comprise words from the list. A number of researchers have looked at what they call 'implicit learning'. In implicit memory tests, the participant is exposed to the material only once and then is given a single opportunity to display what they have learned. In implicit learning tests the participant is exposed to the material a number of times and the researcher looks at the way in which performance improves over a number of trials. The tasks tend to be complex, involving the need to learn rules that are difficult to express verbally. For example, Berry and Broadbent (1984) set up a computer game in which participants had to control sugar production levels in a factory by adjusting the number of 'workers' employed. Unbeknownst to the participants, the computer is programmed with a complex rule linking the number of workers to the amount produced so that the outcome of changing the number of workers is not obvious. They found that people could learn to regulate sugar production fairly accurately, without being able to articulate the rule that linked the number of workers to the amount produced.

Although Jennifer may not be able to recall childhood abuse, implicit memory may mean that situations she experiences as an adult may prime her to think and act in particular ways. However, although implicit memory is a reliable phenomenon in the laboratory it is unclear how durable its effects are, so its impact on the day-to-day lives of our clients is likely to be limited. Most priming effects last for a couple of hours at most, although there is some evidence for effects lasting up to a year (Gardiner, 1986; Schacter *et al.*, 1993). However, studies of implicit memory tend to use emotionally insignificant materials and verbal responses. Perhaps much stronger effects might be observed if emotionally significant events were taken into account and outcomes such as non-verbal choices were considered.

How Can I Use This Information As a Counsellor?

Respect clients' self-reports about their own memories because people are usually very good at judging whether they have genuinely forgotten things or simply mislaid them temporarily. If a client is struggling towards remembering something that they believe they know then it may help to provide them with cues and prompts, but if a client says that they cannot remember at all it would be highly incongruent to force matters.

If someone is in a tip-of-the-tongue state then cues and prompts may help them reconstruct the memory but if they are denying their ability to remember something, the same cues may help them construct a memory to fit in with the cues you are giving. As we have already seen, the balance between the constructive and reconstructive aspects of remembering is very delicate.

People have a lot of information in memory that you may not access if you ask them to report what they remember about their lives, because access to that material will not be linked to the subjective state of remembering. If we are interested in finding out what has happened to our clients we may have to resort to indirect means, to tap memory without relying on conscious recollection. One way of viewing the tactics of psychodynamic counsellors is that they are using a series of procedures, such as dream analysis and free association, that tap into what clients 'know' without getting them to discuss whether they 'remember' it. Any counsellor interested in the past experiences of their clients should consider these techniques as alternative ways of accessing memory.

Section summary

- People are good at judging their own memories. Respect this.

- How well a client remembers something will depend on the questions you ask and the cues you give.

- Clients will have more knowledge *from* the past than knowledge *of* the past.

- Clients may know things they cannot put into words. Indirect methods, like free association, may reveal this knowledge.

Similarity Between Learning and Recall Conditions

Learning and memory turn out to be strongly dependent on context, so that what has been learned in one setting may be poorly remembered in another but recalled very well when the individual is returned to the situation in which the original learning took place. Context can be both external and internal. If someone learns something in a particular, distinctive physical environment, they may be very bad at recalling it in a distinctively different place. If somebody learns something while in a particular mood, they may have difficulty recalling it if their mood changes, and if someone learns something under the influence of a drug, they may have difficulty in recalling it in an undrugged state.

The importance of physical context is discussed by Baddeley (1983), who describes experiments on divers who were asked to learn things either on land or while under water and then tested for recall on land or under water. In one experiment the divers were given lists of 40 words to learn. If the divers learned the list on land, they recalled the items well if tested on land but did badly if tested under water. So far, this isn't surprising since you might expect people to find it difficult to do anything under water, never mind recalling lists of words. What was surprising was that if the divers learned the lists while under water they were good at recalling them if tested under water but poor at it if tested while on dry land. In a second experiment the researchers demonstrated a similar pattern of results when the task was learning to perform a simple skill, namely transferring nuts and bolts from one position to another. The difference between the setting of counselling and the conditions under which any childhood abuse took place may make it difficult for Jennifer to recall abuse when talking to her counsellor.

State dependency is supported by studies by Goodwin *et al.* (1969; cited in Baddeley, 1983) on memory for material which people are taught either when either drunk or sober. If people learn things when drunk, they recall them best when drunk and if they learn them when sober they recall them best when sober. Dependency on emotional state is discussed by Parkin (1987), who describes a study by Bower (1981; cited in Parkin, 1987) in which people kept diaries for one week. At the end of the week either a pleasant or unpleasant mood was induced by hypnosis and the participants were invited to recall events they could remember from the week. Participants remembered more unpleasant events in an unpleasant mood and more pleasant events in pleasant mood. Similar findings are obtained when researchers look at spontaneously occurring variations in mood such as those that occur in depression. Clark and Teasdale (1981) worked with depressed patients undergoing mood swings and found that they recalled more unpleasant than pleasant events when depressed but the situation reversed when the depression lifted. Perhaps Jennifer suddenly recalled her childhood because the counsellor created the same mood as Jennifer experienced during these events.

How Can I Use This Information As a Counsellor?

The conditions of therapy are usually very different from the rest of the client's life. The physical context is usually designed to be unlike the client's home or workplace, comprising an architecturally and aesthetically neutral space which is comfortable without being luxurious. Clients are expected to refrain from drug use before arrival and counsellors often do their best to create a non-threatening mood that contrasts with the often dysphoric state that clients experience in their daily lives. In other words, the counselling setting is designed to minimize transfer of memory from the real world to counselling. We should not be surprised when clients find themselves unable to recall details of their lives, especially of the problematic conditions that have encouraged them to seek counselling. The known effects of physical, pharmacological and emotional context on recall may be enough to explain the reticence of our clients without postulating additional factors like resistance and repression.

What can you do about it? Some counsellors, especially those working in a psychodynamic way probably do a lot to offset these factors by seeking to establish a transference relationship. By facilitating the client's propensity to treat the counsellor as if they are another, more significant person in the client's life, psychodynamic counsellors may be helping to recreate many elements of the context in which problematic events occurred and thus facilitate memory for them.

Those working in other frameworks can adopt other strategies. One approach is to work with a family rather than an individual because the presence of other family members may create enough similarity between the outside world and the counsellor room for the client to recall events accurately. Another approach is to work 'in vivo' rather than in a therapy room, going out with the client into the situations in which the problem actually occurs. A half-way position is to get the client to keep a diary, so that they record events while in the setting and mood associated with them.

If you operate in a problem-oriented framework, context effects in memory can be a serious problem unless you seek to recreate the conditions under which the problem occurs, but these effects may facilitate solution-oriented therapies (Epston and White, 1992; Pare, 1995). In solution-oriented therapy the focus is not on situations in which a problem occurred but on those in which it didn't occur, so that the client can work out the difference between those situations that lead to problems and those that do not. Since it is unlikely that a person will come to counselling unless problem situations pre-dominate in their lives, providing a setting that is unlike their daily life may facilitate memory for these infrequent events.

Pharmacological context may be a significant problem when working with clients who are on concurrent medication. Medication may interfere with memory transfer in a number of ways. Clients who are on mood-altering drugs may find it difficult to recall events associated with anxious or depressed moods, thus reducing access to descriptions of problems. Clients whose problems are drug-related may have difficulties in recalling what happens when they are drugged when in a non-drugged state. A sober alcoholic may genuinely be unable to remember what happens after they have had a couple of drinks. If the pharmacological state during therapy differs from that after therapy, there may be poor transfer of the insights and skills developed during therapy. A depressed client who has learned cognitive behavioural skills while under the influence of anti-depressants may not remember them when drug treatment is terminated. Conversely, an alcoholic who has learned coping skills while sober may forget them once they have had a drink.

Section summary

- **Context effects work against clients remembering events that occurred outside of the counselling setting.**

- **Memory will improve if you can make the counselling setting more like the context in which the initial experiences occurred.**

- **Expect poor transfer from counselling to the outside world, especially when dealing with drug problems and severe mood changes.**

Psychodynamic Considerations

Although experimental psychologists tend to be sceptical about psychodynamic models, they have made a number of efforts to provide experimental evidence for the operation of psychodynamic processes. People working on memory have been particularly struck by the notion of repression and have carried out a series of studies to see whether it is 'real'. I have put 'real' in inverted commas because I am sure that those working with these models view such experiments as trivial and irrelevant, but they are often discussed in this context. All of the work I have seen simplifies the concept of repression so as to equate it with selective forgetting of unpleasant or traumatic events.

As Baddeley (1990) reports, there are a number of psychodynamic case studies describing patients who are unable to recall traumatic events. One of the more famous cases was presented by Pierre Janet, who described a girl whose mother had died under distressing circumstances and while she and the girl were together. The girl consistently claimed that she was aware of the fact that her mother was dead, because she could remember people having told her the fact, but was unable to describe the circumstances surrounding the death.

One case might show that repression is possible but it doesn't indicate how likely it is to occur again. Do people cite Janet's case because it is a particularly clear example of a very common event or because it is one of the few published examples of a very rare occurrence? Researchers have sought to settle this issue by looking for selective forgetting of unpleasant events in other contexts.

In Linton's (1978) diary study it was possible to compare the items she recalled at any time with the items she had reported in her diary to see whether there was a recall bias. Although fairly large numbers of unpleasant events were recorded in her diary, when she looked back over the period covered by the study, she was convinced that her life had been largely happy.

Other workers have looked at physical traumata, such as childbirth, with mixed results. In their study of childbirth, Robinson *et al.* (1980) asked mothers to report on their pain levels as soon as they had given birth and three months later asked them to report how much pain they remembered having experienced. The amount of pain reported immediately after birth was significantly greater than the amount recalled three months later, suggesting that they had repressed their memories for the pain. However, women who had been given a drug to control their pain during birth reported significantly more pain when asked immediately afterwards than those given an epidural block. This difference was present three months later; women who had been given the drug recalled more pain after three months than women given the epidural block reported immediately after birth. If repression were operating, the reverse would be expected and those who had experienced the most pain during the birth would be expected to recall the least pain after three months.

Levinger and Clark (1961) offered some laboratory evidence for repression. They asked participants to learn lists of word pairs. Some of the pairs in the list were comprised of two emotionally neutral words, like window or cow, while other pairs were comprised of one neutral word and one emotional word, like angry or fear. To demonstrate that the emotional words were really emotional, Levinger and Clark carried out additional tests. One test was to measure how long people took to produce associations to the words, using a procedure first devised by Jung. People took longer to say the first word that came into their heads when presented with one of the 'emotional' words than when presented with one of the neutral ones. Shortly after the word association test the participants were presented with the cue words and invited to recall the words that had been paired with them. As predicted by their version of the repression hypothesis, participants were poorer at recalling the associations of the emotional words than those of the neutral words. However, and this is a major qualification, these effects are only obtained if you ask people to recall the associations immediately after learning them. If there is an interval of a month between learning and recall in this type of experiment, then recall of emotionally-biased material is actually better than that of neutral material. Not only that, but exactly the same results are obtained if the emotionally significant words are pleasant, rather than unpleasant.

On balance, the evidence suggests that people are generally good at remembering unpleasant events, suggesting that repression does not occur. In those studies where there is some evidence for selective loss of unpleasant memories, other factors can account for the findings. For example, the effects of emotional context can explain why Linton found herself recording unpleasant events in her diary while remembering the past as being happy.

However, repression is a much more complex concept than these studies imply. According to Freud, repression is linked to desire, being a defence mechanism brought into play to protect the ego against being overwhelmed by libidinous urges and should, therefore, only apply to thoughts and memories that are linked to the object cathexes of instincts. In other words, Freud is saying that you will repress memories only when the presence of those memories in consciousness is associated with powerful libidinous urges with which the ego cannot cope. A further point to note is that, according to psychodynamic models, repressed material is kept out of consciousness in its original form but allowed in in disguised form, following symbolic transformation of some sort. A proper study of repression would not simply look for loss of memory for specific events, it would also look for people knowing or remembering things that are symbolic transformations of the things they are repressing. Since none of the experimental research on 'repression' has sought to arouse libidinous urges in order to create anxiety, or looked for symbolic transformation of repressed material, the jury has to remain out on this matter.

Repression is not a 'thing', it is a concept introduced by a particular theorist, Freud, to make his theory work. When working with clients like Jennifer, there are enough simpler explanations of her failing to recall childhood abuse, including the possibility that none occurred, to demand that counsellors be extremely cautious about proposing 'repression'.

How Can I Use This Information As a Counsellor?

As I have already indicated, people are likely to be biased towards remembering pleasant events if they are in a pleasant frame of mind in a pleasant context. Since a lot of basic counselling skills are directed at inducing this state in clients, we should be careful about misusing concepts like repression to explain gaps in clients' memories. People can remember unpleasant events, although recall is likely to be best when the emotional and physical context in which it is being solicited matches that of the original experience. Given this bias, we should be particularly concerned when clients spontaneously recall large numbers of unpleasant events.

As the appropriate research has not been carried out, and may never be carried out given the ethical issues it raises, we cannot say that repression does not occur. What the research literature does tell us is that it will take more than just unpleasant experiences to create repression. In cases where there does seem to be strong evidence for repression, such as recovered memory for childhood sexual abuse, something else has to be operating.

If psychodynamic theory is to be accepted, repression is most likely to occur when the abuse and the abuser form part of a complex of object cathexes, in other words, when the abusive relationship is desired (subconsciously) by the individual concerned. This could go some way to explaining the, otherwise paradoxical, observation that many instances of 'recovered memory' involve apparently loving families in which there appears to have been a close and satisfactory relationship between the client and the person accused of the abuse.

Section summary

- Only use concepts like 'repression' when you have ruled out simpler explanations for memory failure. Forgetting is the norm, rather than the exception.

- Think about how you would distinguish recovery of memory, following release from repression, from the construction of new ideas about the past.

- Repression implies symbolic transformation of repressed material.

- Repression is a reaction to desire, not pain.

Neurological Considerations

While there is considerable scope for disagreement about whether people forget things for psychological reasons, there is agreement that many people experience emotional distress because of memory problems that arise from neurological disorders. These are particularly distressing because they tend to be progressive and intractable. The technical term for memory loss is *amnesia*. Neuropsychologists find it useful to distinguish between two types of amnesia; amnesia for events that occurred before the trauma, which they term *retrograde* amnesia, and amnesia for events occurring after the trauma, which they term *anterograde* amnesia.

Retrograde amnesia

Most people who suffer head injuries severe enough to make them lose consciousness also tend to suffer memory loss for events prior to the accident. Sometimes the memory loss can be very severe, stretching back many years, while on other occasions it is limited to the events immediately prior to the accident. In cases in which the memory loss is very severe it often recovers as the patient gets better, but there is usually a residual memory loss for the events immediately prior to the accident and there are sometimes gaps in the patient's memory for more remote events. Another reliable source of retrograde amnesia is electroconvulsive shock therapy (ECT), still used on occasion to treat depression. People given this form of therapy usually forget the events prior to the therapy session and may also forget things that took place in the weeks prior to the therapy.

Anterograde amnesia

Anterograde amnesia is found in a number of number of clinical syndromes, including viral encephalitis, Korsakoff syndrome, some forms of brain damage, and dementias, such as multi-infarct dementia and dementia of the Alzheimer type. What these patients have in common is a difficulty in forming new memories. Some patients, suffering from disorders like viral encephalitis, Korsakoff syndrome or localized brain damage, are often considered to suffer from the same type of memory problem, known as the 'amnesic syndrome', in which the memory loss seems largely to affect recall of events and experiences that occur after the onset of the disease. Such patients seem to have relatively pure anterograde amnesia while being able to recall things that have happened to them in the past. However, when careful study is made of their memories of past events, they also typically display retrograde amnesia as well. It is more accurate to say that such patients display much more severe anterograde amnesia than would be expected from their level of knowledge of the past than that they *only* have anterograde amnesia.

Patients suffering from the amnesic syndrome tend to have reasonable short-term memory capacity and seem to have good memories as long as they are able to rehearse material. The memory defect is often only revealed when a patient is distracted, so that they stop rehearsing the material, and are then asked to recall something. Although verbal memory is severely impaired in these patients, they often preserve the capacity to learn new skills, even if they cannot remember having learned them.

Patients suffering from dementia suffer many more global memory failures. Anterograde amnesia predominates in the early stages of the disease, but these patients are distinguished by impairments in short-term as well as long-term recall. In advanced stages of the disease, severe retrograde amnesia becomes prominent and the affected individuals become incapable of recalling important events or figures from earlier in their lives. For example, they may be unable to recognize their husbands or wives.

How Can I Use This Information As a Counsellor?

Increasingly counsellors are working in a range of medical settings, including neurological units, and may work with patients suffering from memory disorders. Working with such patients requires tact, skill and patience coupled with a deep humility about the limits of counselling. You may be able to make life better for such patients but they will still have a memory deficit.

For every person with a clinically disabling memory disorder there are many other people whose lives are touched by the problem. Living with someone with a memory disorder can be exceptionally demanding, so the relatives of such patients often require counselling to help them develop coping skills. Here, the art is to be realistic and optimistic at the same time, acknowledging the limits of your power as a counsellor while identifying those areas where your interventions can make a difference. When working with the relatives of memory disordered patients it is vital to distinguish between what is technically true and what is true for the client. As an outsider, you can apply your knowledge of dementia, for example, to tell yourself that such patients become forgetful and fail to recognize partners with whom they have lived for many years. That is probably not how your client, the partner, may be experiencing it. Memory is intimately bound up in the concept of identity so saying that someone has no memory for their past is another way of saying that they have lost their identity. Faced with hurtful rejection by someone they have cared for and loved for many years your client may be facing a stark choice between interpreting the changes in their partner in moral terms ('My husband is acting forgetfully in order to hurt me') and accepting one of the implications of the technical account of what has happened ('My husband has no memory of me, and, as a consequence, is no longer my husband') and the moral interpretation may be more acceptable to the client. You cannot work effectively with amnesia without knowing how to deal with the issues of loss implicit in the technical accounts.

Section summary

- **Poor memory may be a sign of neurological rather than psychological problems.**

- **Acknowledge the limits of your powers in such cases.**

- **Loss of memory is loss of identity.**

Chapter Summary

Remembering is a complex skill lying at the heart of counselling. Given all of the factors that militate against successful recall, it is remarkable that we and clients like Jennifer are able to reconstruct past events with such facility. Right from the moment you experience something its fate in memory is uncertain. Only those experiences that you attend to and rehearse are likely to make the transition from short-term to long-term memory, and those that make it into long-term memory are likely to fade away from the moment that they were experienced.

Rehearsal and thinking deeply about the meaning of material and events helps protect experiences from loss, but loss takes place nevertheless. When you come to recall things, temporary losses can occur, such as in the tip-of-the tongue phenomenon. Memory is also influenced by our expectations about events. Surprising events are well remembered but commonplace events are recalled poorly. Sometimes memory failure is experienced as a gap of memory, which is particularly likely to happen if one is challenged to recall specific events or pieces of information. However, we have a remarkable capacity for filling in our narratives of the past, using a judicious mixture of what we remember and models of events that tell us what *should* happen in those circumstances, even when we cannot remember specific details.

As we have seen, counsellors can incorporate knowledge of memory into their practice in a number of ways. Awareness of the constructive aspects of memory is vital, especially when clients are likely to act on what they remember in counselling sessions. Awareness of the general fallibility of memory is important when faced with clients who claim they cannot remember things. We do not have any strong evidence against notions like repression and motivated forgetting, but, given the fallibility of memory, much simpler explanations for memory lapses are available in most instances.

Anyone working within a prescriptive framework, such as cognitive behaviour therapy, needs to be aware of the ways in which their clients will have difficulties remembering what they have been asked to do as 'homework'. All counsellors should be aware of the limits of their own memories and the factors that influence those limits.

6

Individual Differences

Following the first session with a new client, John, you are writing a report to his GP. You write:

John is an anxious person who has come to see a counsellor because he is depressed following the loss of his job after the probationary period. There is some dispute about how he came to lose his job. John says that he strongly values honesty and, when he realized that his immediate boss wasn't doing his job properly, he went and shared his thoughts with him. However, in the letter dismissing him, the company said that he had failed his probation because he didn't have the necessary aptitude for the job, and they didn't think he was intelligent enough to learn the necessary skills.

In order to convey your impressions of this client you have used a series of terms that tell us how John is like some people and unlike others. When you write about his being an 'anxious person', you are writing about his personality; when you write about his being depressed, you are writing about his mood; when you write about his value for honesty, you are writing about his attitudes; and when you are writing about his aptitude and intelligence, you are writing about his capacities. These issues form part of what psychologists call individual differences.

Much of the language of psychology is about how people are different from each other and many of the theories with which we work as counsellors are descriptions of those differences and explanations of how they might arise (Mischel, 1993). There are many excellent accounts of all these theories elsewhere, so my goal in this chapter is to look at two of the larger issues relating to individual differences; how psychologists think about them, and how psychologists evaluate them.

How Psychologists Think About Individual Differences

Psychologists divide individual differences into those that relate to how people are disposed to act, those that relate to people's values and those that relate to capacity. The study of disposition has led to research on personality and mood, the study of values has led to research on attitudes while the study of capacity has led to research on aptitude and intelligence. When most counsellors think of individual differences, they probably think of personality, but a lot of counselling work relates to values and attitudes and, in educational and vocational settings, it relates to intelligence and aptitude.

Dispositions

Personality is a disposition to act in a particular way throughout one's life, while mood is a *temporary* disposition to act in a particular way. Both personality and mood entail consistency of action and reaction both within and between people, but the consistency associated with mood lasts for a shorter period.

'Personality' has to be one of the most abused concepts in the whole of psychology and it is, therefore, not surprising that many counsellors are suspicious of the whole idea. Confusion arises because we identify personality on the basis of apparent regularities in peoples' behaviour and then use the concept of personality to explain those regularities (Bateson, 1973)! If somebody asks you why John is tense when he speaks to them, you will say that it is because he is an anxious person. If they ask you how you know he is an anxious person, you will say that it is because he is tense when he speaks to people. Can we have a useful concept of personality that doesn't sink into this quagmire of circularity? I believe that we can.

When we talk about personality we are making three separate claims:

1) people are likely to repeat the way that they behave in particular circumstances;
2) if someone behaves in one way in one situation, they are likely to behave in a predictable way in another situation; and
3) the patterns of consistency are broadly the same for all people.

For example, if John is tense when he talks to you, he is likely to be tense when he talks to other strangers; if he is tense when he talks to strangers, he is likely to be easily startled and inclined to avoid dangerous situations, and you are likely to find other people who display the same combination of reactions. It is this combination of repeatability and predictability from one situation to another, and one person to another, that makes the concept of personality so powerful.

There is good evidence for all of these claims, although most of the evidence comes from capturing self-reports of behaviour in the form of personality questionnaires, and little from direct observation of people. Personality questionnaires depend on the fact that we can spot consistencies in our own behaviour and answer general questions about it like, 'Do you like talking to strangers?', as well as specific ones like, 'Are you enjoying talking to me?', which indicates that we view our own behaviour as being consistent within settings.

Predictability from one behaviour to another is revealed by the way in which answers to one question tend to correlate with answers to other questions. We can show predictability within people because the same patterns arise in many people. This allows us to use complex statistical procedures like *factor analysis*, to show that most people who dislike talking to strangers are also easily startled (Mischel, 1993; Rust and Golombok, 1989). In Eysenck's personality scale (Eysenck, 1973), 'introversion' is identified by the fact that the answers to a group of questions correlate together so that people who say 'Yes' to one are likely to say 'Yes' to another. What is really remarkable is that the questions that cluster together statistically also cluster according to their meaning. On the Eysenck scales, questions about sociability cluster with other questions about sociability, while questions about emotionality cluster with other questions about emotionality.

Researchers applying this approach have disagreed about the number of clusters of ways of acting and reacting, with some authors proposing as few as two and others as many as 16 (Cattell, 1965; Eysenck, 1973). Recently, a number of authors have suggested that there are five fundamental dimensions along which all people vary (Mischel, 1993). These dimensions are: *neuroticism, extraversion, openness to experience, agreeableness* and *conscientiousness*.

Even if it is wrong to say that someone's behaviour is *caused* by their personality, we can use knowledge of personality to predict how someone is likely to act. These predictions are far from perfect and this imperfection is often used to criticize the notion of personality itself. Thus, although you have described John as an anxious person, his anxiety didn't stop him telling his boss where he was going wrong, and you might be surprised to find that John quite enjoys a sport that is considered dangerous, like hang-gliding.

This criticism is only meaningful if we expect psychologists to be able to predict human behaviour with the accuracy with which we can predict the activities of simple machines like clocks. To my mind, a better analogy is between human behaviour and the weather. Weather is broadly predictable; it tends to be warmer in the summer than in the winter and low pressure systems tend to be associated with wind and rain. However, it is a brave forecaster who would claim to be able to predict exactly what the weather will be like over my home at five o'clock this afternoon. Knowledge of personality allows us to predict actions in much the same way as we can predict the weather; we are right more often than we are wrong but we still make mistakes. This isn't because we are ignorant or because we don't understand things properly, it is because weather and human beings are both 'complex' systems that display a fascinating form of unpredictability known as 'chaos'.

We might have more faith in the notion of personality if we understood why consistencies in behaviour appear, in the same way that meteorologists have increased our confidence in their understanding of the weather because they can explain the weather in terms of the behaviour of the atmosphere. However, psychologists are faced with a clamour of competing ideas (Woolfe, 1996) and we don't enjoy the sort of convergence of ideas that meteorologists have experienced. There are two reasons for not coming down on the side of a single theory. First, the accounts of personality offered so far do not constitute theories in the scientifically accepted sense, but are descriptions of factors that the authors have observed as being likely to influence the development of personality. They have the same scientific status as nature study. Second, the way people think about personality has changed.

When Freud (Brown, 1964; Freud, 1943), for example, writes about the mental lives of his patients, what he is doing is similar to a naturalist like Darwin reporting on the specimens he found after visiting particular Pacific islands. Just as it would be ridiculous for two naturalists who had visited different islands to fight over what constituted the 'real' plants and animals on islands, so it is foolish for psychologists who have visited different mental worlds to fight over their descriptions of what they found there.

Originally, personality theories were conceived as grand accounts of the whole of human experience and behaviour, encompassing life, the universe and everything. Such theories are called *broad-band* theories. Recently the focus has shifted to models of personality that focus on facets of human behaviour, such as the way they attribute causes to events (Rotter, 1966). Such theories are termed *narrow-band* theories and we can have many of them encompassing different aspects of mental life.

There are many factors operating in our lives that are likely to ensure consistency and predictability of behaviour. There is evidence to indicate that the bedrock of personality, what we call *temperament*, is inherited and, therefore, has a biological basis (Loehlin, 1992; cited in Shaffer, 1996). However, the genetic impact is modest, accounting for around 40 per cent of the variability in measures of temperament in most studies. This leaves a lot of scope for environmental influences and suggests that genetic factors modulate the impact of subsequent experiences rather than causing personality.

These experiences can take many forms. Psychodynamic writers (Brown, 1964) have drawn our attention to experiences that take place during the pre-linguistic phase of development, or which are not represented in conventional language. They have also drawn our attention to experiences that stem from our efforts to satisfy our desires and to resolve the conflicts that inevitably arise from those desires. Behaviourists, like Eysenck (1973), have stressed the cumulative importance of learning, as behaviour is shaped by the interaction between the individual and the rewards and punishments encountered in the environment. More recently, cognitive accounts have emerged that stress the acquisition of rules for interpreting events (Bandura, 1986).

All of these accounts tell us that each of us should behave consistently every time we experience the same conditions, but they don't explain why there should be consistency *across* conditions. To go back to my example, they can all explain why John might be tense when he meets strange people, but they don't explain why a person who is tense when he meets strangers should also be easily startled and avoid danger. Theories of personality deal with this problem by proposing some form of generalization process to link situations.

In psychodynamic theory, generalization is based on similarity of appearance or action. For example, a snake can stand in for a penis because they both have the same shape, while a pencil can stand in for a breast because you can put both of them in your mouth and suck them. Behavioural theorists, like Eysenck, have concentrated on the interaction between inherited differences in the way the nervous system operates and the experiences of the individual. Eysenck suggested that we all vary in the degree to which the autonomic nervous system, which controls the organs of our body like the sweat glands and the heart, reacts to events. In some of us it reacts strongly, so that we 'feel' situations more strongly than others (but see the chapter on feelings). People whose autonomic nervous systems react most strongly will be easily startled and react strongly to the demands of talking to strangers. An anxious person, like John, is more likely to react to a sudden noise or darkness than someone who is not anxious. Cognitive theorists propose that people generalize according to the meaning of the words they use to think about situations. For example, if somebody labels themselves as 'fearless' , they will seek out new challenges and novel situations, but if they label themselves as 'anxious' they will seek out situations with which they are familiar and which do not challenge their coping skills.

Mood is like a temporary personality. While John is 'depressed', his behaviour will be consistent from moment to moment and certain behaviours will be linked. He is unlikely to smile much and his unsmiling demeanour will be accompanied by lethargy, poor appetite, irritability and thoughts of suicide. You would expect other people who are depressed to act and think in the same way. Mood differs from personality in that it can change abruptly, so there is no reason to presume that John will be depressed tomorrow, just because he is depressed today. If you only meet people for brief periods, or in particular settings, it is easy to confuse mood and personality.

Values

John places a strong value on honesty and has acted on it, apparently to his own detriment. It used to be thought that people's values were always linked this directly to their actions, so that, if you knew what people valued, you would be able to predict how they would behave and if you could change what they value, you could change how they acted. Since those days, we have learned a lot about people's values but we have also learned that there is often a gulf between values and action.

The way that a person evaluates an object or situation is known as their 'attitude'. While values tend to be positive, attitudes can be positive or negative. Thus, John's value for honesty embodies a positive attitude to telling the truth, and a negative attitude to lying and deceit. We would expect that if someone expressed a positive attitude, their actions would be consistent with it. Someone who says they like chocolate would be expected to eat a lot of it, while someone who says that they value the ideas of a political party would be expected to vote for it. It is rarely that simple and people often do things that are incompatible with their attitudes (Baron and Byrne, 1997). British people were treated to an example of this in the 1992 General Election. Opinion polls put the Labour Party ahead of the Conservatives but, on polling day, the latter won more seats.

Another example is provided by LaPiere (1934). He arranged for a Chinese couple to visit a large number of restaurants and hotels throughout the USA and monitored whether or not the couple were served. He found that they were served nearly everywhere they went. He then wrote to the same places and asked whether they would serve a Chinese couple if they visited their hotel or restaurant. Nearly all of them said that they would not.

More recent work has shown that attitudes do predict behaviour when you take other factors into account. According to Fazio and colleagues (Fazio and Roskos-Ewoldsen, 1994), people are more likely to behave consistently with their expressed attitudes when they are forced to react quickly to situations and don't have time to think through how to react. If you give people time to think, other factors come into account, particularly the person's notion of what other people think is appropriate behaviour and the degree to which they think that their actions can influence a situation. John may have been caught out by something his boss had said and found himself talking in a way that was consistent with his attitude towards truth before he could consider the consequences. Had he been given time to reflect on the consequences, he might have kept his thoughts to himself.

What happens if someone's behaviour is inconsistent with their expressed attitudes? According to Festinger (1957), they will experience an unpleasant state which he called *cognitive dissonance*. Getting people to behave inconsistently with their attitudes induces physiological arousal similar to that seen in emotional state (Elkin and Leippe, 1986; in Baron and Byrne, 1997) and Elliot and Devine (1994) found that students who had been invited to write an essay in favour of increasing their fees felt more uncomfortable immediately after writing the essay than those who had to write an essay supporting their own views about tuition fees. John may have found himself becoming unhappy at work as he struggled to deal with the inconsistency between his attitude towards truth and the way that he had to act towards his superior.

Since attitudes can predict how people will act, it is worth asking how attitudes can change. The obvious approach is direct persuasion by reasoned argument, but this only works under certain conditions and often the format of the communication is more important than the content. People are more likely to change their attitudes if the person trying to persuade them is attractive or speaks quickly than if the persuader is unattractive or speaks slowly. Messages that do not seem designed to change attitudes are often more effective than those that tackle the issue straight on. Your degree of susceptibility to the style of the message as opposed to its content depends on the mental resources you have available to devote to it (Petty *et al.*, 1994). If you find the content of a message interesting and important and nothing distracts you from thinking about it, you will attend to the content. If the message is uninteresting, or you are distracted, you are more likely to react to the style of the communication. John is unlikely to change his attitude towards being honest at work as a result of direct persuasion.

People value the attitudes they currently hold and are usually reluctant to change them. As a consequence, there are a variety of processes that lead us to resist attitude change. The simplest way is to avoid communications that might lead us to change attitudes. If you were to try to tell John to change his attitude, he could simply stop coming for counselling. If John feels obliged to sit through a persuasive message from you, he can resist its impact by rehearsing counter-arguments before he gets the message. If neither of these mechanisms work, he may still not change his attitude in the expected direction. Instead, he may display 'reactance' and stick more strongly to his original view.

Attitude change can be facilitated by encouraging people to change their behaviour. A number of studies have shown that if someone can be persuaded to do something that is contrary to their current attitudes, they will tend to change their attitudes to make them consistent. If you do a boring and repetitive task, you are likely to say that it is interesting and pleasant! If John could be persuaded to spend time with people without telling them what he thought was the truth, he might find that his negative attitude to dishonesty diminished.

Two factors modify this effect. One is introducing new information that makes the behaviour sensible without having to change the attitude, the other is having the opportunity to play down the inconsistency. For example, if you are paid a large amount of money to do a boring and repetitive task you can explain your own actions in terms of the financial incentive, so your attitude towards the task doesn't have to change. On the other hand, if you are induced to do the task for no obvious reward, you can only achieve consistency by changing your attitude. If John acts differently at work because he thinks it will please his counsellor, there is unlikely to be much attitude change. Playing down the inconsistency is called *trivialization*. If John changes his behaviour at work, but tells himself that it is 'only an exercise' and that 'it isn't real', he is trivializing and change in attitude is unlikely.

Capacity

Aptitude is your ability to do specific things, like play musical instruments, operate complex machinery or solve intellectual puzzles. Intelligence, in contrast, has tended to be viewed as a general capacity for problem solving that underpins successful performance in a number of different areas. If, for example, one is good at mathematics but poor at everything else, one is said to have an aptitude for maths. If one is good at maths and everything else, one is said to be intelligent (Kidd, 1996; Kline, 1991). John's employers have commented on his aptitude and his intelligence.

In practice, intelligence has become defined as general scholastic aptitude. Someone who can pass written examinations, write theses and get papers published in journals is considered 'intelligent', even if they get lost every time they visit a strange city, cannot fix their car when it breaks down and cannot sustain social relationships. Someone who can fix cars and other machines, who has a good sense of place and gets on well with people, but who does badly on things like examinations is not considered intelligent. This often leads psychologists into the embarrassment of having to explain why apparently intelligent people have done foolish things while apparently unintelligent people have done seemingly clever things. Even if it is true that John does not have very high intelligence, that is no reason to presuppose that he will not benefit from specific skill training. Conversely, his lack of aptitude for particular aspects of his job is no basis for assuming that he lacks intelligence.

How Can I Use This Information As a Counsellor?

You cannot stop yourself making use of models of personality, but you *can* work on making your assumptions more explicit to yourself. By making the assumptions explicit, you can begin to separate personal prejudices from personal experience, and you can also take advantage of the experience of other people. For example, if you note that when you hear clients like John described as 'anxious', you find yourself assuming that he will also be unfriendly, you might want to consider why you are making this connection. Is this link well-documented in the literature? Is it based on your personal observations, and if so, which ones? Is it based on your experiences of your own life?

Egan (1994) distinguishes two forms of empathy, *ordinary* and *advanced*. Advanced empathy involves going beyond paraphrasing what your client has just told you to offering an understanding of their experience based on a broader knowledge of people. It presupposes the existence of personality because it involves extrapolations that can only be made if you assume some consistency of behaviour within and between people. Assuming that your client is consistent across situations allows you to make the jump from their accounts of what happened in one setting to how they might feel or act in another. For example, you might react to a comment about how a client feels at work by offering a suggestion about how they might feel when dealing with family problems. Assuming consistency across people also provides the information about the types of consistency you might see within a single client. If, for example, you make a connection between a client having difficulties relating to their boss at work and their relationship with their father, this is only possible if you assume that people, in general, tend to treat bosses like they treat fathers.

Good counselling practice incorporates everything that we have learned about attitude change. People tend to protect their attitudes by selective avoidance of persuasion and the development of robust counter-arguments, so direct argument with our clients is unlikely to foster attitude change. Furthermore, direct assault on someone's attitudes is likely to generate reactance and further resistance to change. Counselling practice avoids direct confrontation and usually relies on the client to supply their own arguments for change. Great emphasis is placed on developing the relationship between client and counsellor, so that the client sees the latter as trustworthy. When we discuss matters with clients we usually adopt an even-handed approach to issues, rather than pushing a particular point of view. All of these factors foster attitude change.

Attitudes can be changed by changing behaviour, providing the individual doesn't have alternative ways of explaining away their actions. Thus, behaviourally oriented counsellors who encourage their clients into trying new ways of acting and thinking are likely to be effective in changing attitudes as well as behaviour, but only if the individual cannot discount the change as mere obedience to the counsellor. The less pressure we put on clients to change, the more comprehensive the change will be when it happens. These issues are particular critical where legal sanctions may be applied to clients, such as drug users and sex-offenders, if they do not co-operate with counsellors.

People are not all equal in their aptitudes, and aptitude, or lack of it, may be at the heart of many of the problems that our clients present. When listening to a client's story it is worthwhile asking whether it is a story about disposition, aptitude or the combination of the two. When a student reports being unhappy on a course, is that because they lack the aptitude for study, because their course does not fit with their personality, or because their personality involves a disposition to select a course of study for which they lack aptitude, even though they have the aptitude for something else?

Section summary

- The questions we ask our clients and the comments we make to them depend on us having notions about personality, of what people are like in general and of consistencies in their actions.

- We can choose between basing our ideas on other people's studies of personality or rely on our own experiences and prejudices.

- Advanced empathy depends on notions about personality.

- Good counselling practice embodies most of the practices that foster attitude change.

- Attitude change occurs most readily when the individual is not under pressure to change.

- People vary in their abilities as well as their dispositions and ability should be taken into account when helping clients chart their futures.

How Can We Assess Individual Differences?

There is a constant tension in discussions of personality, between those who see it as what makes each person unique and those who see it as what individuals have in common with some people but not others. The first approach is called *idiographic* while the second is called *nomothetic*. Each of them is right in its appropriate context; it depends on what you are going to do with the information that you obtain. An analogy from my favourite pastime, sailing, might help illustrate the point. When I plan a passage from one harbour to another I need two types of knowledge. One type of knowledge concerns the general properties of the harbour, such as its position relative to my starting point, how fast the tide flows between the two harbours, how high the tide rises and how low it falls. This sort of information is available for all harbours, and is used for navigating between the ports. When I get to the strange harbour, this sort of general information is useless. What I need is specific information about that particular harbour, where the dangerous rocks are, where it is safe to anchor, where there is shallow water in which I can go aground, where ferries are likely to be manoeuvring.

I have trouble getting up in the morning	Yes	No
My appetite is always good	Yes	No
I have much to look forward to	Yes	No
People do not like me	Yes	No
I often get angry over small things	Yes	No
I get pleasure from seeing friends	Yes	No

Figure 5: Examples of items that might appear in a self-report questionnaire on depression (please note that, because of the need to ensure that questionnaires are not misused, these are not from a real questionnaire). The client would be expected to circle the answer that best corresponded to their typical experience and the counsellor would count up all of the answers that were associated with depression.

I use this specific knowledge for pilotage. In personality, nomothetic information is useful for 'navigation', giving you ballpark estimates of what you are likely to expect. Idiographic information is necessary for 'pilotage', negotiating your approach to the individual client. Navigation and pilotage are both needed to make successful contact with a client.

Tests

Constructing nomothetic assessments is a technically complex business that has given rise to some misunderstandings (Rust and Golombok, 1989). The first stage is to collect examples of how the individual acts in a range of situations, or how they feel about them. This can be done in two ways. The simplest is to rely on self-report by the person and ask them to state or rate how they have reacted or felt in the past. If you wanted to find out whether John was an anxious person, as opposed to just tense in the unfamiliar setting of counselling, you could ask him about his habitual behaviour in a variety of settings. *Figure 5* shows examples of items used on self-report questionnaires.

These so-called 'objective' tests are very easy to use and score but assume a considerable amount of insight and knowledge on the part of the individual. They are also fairly transparent about their intent and therefore liable to falsification by people who want to create a particular image. For example, John might want to use evidence from a personality test in court to support his claim that he had been sacked unfairly, in which case he would have an incentive to produce the most extreme score possible. An alternative approach is to use 'projective' techniques, in which the client is shown ambiguous images, such as ink-blots or cartoon frames without dialogue, and asked to indicate what they see or what they think is happening. Projective tests are very difficult to score, and require a considerable amount of training to use properly, but they require little self-knowledge on the part of the client and make it difficult to falsify answers (Mischel, 1993).

Reliability and validity

Typically, many more items (questions or images) are generated than are used in the final test. Items are then weeded out on the basis of statistical criteria to ensure that the final version of the test works as it is intended. A good test meets two criteria: it is *reliable* and it is *valid*. The simplest way of thinking about reliability is that a reliable test will produce the same score for a person every time it is used. When used twice on a large group of people, the correlation between their scores on the two occasions will be very high. If this were the only way of assessing reliability, Kelly's reputed claim that reliability is the measure of a test's insensitivity to change (Bannister and Fransella, 1971) would be justified. However, this form of reliability, known as *test-retest reliability*, is only useful when we are looking at characteristics that we don't expect to change. A better definition is that a test is reliable if changes in scores reflect real changes in what it is you are trying to measure. A test on which *scores* change a lot is not necessarily sensitive to change.

An analogy might help. Imagine you want to measure how your waist size changes with diet. You might take a long piece of material, mark off units of equal size, and count off the number of units around your waist. Now suppose that you had two measures, one on elastic and one on an inelastic material, like linen. If you took two measurements with the elastic measure you wouldn't know whether any difference was due to differences in waist size or whether it was due to the measure being stretched differently between measurements. If you took the measurements with the linen measure, which doesn't stretch very much, you would be safe to conclude that differences in the measurements reflected real differences in waist size. Reliable tests are like measures printed on linen; unreliable tests are like measures printed on elastic.

Tests also need to be valid. This means measuring what they are supposed to measure. Validity seems to be paradoxical because, to establish that a test measures what you claim it will measure, you must already be able to measure that characteristic. To be able to show that a test measures 'anxiety' you already need an independent measure of anxiety. As with reliability, the situation is much more complex than this. Establishing validity is what is known as a 'bootstrapping' procedure, in which the process of validating the test enables you to define what it is you are trying to measure. To put it simply, a test is valid when it works in the way that you would expect it to work, and this can be established across a number of settings in a number of ways. For example, if you are trying to measure the degree to which a person is prone to experiencing anxiety you could subject your 'anxiety' scale to a number of tests of its validity. Do its items relate to anxiety (content validity)? Do people who score high on the test avoid dangerous situations more often than people with low scores (criterion validity)? Do the items correlate highly with each other, but not with items relating to other characteristics, such as sociability (factorial validity)? A test is validated every time someone uses it, so the process of validation is cumulative.

The procedures that have been used to construct personality tests have also been used to construct measures of state, mood and attitude. Some scales come in two forms, a state and a trait measure, where the trait test corresponds to a conventional personality test, seeking to establish the degree to which someone possesses an enduring characteristic while the state test is aimed at assessing change in the same characteristic. For example, Spielberger has developed a widely used *State/Trait Anxiety Inventory* (Spielberger *et al.*, 1987) that allows you to assess how anxious a person is in general and to distinguish that from their degree of anxiety at a particular moment. You could use this with John to see whether he was habitually anxious or just anxious when seeing you. As you might expect, the two anxiety measures tend to correlate together but there are enough differences between the scores on the two parts of the test to make the distinction useful. Attitude scales are constructed in the same way, but incorporate items about how people evaluate particular objects or situations.

Aptitude tests require banks of items that sample the aptitude under study (Rust and Golombok, 1989). In the case of scholastic aptitude tests, like intelligence tests, this is fairly straightforward because scholastic skills usually involve completing written tests. It is more problematic when assessing aptitude for technical or artistic skills, like operating complex machinery or playing a musical instrument. In cases like these, aptitude tends to be assessed indirectly by using items, performance on which tends to correlate well with performance of the real skill. When John's employers say that he lacks both aptitude and intelligence, have they given him appropriate tests? Is it possible to devise a test to assess the aptitudes they think are necessary for the job?

Once you have the items you have to decide whether you are going to have a speed or a power test. In speed tests, all of the items are of the same difficulty, and performance is measured in terms of how many the person gets right. In power tests, the items are graded in difficulty, and aptitude is measured in terms of how far the person gets through the test. Having generated the items, aptitude tests have to be subjected to the same procedures to demonstrate reliability and validity as personality tests.

Most of the criteria for developing nomothetic tests require statistical comparisons involving large groups of people. These criteria are, therefore, inappropriate for establishing idiographic tests, which focus on consistency *within* individuals. Two systematic procedures have been developed for idiographic assessment, the Q-sort (Stainton-Rogers, 1995) and the repertory grid test (Smith, 1995). You might use these to track how a client like John's views and values are changing during counselling.

In the Q-sort you would give John a large number of statements (around 100), such as 'I am likeable', 'I am energetic', and ask him to sort them into nine piles according to the degree to which the statement is true of him, running from one pile for 'Completely unlike me' to another for 'Completely like me'. The number of items he is allowed to sort into each pile is limited, so that he has to put most cards into the middle of the range, giving the nine piles a bell-shape. The ratings given to each statement can then be compared at different stages of therapy or with the ratings given when he sorts the statements according to a different criterion. For example, John might do one sort according to how he thinks he actually is and another according to how he would like to be.

The repertory grid approach is a two stage process. In the first stage John would generate a set of concepts or 'constructs' through which he interprets the world. In the second stage he would rate people or events according to the degree to which the constructs apply to them. The construct generation stage is strongly disciplined. It involves the tester presenting the client with triads of people or situations, such as self, mother, father, and asking them to indicate one way in which two of the elements are similar to each other but dissimilar to the third. For example, John might say that he is similar to his father in that he is male and dissimilar to his mother in that she is female. This would yield a construct which could be labelled 'gender', with two poles, male and female. Another comparison might yield the construct 'temper', with the poles 'angry' and 'calm'.

133

In the subsequent stage John would be given the names of a number of people, objects or events, and would be invited to indicate whether they were male or female, angry or calm, and so on. Once one has this grid it can be subjected to a statistical procedure similar to factor analysis, which enables us to see whether constructs correlate into clusters. For example, this procedure might reveal that when John rates people as 'male' he also tends to rate them as 'angry' and 'distant'.

The problem with these techniques is that it is difficult to establish their reliability. You may well observe change in someone's Q-sort or in how they complete a repertory grid, but it is difficult to separate change in the person from inherent error in the test. There is a way round this, which is to use the procedures a number of times within a single case design so that you can show that change is consistent and only occurs during therapy (see *Figure 6*).

All current measures of individual differences rely on language and most of them are also culture specific. It is, therefore, dangerous to assume that tests that have been developed in one language or culture will be valid and reliable when translated into another language or used with another cultural group. These problems don't just arise when you translate from American to Japanese, for example. They can also arise when you use tests developed in the USA with people living in the UK and vice versa.

How Can I Use This Information As a Counsellor?

It is *possible* to assess individual differences, the question is whether you, as a counsellor, can make use of these assessment tools. On the one hand, it would be naive to assume that you do not assess individual differences when you meet clients, so the choice is between basing them on intuition and basing them on empirically validated scales. On the other hand, tests of individual differences are difficult to fit into counselling protocols and may disrupt formation of the therapeutic alliance. To some degree the choice may be taken out of your hand by commissioning agencies that want value for money and require counsellors to provide 'objective' evidence of change in clients.

Tests of individual differences are not a substitute for clinical skills, but they may be useful in speeding up the assessment process. Given the pressures towards brief therapies, this may be an advantage that offsets the problems of incorporating tests in practice. If you do decide to use tests, you need to be sure that they are

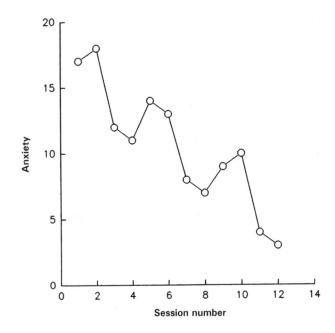

Figure 6: The results of a single case study in counselling. This graph shows a hypothetical study in which the counsellor attempts to help someone with anxiety, which is being measured at the end of each session using a standardized anxiety questionnaire. During sessions 1, 2, 5, 6, 9 and 10 the counsellor works on interpersonal issues, while during sessions 3, 4, 7, 8, 11 and 12 the counsellor focuses on the client's anxieties. Note how the anxiety improves during the sessions that focus on it and gets slightly worse during the other sessions. Note also the gradual improvement in anxiety levels during counselling. These results suggest that the counsellors's interventions are having very specific effects.

reliable (with a reliability coefficient of around 0.9 or better) and valid (correlating with other criteria at a level of 0.7 or better). Ideally they should also be short, although some of the most effective clinical assessment tools, such as the *MMPI (Minnesota Multiphasic Personality Inventory)*, are very long.

Some measures of individual differences are so straightforward you can learn how to administer and interpret them just by reading the instruction manual. Others are so complex that you need to be properly trained. In order to prevent untrained people using measures of individual differences, you can only get access to these if you register as a user and show that you have undergone appropriate training. Do not attempt to use tests which you are not trained to administer.

Psychological tests must be used ethically and The British Psychological Society has published a set of standards, to which all professional psychologists are expected to adhere, to help people do so. Clients have a right to know the results of tests that you have given to them and for you to interpret the results. This means that, if you cannot interpret a test properly, you should not use it and, since feedback about the test will become an intervention, you have to decide whether it will be therapeutic to provide it. If you think the information obtained from a test will be counter-therapeutic, do not use the test.

For example, you might decide to explore John's intelligence and aptitudes to help him discover whether he really did have the skills for the job he has just lost. What do you do if the company turn out to be correct, and he gets low scores on both tests? The best way of dealing with this problem is to discuss the implications of all testing with clients like John *before* you administer tests, and get their consent *in writing*. This is particularly important if you are using tests of ability where certain scores might constitute bad news for the client or where you might be obliged to disclose the result to a court.

When selecting tests to monitor the progress of therapy, look for state rather than trait tests. Trait tests are developed to be largely insensitive to change and may miss the subtle but real benefits of therapy. Ideally you should use tests that have been validated on samples that include people like your clients. For example, if you are trying to assess eating behaviour in somebody with the symptoms of anorexia nervosa it is important that the test has been validated on a sample that includes similar individuals. If you use tests that haven't included people like your client, you may find that your client has such extreme scores on the scale that it is insensitive to change in your client. If a client scores 20/20 on a scale, you don't know whether that is because it is their real score or because they simply cannot get a larger one. To go back to the tape-measure analogy, if you try to measure the height of a group of basketball players with a tape-measure that was developed on a group of jockeys you may find that the scale doesn't extend far enough to include the basketball players and they all come out as being 6 feet tall!

One of the problems with using psychological tests in clinical practice is knowing how to translate numerical change into clinical significance. All good tests come with data about the average score for different subgroups of the population, and the best strategy is to compare your client's score with the average for the relevant group.

For example, if John scores 15/20 on a scale of depression at the start of counselling and 10/20 at the end then the change is clinically significant if non-depressed males of similar age and background score around ten, but it is probably not clinically significant if the reference group score around 5.

Section summary

- Psychological tests can be useful for checking your insights about clients.

- Psychological tests can be difficult to incorporate into practice and should not be introduced without consideration of how they fit with your model and their impact on the therapeutic alliance.

- Only use good tests, that have high levels of reliability and validity.

- Only use tests for which you have been trained.

- Be prepared to give feedback to clients about their test results and consider the impact of this information on therapy.

- Prepare clients for the outcome of the tests you administer and only use them with the client's consent.

- If you use tests to monitor the progress of therapy, use state rather than trait versions, as the latter are designed to be less sensitive to change.

- Pick tests that have been validated on people like your client.

- Distinguish between numerical change and clinically significant change in test scores.

Chapter Summary

It is a commonplace that people are different from each other. Psychological research confirms our common sense view that there are regularities in the differences between people. People tend to behave in the same way every time they encounter a particular type of situation and those who behave in a particular way in one situation are likely to behave in predictable ways in other settings. People who turn down one invitation to a party are likely to turn down others. They are also likely to avoid noisy pubs and like spending time by themselves reading. People who solve this morning's crossword are likely to do well on tomorrow's, and they will probably also do well on other forms of problem-solving.

Personality does not mean that our actions are determined in a mechanical way. A useful analogy is with the weather. No two showers are exactly the same but showers have enough in common with each other for us to have a reasonable expectation of what the weather will be like if a shower is in the offing: there will be a sudden darkening of the sky, intense rain for a while and strong winds with the rain. Showers are different from ordinary rain, since rain follows a gradual darkening of the sky, it is usually less intense and there is no marked change in wind strength.

People also differ in their values and attitudes, which are often the focus of counselling. Much of our work focuses on attitudes to the self but there are quite often issues about client's attitudes towards other people. Psychologists have learned much about the factors that facilitate attitude change and most of these are incorporated in counselling practice.

We can identify these consistencies using psychological tests like personality inventories and ability tests. A wide range of tests that offer high *reliability* and *validity* is commercially available for use in practice. Tests can be a useful adjunct to counselling, allowing you and the client to test out hypotheses and offering a means of assessing the progress of counselling that does not depend on the, possibly biased, judgements of clients and counsellors. However, they have to be introduced sensitively and clients have to be prepared for the information they might yield.

7

Growing

Your client is called Mary. She has been referred to you for counselling because her father has just died and she has temper tantrums and gets upset when her mother goes out and leaves her by herself. Mary is reluctant to engage with you, and prefers to scribble all over your notepad or run around the room. When she does talk to you, her speech is very simple and she has difficulty understanding some of the things you say to her. Mary is three years old. Now imagine how you would have reacted if I had told you that Mary was 33.

People do not remain the same throughout their lives; as they grow from babies into adults, their abilities and dispositions change in fairly predictable ways. Change occurs in both *disposition*, what people are inclined to do, and *ability*, what they are able to do. For example, infants may display a fear of strangers which is appropriate in a young child but not in an adult, while adults can express themselves in language in a way that one would not expect of a three-year-old. Thus, the counsellor needs to know where someone is in the developmental sequence before intervening with regard to fear of strangers or relying on the client's verbal skills.

With the emergence of dispositions and abilities we see the emergence of personal identity, an awareness of being a separate individual with unique psychological characteristics and a place in the social framework. People come to describe themselves in psychological terms, such as 'sociable' or 'lazy' and predict their future behaviour, and other people's future reactions to them, on the basis of them. They also come to anticipate what they will and will not enjoy, and modify their behaviour accordingly. People who describe themselves as 'sociable', for example, anticipate that they will seek out other people, that other people will probably respond positively to their advances, and that they will enjoy interacting with people so that they develop a preference for being with people.

Alongside the development of awareness of psychological identity we see the emergence of a social identity, an awareness of where one fits into the social world. This is linked to a number of factors, including family of origin, educational experiences and occupation, but one of the most significant determinants of social identity is one's sex. The structure of a person's genitals at birth profoundly influences the social environment in which the individual is raised. In most societies there are different expectations for how boys and girls will behave, and they get treated differently, right from birth. Since the society is a world of values, increasing social awareness is coupled with increasing awareness of one's value to other people, and a desire to find a social niche that reflects positively on one while being true to one's psychological identity.

Developmental ideas are of particular relevance to counsellors because many models, such as psychodynamic theory and Roger's person-centred approach, are developmental theories that explain the distress experienced by our adult clients in terms of aberrations in the unfolding of a normal developmental sequence. For example, according to Freud (Brown, 1964; Freud, 1943), all children pass through an Oedipal phase, but inappropriate resolution of the Oedipus complex results in the development of phobias and other neurotic symptoms. According to Rogers (1961), children develop a concept of their ideal self, based on their experiences of conditional and unconditional positive regard from their parents. If they are exposed to an excess of conditional positive regard, they entered adulthood encumbered with an excess of 'conditions of worth' that lead to distress. In both instances, the goal of the counsellor is to allow the client to experience a relationship in which the damaging effects of these past experiences can be mitigated, either through interpreting the 'transference' relationship or allowing the client to experience a relationship with a counsellor who offers unconditional positive regard.

Counselling itself is a developmental process. Through counselling, clients acquire new ways of viewing themselves and the world they inhabit and new ways of relating to them. Whether one approaches counselling optimistically or not depends on one's view of the scope for psychological development once childhood is over. If psychological development is a rigid, age-related process, then one should be pessimistic about the benefits of counselling but if, as most of the current evidence suggests, development is a process that goes on throughout life then there is plenty of scope for change in adulthood.

I will start with an outline of the major concepts in developmental psychology before turning to the development of dispositions, competencies and identity.

Major Concepts in Developmental Psychology

Irrespective of the aspect of development with which one is concerned, there are certain key ideas in developmental psychology that are worth exploring separately because they suffuse work on specific aspects of development. From the counsellor's perspective, I think the most important concepts are *developmental stage*, *critical periods* and *genetic determination*.

Stages

Two of the most influential writers on human development, Freud and Piaget, advanced the idea that we develop through a series of qualitatively distinct stages, in much the same way as a frog starts off as a bit of spawn, turns into a tadpole and then into an adult frog, or a butterfly starts off as a caterpillar and then pupates before becoming an adult butterfly. As we enter a particular stage, entirely new dispositions and capacities come into play that are not merely increments on what appeared at an earlier stage. For example, Freud (1943; Brown, 1964; Shaffer, 1996) held that we pass through a series of stages related to different erogenous zones, starting with the mouth and working through to the genitals while Piaget (Flavell, 1963; Shaffer, 1996) held that our intellectual development passed through a series of stages related to the ways that we represent knowledge (through actions or words) and the logical rules we have available to draw conclusions from that knowledge. What happens at Freud's anal stage does not reflect what happened at the preceding oral stage and the cognitive abilities of a child in Piaget's 'concrete operational' stage do not reflect the abilities developed during the preceding 'pre-operational' stage.

Freud would have placed Mary at the transition between the anal and phallic stages, where she would have started to develop an incestuous interest in her father. Piaget would have placed her in the 'pre-operational' stage, in which she would have language and mental images to represent the world but would not be able to manipulate these images logically to draw conclusions that were not obvious from what was immediately visible. As a three-year-old, Mary's behaviour is appropriate to her stages of development.

If she were 33, her behaviour would cause great alarm. As counsellors we are concerned that an experience like bereavement during an early stage will derail subsequent development, having far greater impact than the same experience at a later stage.

As we move from one stage to the next, we do not necessarily forget what happened at the previous stage (indeed, psychodynamic theories are expressly based on the idea that we remember) but that knowledge may not be accessible to the mental apparatus that has emerged. According to Freud, frustration at the oral stage of development leaves a lifelong residue that significantly affects adult behaviour while, according to Piaget, the capacity to represent ideas symbolically and to apply logical reasoning to those ideas does not rule out knowledge that can only be expressed through action, such as riding a bicycle. However, knowledge of oral frustration is not directly available to adults; it is expressed symbolically through behaviours like chewing pencils and being sarcastic. Knowledge of how to ride a bicycle cannot be expressed in words and no amount of logical reasoning can make you a better cyclist. Later in life, Mary may not remember much of her father's death, but it may leave an indelible mark on her style of thinking and acting.

Stage ideas are attractive because they summarize development by breaking up a lengthy and complex sequence of events into a small number of large chunks. Describing a child as being in the phallic or pre-operational stage conveys a wealth of information in a very straightforward way. It may, however, be misleading. The largely retrospective nature of the investigatory procedures used by psychodynamic writers precludes direct evaluation of their stage concepts. In the case of Piaget's work, 'stages' are much less clear-cut than simple summaries of his work suggest. There are two problems. The first is that stages are demonstrated in studies that use tasks that a child can only either get right or get wrong; they cannot be 'a little bit' right. For example, one of Piaget's most famous studies involved investigating whether young children could recognize that, when you pour water from a tall, thin beaker into a short, wide one, the amount of water does not change. Pre-operational children say that the water gets less but children in the concrete operational stage recognize that the amount stays the same. A child either gets this right or wrong so that there is no way that one pre-operational child can show that she understands more about what is happening in this situation than another. Using this sort of task is a bit like measuring how high children can jump by setting a hurdle at four feet and inviting them to try to jump over it. Some children will succeed and some will fail but it would be meaningless to say that all children who failed had the same jumping ability because some might just fail to clear the hurdle while others may not get six inches off the ground.

The second problem with Piaget's stages is that whether or not the child clears the hurdle depends on how you set it up. Children who fail the two beaker test when it is presented in one way are found to succeed when it is presented in another. Children who pass the two beaker test may then go on to fail another test that, according to Piaget, requires exactly the same logical abilities, suggesting that logical reasoning does not develop in discrete stages.

A further problem with all stage theories is that it is difficult to separate the psychological from the social, physical or the logical. For example, Erikson (1982; cited in Shaffer, 1996) outlined eight stages of human development, built around different types of crisis, running from the crisis of 'basic trust versus autonomy' in the first year of life, through 'intimacy versus isolation' in early adulthood to 'ego integrity versus despair' in old age. Erikson's sequence of crises illuminates the problems we have to deal with as we grow, but it reflects the social and physical status of the individual and the logical relationship between the concepts, rather than reflecting underlying psychological processes. We have to be physically and sexually mature to experience the crisis of 'intimacy versus isolation', so it is inevitable that it will follow other crises that arise from immaturity, such as 'basic trust versus mistrust'. 'Ego integrity versus despair' logically presupposes that one started with an integrated ego which has to have developed out of earlier experience. Some of Erikson's stages seem rooted in Western, industrialized social structures. If Mary lives in a rich, industrialized nation she will have the benefit of a stage of 'industry versus inferiority' during which to develop social and academic skills, followed by a stage of 'identity versus role confusion', during which she could develop her adult identity, that would be denied to her if she lived in a developing nation where she had to start work at the age of six.

Critical periods

One of the reasons to be concerned for Mary is that she might be passing through a phase of development during which a particular experience, such as forming an incestuous attachment to her father, has to occur for development to proceed normally and the individual will only accommodate the experience if it happens at that time. Such phases are known as *critical periods*.

The strongest evidence for critical periods comes from the study of 'imprinting' in birds that are physically mature and mobile on hatching, such as ducks and geese. As Lorenz (1937) discovered, goslings develop a habit of following around whichever animal they happen to see shortly after hatching. Normally this is the bird that has hatched them, but Lorenz discovered that, if goslings are hatched artificially, they will follow the humans they see after hatching. Subsequent research demonstrated that this tendency to follow things around could be attached to almost any moving object seen shortly after hatching; it didn't have to be alive. The research also showed that, if ducklings or goslings were left for long enough after hatching and then allowed to see a moving animal or object, they did not follow it around. The tendency to 'imprint' on an animal or object only occurred if it was seen during a 'critical' period.

Critical periods can also be seen in the development of the nervous system (Shatz, 1993). One of the most remarkable features of our visual systems is that, although we have two eyes, we see one world in three dimensions. This is possible because input from the eyes to the brain is routed in such a way that the nerve fibres linked to corresponding areas in the two eyes end up being routed to make contact with the same cells in the visual cortex. This linkage depends on appropriate sensory experience during development. If the inputs from each eye are simultaneously active, they will both maintain their contacts with the same nerve cell in the visual cortex. If one of the inputs is active without the other one, such as happens if a child grows up with a squint, then only one of the inputs survives and the capacity for binocular vision is lost. Experimental studies have shown that this simultaneous input has to take place within a limited period of time after birth. If the experience of appropriate binocular activity is delayed then the capacity for binocular vision is lost and is rarely recovered completely, even with extensive treatment.

It is one thing to show that there are critical periods in development for birds and brain cells but it is another matter entirely to show that they occur in human intellectual, social and emotional development. The idea of critical periods is central to models of attachment, particularly Bowlby's (1969) psychodynamic approach. According to Bowlby, infants need a warm, close and continuous relationship with a primary caregiver (ideally the biological mother) during the first three years of life and those who do not experience such a relationship during this period grow up anxious and find it difficult to form close relationships later in life. Moreover, according to Bowlby, subsequent experience of such a relationship cannot overcome the damage done by the initial deprivation.

While most authors accept the importance of early experience in development, much of the evidence suggests that warm, close and supportive parenting of children older than three years can considerably offset the effects of initial deprivation. Thus, the notion of *critical* periods in emotional development has been largely abandoned, although it is recognized that there may be periods during which developing infants are more *sensitive* to certain experiences. Most developmental psychologists would acknowledge that, because of its timing, Mary's bereavement could seriously damage her subsequent development, but they would maintain that appropriate support and parenting could mitigate the effects.

Genetic determination

For over a century psychologists have debated whether our behaviour is determined by our genes or by our experiences following our birth (Shaffer, 1996). Most counsellors are inclined to the latter view and tend to play down the possibility of genetic influences, because counselling doesn't make much sense if our actions and thoughts are largely determined by the chromosomes we inherited from our parents. If I, as a male, am destined to be aggressive and violent towards women because I carry a Y-chromosome, then no amount of counselling or therapy is going to change that. If my sexuality is determined by another gene then, no matter how much I admire my homosexual friends I am never going to be able to be like them. On the positive side, if Mary's temperament is genetically determined, she will be insulated from the effects of her bereavement.

The problem with this argument is the use of the word 'determine'. In development, nothing is determined; things are *constrained* because development relies on an interaction between genetic information and the environment in which development takes place. The process is similar to the way that landscapes form through the interactions between the structure of rock formations and the impact of water.

Imagine a newly formed continent where the rock consisted of an absolutely level plateau of totally uniform rock. Over the millennia, rain falls on this surface and washes little bits of rock away, creating little grooves in which subsequent rainfall can collect and run. Over the subsequent millennia, falling rain gets channelled into these grooves, cutting them deeper and deeper until river valleys form. If you could restart the process and let the film run again, you would end up with a completely different landscape each time. This is a world in which the environment holds sway and inheritance has no impact.

Now consider a continent where the rocks are solid granite that has been spewed out by volcanoes over many millennia. The surface is uneven and the rocks unyielding, so all of the rain that falls is channelled into the hollows, and grooves between the rocks and runs in predetermined channels that change little over the millennia because the rocks are so hard. This is the world of genetic determinism.

Now imagine a more realistic continent, in which the rocks are slightly folded and uneven in texture, being soft in some places and hard in others. As the rain falls on this landscape it will be channelled into the pre-existing grooves and cut them deeper and it will erode away the soft rock faster than the hard. After a number of millennia, deep valleys will have been cut between the peaks of the original folding and mostly only hard rock will remain. If you restarted this process, you would end up with a different landscape each time but there would be similarities between them, reflecting the inherent fault-lines in the original landscape.

Our development is like the formation of the landscape in the folded, uneven continent. Genetics endow us with the rock formations with their folds and flaws, and our physical and social environments constitute the weather that moulds the landscape. Without the weather, nothing happens, but its impact is channelled by inherent folds and flaws. Even if people have exactly the same genetic endowment they do not turn out the same unless they experience the same environmental forces; they do become similar because the impact of the environment is constrained by the genetic factors. Neither genetics nor environment is responsible for development; the impact of one is constrained by the other. The Mary who emerges after her bereavement will be different from the Mary we would have seen had her father lived, but the two Marys would have much in common.

How Can I Use This Information As a Counsellor?

Be careful of big ideas like 'stages' or 'critical periods'; development is a very complex process. Stage models are useful summaries of what you might expect of someone at a particular age, but they gloss over a lot of the fine detail that may be relevant to counsellors and they probably tell us more about the constraints on what we can do as we grow up, and the resources we have available to do things, rather than illuminating fundamental psychological processes.

The temptation to treat stages as plans for how clients should develop can make you insensitive to clients' descriptions of their own histories. You may fail to ask questions because you think you already know the answer, you may misinterpret what your client is saying, or you may actually end up fighting with clients as you try to impose your model of 'normal' development on their experiences. The notion of 'critical periods' may be unhelpful to counsellors because it focuses on what may have 'gone wrong' with someone's development, rather than offering clues as to how they can come to live fulfilling adult lives.

On the positive side, stage theories are an aid to problem-solving, indicating sub-goals in helping clients move towards their goals in counselling. Intellectual abilities are built on other intellectual capacities and mature social competence depends on having developed other interpersonal skills. To take a very simple example, a client experiencing low work satisfaction might benefit from further training but will be unable to get it if they haven't mastered the earlier intellectual skill of reading. At the social level, it is unlikely that an adult who has difficulty trusting people is going to be able to negotiate intimate adult relationships. In both instances, thinking in terms of stages helps us identify what might benefit the client before focusing on the problem that has brought them to counselling. Going on a vocational training course is not going to benefit the client who cannot read and offering social skills training to a client who cannot trust the trainer is likely to be fruitless.

For counsellors who work eclectically or integratively, stage models offer a way of deciding which approach is most appropriate. Some models, such as psychodynamic and client-centred approaches, focus on the effects of very early developmental experiences and may be most appropriate when clients experience difficulties like lack of trust, that pervade all of their adult experiences. Other models, such as Egan's (1994) skilled helper approach, implicitly presuppose that early stages of development have been negotiated appropriately and that the client needs help dealing with crises of adulthood.

It is possible to acknowledge the importance of genetic endowment in guiding a client's development without falling into the pit of genetic determinism. Genetic influences do not determine who you become, but they make it more likely that you will develop in one way than another and they will make it harder for a counsellor to facilitate some sorts of change than others. For example, someone born with an innate disposition to be anxious may be raised in an environment in which that disposition gets little chance to flourish, so ending up quite fearless. However, there are fewer ways in which someone born with this disposition could end up as a

147

non-anxious adult than someone born without it, and fewer ways of enabling the individual to cease to be anxious.

Section summary

- Developmental ideas are descriptive of the average child, not prescriptive for your client. Do not let your ideas about development stand in the way of listening to your client.

- Childhood is an important time in development, but development continues throughout life. Be optimistic about your client's capacity to change.

- Developmental ideas help you think about the order in which clients may have to deal with problems to achieve their goals. Establishing trust is fundamental in development and it must be the first stage in counselling.

- Genetic factors constrain development, they do not cause it. There is always scope for change if the environment is appropriate and the job of the counsellor is to provide the context in which change can occur.

The Development of Dispositions

As we grow, we find ourselves more inclined to do some things and less inclined to do others. At two, Mary may well have clung shyly to her father when family friends came to visit but, twenty years later, she would probably face the same people with self-confidence. At two, Mary may cheerfully have wandered onto a busy road, oblivious of the risk of serious injury, but the adult Mary would be expected to show a healthy respect for moving cars and be very cautious when crossing roads. At two, Mary probably had no interest in genital sex but at 22 she would probably spend a fair amount of time thinking about sexual encounters. For convenience I will consider the development of feelings and desires separately.

Feelings

Feelings are there from birth, and most of an infant's behaviour that is likely to be noticed by adults can be crudely classified as 'emotional'. Izard (1993; cited in Shaffer, 1996) filmed the reactions of babies as young as 2.5 months to events like being given an ice-cube to grasp or seeing their mother return after a separation and showed the pictures of the babies' expressions to raters, who had to name the emotion exhibited by the baby without knowing what had happened. Positive emotions, such as joy or interest, are very clearly communicated. Negative emotions, such as anger or fear, are readily distinguished from positive emotions but are difficult (but not impossible) to distinguish from each other.

Three important things happen to our emotions as we get older. The first is that we move from having emotions that reflect what the world has done to us, such as anger, disgust or joy, to having emotions that reflect what we have done to the world, such as pride, shame and embarrassment, the 'self-conscious' emotions. At three, Mary would have been able to feel guilt about her father's death if she had ever wished him ill, as well as anger at her loss. The second is that we learn to control or hide our feelings in accordance with social expectations and their impact on other people. A good example is children's reactions to presents. Very young children react very openly and negatively to presents that they don't want but, as they get older, they learn to suppress their anger and express thanks to the giver. Mary may be *feeling* no worse than her mother, but she has yet to learn how to hide her feelings. The third is that we become sensitive to the emotions of others, learning to read them from their expressions and behaviour. Not only do we learn to identify the emotions of others, we also react sympathetically so that we experience fear if another person displays fear in a particular setting. For example, a one-year-old will approach and play with an unfamiliar toy if a nearby stranger is smiling, but will avoid it if a stranger is exhibiting fear (Klinnert *et al.*, 1986; cited in Shaffer, 1996). Mary's reaction to her loss may be mirroring her mother's, even though she does not fully understand what has happened.

Awareness of other people's feelings develops very early, suggesting that it is a fundamental aspect of human development like learning to speak, but what strikes me when working with clients is how often they seem to be unaware of what others are feeling. How can we fit these ideas together? I think that adult emotional sensitivity is different from that which has been described in infants. First, the emotions to which infants are sensitive tend to be the ones that develop earliest, like fear or joy, rather than the more subtle social emotions like shame or pride, but our adult lives are much more dependent on recognizing social emotions. Second, adults are good at hiding their reactions, so the cues available to us may be much more subtle than those that are revealed to infants. Third, you can only notice that to which you are attending, and adults who are insensitive to other's feelings may simply not be attending to other people, either because they haven't learned the strategies involved or because their mental capacity is fully occupied attending to their own concerns and feelings in a situation. Finally, the ability to recognize emotions depends on the ability to anticipate them, which requires some sort of 'mental model' of how other people are likely to react. A child may acquire a fear of dogs by observing that his father is also afraid of them, but he is more likely to learn from his father's reaction if he knows that fear is an *appropriate* reaction to large animals and looks for signs of fear in his father when they encounter dogs together. An adult who does not anticipate that their actions may frighten other people will not be looking out for fear and may interpret what they do observe in other ways.

Desires

Our desire for food, water and warmth remains fairly constant throughout life, unless we are ill, but other desires emerge and change as we get older. These tend to be social desires. New-borns desire to be looked after but they don't seem particularly concerned about who does the caring, providing it reaches an acceptable standard. After a few weeks, babies develop a preference for the presence of other people but it is only after about six months that babies come to desire the presence of *specific* other people, usually their primary caregiver. Subsequently, babies develop attachments to other people, such as their fathers, siblings or playmates, while retaining their primary attachment to their main caregiver. During adolescence our attachments to other people undergo major upheavals, partly related to the emergence of the peer group as the major focus, and partly due to the emergence of mature sexual desire (Shaffer, 1996).

Attachment is a complex process because it is a two-way street; caregivers have to become attached to their infants in order for infants to become attached to their caregivers. During the phase in which infants are indiscriminate about who cares for them, they have a number of features and engage in a range of behaviours that seem to enhance the attachment of their caregivers.

The physical appearance of babies encourages attachment. Humans show a remarkable capacity for becoming attached to non-human animals like cats that have the same shape of face (round, with big eyes and a flattish nose) as babies, and mothers of unattractive babies spend less time playing with and cuddling them than mothers of attractive infants spend with their babies (Barden *et al.*, 1989; cited in Shaffer, 1996). The emotional reactions of babies that I mentioned earlier are also likely to foster attachment. Few of us can resist a baby's smile and even crying can generate attachment if it stops when the caregiver does something.

It used to be thought that the attachment of the child to the caregiver depended on very little other that the continued presence of the caregiver and a reasonable level of physical care but it is now recognized that the quantity and continuity of care is less important than the degree of sensitivity displayed towards the child's needs and emotional state. The degree of sensitivity that can be attained is revealed in the detailed observations of caregiver/baby interaction that can be obtained by filming interactions between mothers and babies and playing them back in slow motion (Shaffer, 1996; Trevarthen, 1979). This typically reveals an exquisitely choreo-graphed sequence of actions by the child and caregiver in which each attends to the behaviour of the other and adjusts their actions accordingly. For example, mother and baby may play an apparently repetitive game of peek-a-boo, but detailed analysis reveals that the child sometimes turns away abruptly from the mother and becomes impassive. If the mother stops playing and waits a few seconds the child turns back and the game resumes. If the mother does not wait, but pursues the child's gaze and insists on continuing the game, the child is likely to turn even further away and make its rejection of its mother even more overt. Two mothers may appear equally caring and sensitive to their child but, at this fine-grained level of analysis, only one may be sensitive to the child on a moment-to-moment basis.

According to Ainsworth, variations in the sensitivity and consis-tency of mothers' reactions to their children are associated with variations in the child's attachment to its mother. Ainsworth *et al.* (1978; cited in Shaffer, 1996) developed the *strange situations* proce-dure to study variations in the way children are attached to their mothers. It is a complex procedure but, in essence, it involves the child being left in a room for brief periods, either completely alone or with a stranger. The type of attachment the child has for its mother is assessed from the way the child reacts when left alone and how it reacts when the mother returns. Using this procedure, Ainsworth and her colleagues have identified a number of types of attachment, the most common of which are *secure attachment* and *avoidant attachment*. Securely attached infants play happily with their mothers present and seem happy to have the stranger present with the mother. They are clearly upset when the mother leaves but seem pleased when she returns and seek out her company. Avoidantly attached infants try to stay close to their mothers and explore very little during this phase of the test. They show little reaction when the mother leaves and ignore her or avoid contact when she returns. These infants are neither particularly afraid of the stranger nor interested in them. Subsequent work indicated that the mothers of securely attached infants tend to be sensitive to their social cues, enjoy their company and encourage them to explore while the mothers of avoidant infants seem to fall into two camps, those who neglect their children and those who spend a lot of time with them but are insensitive to their social cues, so that they give them attention that they do not want (Ainsworth, 1979; Isabella, 1993; Isabella and Belsky, 1991; all cited in Shaffer, 1996).

It is widely assumed that one's attachment with one's mother sets the pattern for all other relationships later in life, but recent evidence suggests that although the type of attachment experienced in infancy carries on into later childhood, it does not have an inevitable effect on adult social relationships. If a child continues to experience the same type of interaction in childhood as it experienced in infancy, then the evidence suggests it will exhibit the same patterns of attachment to peers and adults other than its parents. However, if the pattern of care-giving changes or the individual is exposed to other social influences, such as a significant peer group, then the effects of the earlier relationships can change. Avoidant individuals can become secure in their attachments while securely attached infants can become avoidant adolescents and adults (Shaffer, 1996). By three, Mary may have developed a strong attachment to her father and, in some circumstances, that attachment may have been more important than her relationship with her mother.

Adolescence sees a major shift in attachment patterns, as the focus shifts from the family to potential sexual partners. The desire for sexual stimulation seems to be present from a very early age, as witnessed by the fact that toddlers and young children often masturbate and play sexual games with each other such as 'doctors and nurses'. Sexuality changes radically with the onset of puberty in that the desire for sexual stimulation becomes linked to the desire to experience it with specific people, typically members of the opposite sex. With puberty, sex takes on a personal dimension and personal relationships take on a sexual dimension. These changes are linked to increases in the output of sex hormones in adolescents and the development of a cyclical pattern of hormone release, the menstrual cycle, in girls.

In both sexes, the increased hormone levels also trigger the development of secondary sexual characteristics, such as lowered voices and facial hair in boys, and the development of breasts in girls, that mark the onset of sexual maturity. Boys also undergo a significant change in facial appearance, as their chins and foreheads thicken and their noses grow, so that by the end of puberty boys develop a distinctive masculine appearance. The desire for a sexual partner is a complex one to fulfil, since it requires you to attract a potential partner and to negotiate the fact that you are intending a sexual relationship. With adolescence comes the need for a new set of social skills that enable us to establish such *sexual* relationships (Levin, 1994; Shaffer, 1996).

Most of us experience the desire for the company of other people throughout our lives, but the objects of that desire change systematically with age. Infants and young children seek the company of reliable caregivers who will provide them with sustenance and protection. As they grow, children lose their dependence on their caregivers and become more interested in their peer group, particularly members of their own sex. However, with puberty and the onset of mature sexual desire, the situation changes again and adolescents desire the company of potential sexual partners.

How Can I Use This Information As a Counsellor?

Emotional maturity has two parts, controlling the expression of our own feelings and being aware of the feelings of others. Self-control is something that takes a considerable amount of effort and relies on appropriate feedback from other people to teach the growing child the contexts in which particular emotions are appropriate and the strategies for achieving self-control. Beyond the first two or three years of life, self-control should be the norm rather than the exception and this should be reflected in your practice with families and children. A counsellor working with children who does not address issues of emotional self-control may have a difficult time justifying their practice to outsiders. Interestingly, many of the strategies used by children to master self-control, such as verbal self-instruction, are the basis of adult therapies such as cognitive behaviour therapy.

Clients may fail to develop sensitivity to other people's feelings for any of three reasons: an inability to read the cues properly; developing strategies of social interaction that occupy so much mental capacity the client is unable to attend to the cues; and failing to develop appropriate models of social interaction that enable them to anticipate other people's feelings successfully. When working with clients who have difficulties in social interactions, it is important to identify where the difficulties have arisen and what their other consequences may have been. For example, psychodynamic approaches centre on the third area, the development of inappropriate models which are revealed through interpreting 'transference'. Such an approach may have limited success for two reasons:

first, the client's difficulties may be the result of failing to learn to read social cues, or being too preoccupied during social interactions to attend to them; and, second, even if the core problem was the failure to develop an appropriate model of how others react, the client will probably also have failed to learn to read the social cues successfully because they will have no meaning within the model that the client had developed. After you have completed psychodynamic therapy, social skills training may still be required.

Becoming a counsellor involves continuing your own emotional development. Emotional self-control is fundamental to counselling practice, and much of the work in supervision and training involves enabling counsellors to detach their emotional *expression* from what they feel when they hear their clients' stories. At the same time as having to learn to control the expression of their own emotions, counsellors have to acquire greater sensitivity to clients' feelings. The fact that counsellors can acquire and heighten these abilities should make us optimistic about what our clients can achieve, given appropriate support by us.

The recognition of other people and the desire to be with them develop very early, suggesting that sociability is inherent in being human, rather than something we learn out of the frustration of egocentric desires. How caregivers respond to these early social desires has a huge impact on the way that we subsequently relate to other people and being raised by caregivers who are sensitive to a child's emotional state and needs gives that child a great advantage in being able to achieve satisfying, trusting relationships later in life.

Current evidence indicates that we should not be too pessimistic about this situation, as warm, supportive relationships later in life can help people overcome the impact of damaging early social relationships. I think it is interesting that many of the features of the core counselling relationship, such as empathy, congruence and warmth, are precisely what have to be present in relationships with caregivers early in life to ensure confident attachment and encourage trust in relationships with others. This, in turn, suggests that the style of the counselling relationship is, in many instances, going to be much more important to the client than the content, and counsellors who put approach before relationship style may have great difficulty in working with clients who have failed to establish confident, trusting relationships.

Translating sexual desire into adult sexual relationships is extraordinarily difficult because some many things have to be got right. It is not surprising that many of our clients have difficulty with sexual relationships and it may be worthwhile viewing sexual problems through a developmental perspective to identify the point at which things might have gone wrong. For example, sexual behaviour depends on trust so it is unlikely that a person who has failed to learn to trust will be able to establish satisfactory sexual relationships. It also depends on learning social rules that are likely to be culture specific, so clients who trust other people may fail to establish satisfactory relationships if they have not learned the rules, sometimes termed 'sexual scripts', for establishing intimacy.

Section summary

- Expect emotional self-control even in young children and worry about it if it is absent.

- Expect clients to be sensitive to the feelings of others, as this typically develops quite early.

- Consider making emotional self-control and sensitivity to others explicit goals of therapy, since many problems may be the result of clients having failed to develop these basic social competencies.

- Becoming a counsellor involves continuing your own emotional development. If you can do it, so can your clients.

- Being around people who are sensitive to your emotional state and needs helps you develop trust in others. Sensitivity to clients may be more important than the model you use.

- Clients who can establish trust may fail in relationships because they have not learned the rules for particular types of social interaction, such as sexual encounters. Social skills training may be a useful adjunct irrespective of your model.

The Development of Abilities

It is well established that children's perceptual, manual and intellectual abilities improve with age and the changes that are reliably observed in ability are well documented in a number of sources (Shaffer, 1996). Development involves two processes. One is the generalization of cognitive and perceptual skills across a wider and wider range of contexts and media of expression, the other is the acquisition of entirely new abilities. Infants have a surprising range of perceptual and intellectual skills, but they are expressed solely through movement, such as directing the gaze towards interesting or surprising visual scenes, and it is not clear that the knowledge expressed in one context can be applied in others. As children get older, their knowledge is less strongly dependent on context and can be expressed in a variety of ways but particularly through language. The other is that new abilities come with age, the most obvious example being language but social knowledge also emerges as children grow. In this section I want to focus on two issues that I believe are most relevant to counsellors, the processes that facilitate cognitive development and the development of knowledge about other people.

What prompts cognitive development? Most authorities agree that cognitive development is encouraged by a mismatch between the current competence of the child and the demands of the problem facing it, providing the mismatch is not too great. In learning language, for example, children can acquire new vocabulary by hearing words that they don't understand in the context of words that they do. If they hear only words they understand, there is no stimulus for learning new words and if they hear only words that they don't understand, they are likely to give up the pursuit of meaning altogether. There is no reason to presuppose that this principle applies only to children and it would be safe to conclude that, if you wish to foster cognitive development in individuals of any age, you need to contrive situations that are just beyond their current ability to cope, placing them in what Vygotsky (1978; cited in Shaffer, 1996) termed the 'zone of proximal development'.

Mary's experience is unusual for a three-year-old and she is unlikely to possess the cognitive apparatus to deal with it. Adults will be acting strangely and using language that is either unfamiliar, or unfamiliar in its present context. Mary will be able to cope if these experiences slightly exceed her ability but not if they exceed them dramatically. Her mother and counsellor will have to work hard to find ways to enable Mary to understand.

What resources support cognitive development? Cognitive development takes place against the background of a maturing central nervous system, so a lot of it is likely to follow a genetically programmed sequence. Thus the emergence of language is believed to depend on the maturation of specific neural mechanisms, often described as a 'language acquisition device'. Some authors believed that cognitive development was largely a matter of appropriate experiences encouraging this innate sequence to unfold (Chomsky, 1968) so that, in the absence of such experiences, individuals remain arrested in early stages of development while, in the presence of these experiences, cognitive development proceeds in the same way in every individual.

A number of authors have argued that, once we acquire language, a lot of our cognitive abilities are embedded in language rather than in our brains. Language structures our thinking and gives us a set of tools with which to carry it out (Bruner, 1986;

Hutchins, 1996; Vygotsky, 1962). For example, people of my generation were taught to do arithmetic by rote learning of multiplication
tables so that, even without understanding why, I can tell you
instantly that 11 times 11 is 121 and 12 times 11 is 132. Some of the
best evidence for the relationship between language and thinking
comes from listening in on pre-school children who are problem
solving. At this age, they tend to talk to themselves about what they
are doing and detailed analysis of this speech reveals that they talk
more to themselves about difficult problems than simple ones and
the sorts of things they say to themselves are very similar to the
things that adults have previously said to them when guiding them
through similar problems. At a later stage, children no longer say
these things out loud but most children and adults will admit that
they engage in a similar, but internal, monologue when dealing
with difficult problems. Sometimes adults revert to talking to
themselves out loud when problems become very difficult (Hutchins,
1996).

There is no reason to suppose that these two approaches, the
unfolding of innate capacities under the guidance of appropriate
experiences and the acquisition of knowledge and cognitive skills
embedded in language, should be mutually exclusive. The fact that
language seems to arise at about the same age in all cultures and
that there seems to be a consistent lag between acquiring the ability
to speak and acquiring the ability to use language as a vehicle for
problem-solving suggests that our ability to use language as a
medium for thinking itself depends on the unfolding of innate
capacities.

A huge amount of research has been conducted on the development of the ability to think about objects and ideas, but there are
good grounds to believe that this neglects the most intellectually
challenging aspect of our lives, which is social interaction. If you
think about a typical day you will probably find that the most
demanding decisions you had to make involved thinking about
other people. Even as I sit here and write this book I am having to
think about people because I have to consider how my readers are
going to react to what I am writing. Will you understand it? Will
you agree with it? Will you enjoy my style of writing? In order to
think about my readers I have to understand that you have minds
that exist independently of me, that you know and believe things
that I might not know and believe and that you might be ignorant
of things which I take for granted. Young children don't know any
of these things and they assume that other people must know
exactly what they know (Mitchell, 1997).

Children's understanding of other people's minds is explored using 'false belief' tasks, a good example of which is the following story:

A boy puts some chocolate in a blue cupboard and goes out to play. In his absence, his mother moves the chocolate to the green cupboard. When the boy returns, he wants his chocolate. Where does he look for it?

If you tried this story on three-year-old Mary, she would probably tell you that the boy will look in the green cupboard, suggesting that she assumes that everyone must know what she knows to be true. By four or five, she would probably tell you that the boy will look in the blue cupboard because that was where he placed the chocolate, suggesting that she can distinguish between what she knows and what she recognizes other people might know. This is a liberating discovery for children because it means that they can lie! Interestingly, children diagnosed as 'autistic' usually fail these false-belief tests.

Cognitive development is a complex process that involves maturation, the unfolding of innate capacities under the guidance of the environment, and the acquisition of problem-solving strategies that are built into language. Most research on cognitive development has focused on thinking about the non-human world, but there is now considerable interest in the development of social intelligence. Cognitive development is encouraged by experiences that go a little bit beyond the child's ability to cope intellectually.

How Can I Use This Information As a Counsellor?

Intellectual development is linked to the development of language, but linguistic ability usually exceeds understanding during early childhood so children may use words that they do not understand in the ways that adults do. A good example is that toddlers understand the differences between males and females but it is only later that they realize that gender is fixed for life . This means that, when working with children you have to be very careful that you understand each other properly and do not assume that they are using words in the same way as you. For example, young children may not understand that death is permanent (Baker *et al.*, 1992) or that gender is permanent.

Understanding is best fostered by presenting a person with challenges that are a little way beyond their current capacity, placing the individual in their 'zone of proximal development'. For the counsellor, this means ensuring that the challenges with which we present our clients are carefully matched to their current position. If you are reinterpreting clients' experiences, as one does as part of many approaches, it is important that the new interpretations are fairly close to the clients' own views, otherwise the result will be blank incomprehension rather than therapeutic gain. For example, if a client divides his experiences of the world into a stark contrast between winning and losing, viewing one experience as 'winning' and another as 'losing', then you are more likely to be understood by your client if you introduce a modification of this theme, such as 'winning in the short-term' versus 'winning in the long-term,' than if you try to develop a radically different view of the world in which winning and losing are unimportant elements.

Section summary

- **Children often use the same words as adults but don't mean the same things. When working with children and young people, do not make assumptions about their understanding.**

- **People are much better at taking in ideas that are related to what they already understand than those that wildly exceed their understanding. Make sure your feedback to clients lies in their 'zone of proximal development'.**

Identity

Our identity is important because it affects how we act. If we see ourselves as unattractive or socially unskilled, we are unlikely to enter social situations with great enthusiasm. If we see ourselves as intelligent, we are likely to go in for academic pursuits and will probably persist at intellectually challenging tasks, because we believe that we have the ability to cope with them. When we talk about the development of identity we are usually dealing with a number of distinct, if overlapping, ideas:

1) the development of a sense of self as distinct from other objects or people;
2) the identification of regularities in our actions and the way that people react to them;
3) a desire for consistency in our actions across settings; and
4) a desire to attribute socially valued characteristics to ourselves.

At around 18 months, babies start to recognize themselves in mirrors and photographs and use personal pronouns when talking about themselves. Self-recognition in mirrors was demonstrated by Lewis and Brooks-Gunn (1979; cited in Schaffer, 1996) by asking mothers to put a smudge of coloured make-up onto their infants' noses and then placing them in front of a mirror. Children younger than 18 months tend to treat the image in the mirror as if it is another child with a smudge on its nose but those older than 18 months tend to reach for their own noses and touch the mark, indicating that they have recognized that the image in the mirror is them. This ability does not seem to require any prior experience with mirrors, since infants raised in nomadic cultures that lack mirrors react in the same way as other children (Priel and deSchonen, 1986; cited in Shaffer, 1996).

Quite young children, like Mary, have a sense of who they are and can identify consistencies in their own behaviour, but the way that they talk about themselves and those consistencies tends to change as they get older. If you ask three- to five-year-old children who they are, they don't seem to find it an odd question, but they will tend to answer in very concrete terms, such as having green eyes or brown hair, or in terms of possessions, such as owning a bicycle. According to Eder (1989, 1990; cited in Shaffer, 1996), children as young as three years six months will report on how they act in different situations, but they couch their descriptions in behavioural terms, such as 'I like to play by myself'.

As children get older, these physical and behavioural descriptions tend to get replaced with statements about personality traits. Characteristics that were considered important by pre-schoolers, such as owning a bicycle, do not get mentioned at all and specific behavioural descriptions, such as, 'I like to play by myself', are replaced with personality traits like 'I am not very sociable'. As we move from very specific to very general descriptions, from 'I like to play by myself at playgroup' to 'I am not very sociable', so their impact on our behaviour increases. A child who likes to play on their own at playgroup may well play happily with siblings at home, but a teenager who describes him or herself as 'not very sociable' is likely to withdraw from a wide range of social situations.

Children learn to apply psychological descriptions to themselves by applying the descriptions that others, particularly significant adults like parents and teachers, use when talking about their actions. Dweck (1978; cited in Shaffer, 1996) has explored how this process works in influencing how children think about their own success and failure in school. Imagine two children, both of whom have just completed an exercise in class. The teacher of one of them praises the child for having worked hard while the teacher of the other praises the child for being clever. Now imagine them have failed to complete an exercise. The teacher of the first child criticizes them for lacking ability while the teacher of the second child criticizes them for being lazy and not trying. According to Dweck, the first child will learn to label him or herself as academically unable, the second will learn to label him or herself as clever.

We know that the sense that other people make of a child's failure is important because Dweck (1975; cited in Shaffer, 1996) was able to change the way that children worked on tasks by giving them verbal feedback about their failures. She set up a situation in which a group of children was asked to solve a series of very complex maths problems, on most of which they failed. Not surprisingly, the children started to lose heart and gave up fairly quickly when presented with a new problem. The group was then divided into two. One group was given easy tasks and given tokens as rewards each time they got one right. The second group was given a mixture of easy and impossible problems and, after each failure on an impossible problem, they were told that they had failed on it because they had not tried hard enough. Both groups were then given some more impossible problems. Children who had received rewards gave up on the impossible problems as quickly as they had done at the end of the first phase, but children who had heard an adult label their failures in the second phase as resulting from lack of effort worked much harder in the third phase, suggesting that they had taken on board the adults' comments and applied them to their own actions.

The important feature of psychological language, in which we use terms like 'sociable' , 'anxious' or 'unlikeable' to describe ourselves, is that we .cannot use it unless our actions and the reactions of other are consistent across a range of settings. The only terms we have in English to describe people whose behaviour is inconsistent across settings, such as someone who is withdrawn in one social setting and the life and soul of the party in another, come from the psychiatric literature. As we grow into describing ourselves in psychological terms we come under increasing pressure to find ways of identifying consistency in our actions. We can do this in two ways:

1) by being creative in construing our actions so that what is inconsistent in one set of terms becomes consistent in another;
2) by changing our behaviour so that it becomes consistent with the descriptions we apply to it.

For example, someone who recognizes that they are sociable in one setting but reclusive in another might deal with the problem by qualifying the situation in which they are withdrawn as having special features, such as the company being boring, that would merit withdrawal by a sociable person, or they might resolve to change their behaviour so that they become reclusive in all settings. In either event, the pursuit of consistency is likely to create conflicts and problems.

According to Harter and Monsour (1992; cited in Shaffer, 1996), the desire to be consistent develops with age. They asked cohorts of 13- , 15- and 17-year-olds to describe themselves in a number of settings, such as when they were with parents or with friends. Participants were then given their descriptions and asked to note inconsistencies in their accounts of themselves in different settings. Thirteen-year-olds noted very few inconsistencies, 15-year-olds noted nearly twice as many as the younger group and 17-year-olds noted an intermediate number. Not only did 15-year-olds note more inconsistencies than the other groups, they were also more upset about them as well.

Psychological identity develops in a social framework that gives us a social identity. Our social identity relates to the roles that we occupy in society and the ways in which we occupy those roles. Some of those roles are linked to our age, so that British children aged between five and 16 are legally required to fulfil the 'school pupil' role. Other roles are a matter of individual choice, so that adults in most Western countries have a choice of occupational roles. Social identity interacts with psychological identity in two ways. The first is that the social framework attaches values to the labels that we give ourselves, so that some self-descriptions are more socially favoured than others, and the second is that our actions have to be consistent with our social roles, and particular social roles are more consistent with some self-descriptions than others.

As we grow, we seek out self-descriptions that are approved of by our families and by our peers, creating two sources of conflict. One is between the ways in which we see ourselves and the values expressed by those around us, the other is between the values held by different groups of significant people. For example, Mary may grow up timid in the company of other people, preferring her own company and enjoying solitary pursuits like reading or single-handed sailing. However, Western society does not prize timidity or shyness, valuing sociability and self-confidence much more. An adolescent who interprets his behaviour as 'timid' or 'shy' comes under strong pressure to change his behaviour so that he becomes more sociable. Another child might like saving all her money. Her parents might view this in a favourable light, seeing her as thrifty or sensible, but her friends might see it negatively, viewing her as mean and ungenerous.

As I have pointed out in an earlier chapter, social roles provide rules for how we should act, and how others should react towards us, that are independent of our identity. Roles are linked to our psychological identity in three ways. The first is that they expose us to particular experiences that give us feedback about ourselves, the second is that our notions of who we are are likely to influence the ways in which we choose our roles as we grow up, and the third is that the need to be able to talk about ourselves in psychological, rather than sociological terms, means that we are likely to look for roles, or ways of occupying roles, that allow us to retain a psychological identity.

In practice, all three of these processes will be linked. Take, for example, the role of school pupil. This role exposes children to feedback about scholastic aptitude that is likely to influence how they view themselves and the subsequent choices they make. A child who labels him or herself 'clever' is more likely to pursue further academic study than one who labels him or herself 'dull', so that the former may go on into a profession like medicine or law that requires high levels of academic attainment while the latter may pursue manual trades. Had these individuals not been in school and exposed to this feedback, they may have developed different self-concepts and had totally different career trajectories later in life.

One of the ironies of Western society is that the emergence of psychological self-description coincides with being institutionalized into roles, such as school pupil or employee, that confer no psychological identity. In order to have a sense of self, the individual has to occupy the role in a way that is unique to themselves, which can be difficult in large institutions that expect considerable uniformity in the behaviour of their participants. We would, therefore, expect adolescents to experience conflict between their desire for psychological uniqueness and the need to learn appropriate social roles.

Right from birth, one's sex influences how people behave towards us and how we are expected to behave. Psychologists conventionally distinguish between three aspects of sexual identity; gender identity (whether one sees oneself as a boy or a girl), the acquisition of non-sexual behaviour considered typical of one's sex, and sexual orientation. A soon as a child is born, its genital sex is a matter of interest to everyone and parents tend to attend to the strength and vigour of male babies but to the softness and 'cuddliness' of girls. By the time they reach adulthood, males are expected to be 'active', 'adventurous' and 'creative', while girls are expected to be 'aware of others', 'considerate' and 'creative', and these differences are considered to be 'natural' and, by implication, genetically inevitable. Of course, the real picture is much more complex than this. There are small numerical differences between males and females on some tests of cognitive ability, such as verbal fluency and spatial ability, but there is massive overlap between the distributions of scores of the two sexes, so much so that it is impossible to justify the quite rigid gender stereotyping typical of our society on the basis of biologically determined differences between boys and girls. To take a concrete example, if we accept the evidence for a gender difference in mathematical ability, that difference is far too small to explain the under-representation of girls studying sciences at school and university or going on to become engineers or doctors. Similarly, a small advantage in verbal ability amongst females (Shaffer, 1996) is not sufficient to explain the predominance of female counsellors.

Gender identity and sex-typical behaviour

How do physical differences in genital structure at birth lead to such large differences in social role in adulthood? Gender identity emerges first, as children as young as two years six months can accurately identify themselves as boys or girls and can tell you what the differences are in terms of behaviour, so Mary would know that she was a girl, and would be able to tell you what that meant. However, it isn't until children are about six that they recognize that gender is fixed, rather than a matter of choice. Along with the emergence of gender identity we see the development of an awareness of sex-typical behaviour and an interest in behaving appropriately for one's sex. This means playing with the right toys, expressing the right attitudes and preferring to play with children of the same sex. Emerging attitudes to sex-typical behaviour are both descriptive and prescriptive. Young children know how boys and girls are expected to behave and they are also censorious of children who violate the rules for their sex, such as boys playing with female dolls. As they get older, they may become more tolerant of violations of sex-roles but they become very intolerant during adolescence.

A number of factors contribute to this process. Labelling by parents and other adults undoubtedly contributes to the development of gender identity and parents tend to reward children for gender typical behaviour and punish them for atypical acts. Children are not passive in this process and there is evidence that they actively seek out information about the behaviours and choices that are appropriate for their genders. For example, Bradbard *et al.* (1986; cited in Shaffer, 1996) gave four- to nine-year-old children boxes of things like hole punches or pizza cutters and told them that the objects were either things that boys used or things that girls used. Boys who were told that a particular object, say a pizza cutter, was a 'boy's thing' attended more to it than if they were told the same object was a 'girl's thing', while girls showed the reverse preference. A week later, the boys remembered more about the objects that had been labelled 'boy's things' than the objects that had been linked to girls. The pattern was reversed in girls.

Preference for playing with members of the same sex may reflect differences in style of play. Maccoby (1990; cited in Shaffer, 1996) reports a study in which 33-month-old boys and girls were dressed in gender neutral clothes and placed in pairs to play together. Same sex pairs played together more than opposite sex pairs, even though there was no obvious sign of the sex of their playmate to the children, which suggests that there might be differences between boys and girls in the style of their play.

Sexual orientation

Gender identity is closely linked to the emergence of sex-typical behaviour, but both can be uncoupled from sexual orientation. Having a masculine or feminine gender identity does not mean that one automatically feels sexually attracted to members of the opposite sex, nor does being attracted to members of the same sex mean that one engages in inappropriate sex-typical behaviour. The origins of sexual orientation are currently poorly understood. Most of the work seems to take it for granted that the majority of us will be sexually attracted to members of the opposite sex and focuses on explaining the incidence of homosexual preferences, but exclusively heterosexual preferences are equally puzzling from a scientific point of view.

Overview of identity

Forming a coherent sense of who you are and how you fit into your social world takes time and can be a source of unhappiness, although the current view is that most people achieve a sense of identity without undue personal distress and may actually enjoy the process of discovery involved as they try out different ways of relating to the world. It is generally believed that issues of identity formation come to the fore during early adolescence and may take until early adulthood to be resolved. The timing of this process probably reflects a number of factors, including intellectual maturation, sexual maturation and changes in the social roles and opportunities that present themselves as one gets older. Actively forming an identity means being able to think about the future, to recognize that the future will not be like the present and to imagine different futures, all of which require sophisticated intellectual abilities (Shaffer, 1996). Puberty usually brings with it an awakening sexual desire that requires one to restructure one's social relationships, and acquire new social skills, to fulfil. Intellectual and sexual maturity are likely to occur at similar ages in different cultures but changes in social roles and opportunities are likely to be culture-specific. People in societies in which one starts working as a teenager and has little choice of career probably form stable identities younger than people in societies where higher education is the norm and in which career choices and the establishment of stable relationships are often delayed into one's early twenties.

How Can I Use This Information As a Counsellor?

My four-part distinction between aspects of identity (the development of a sense of self as distinct from other objects or people; the identification of regularities in our actions and the way that people react to them; a desire for consistency in our actions across settings; and a desire to attribute socially valued characteristics to ourselves) may be helpful in thinking about how identity-related problems might have arisen. Most people achieve differentiation between themselves and others, and most of the people we see as clients are probably able to identify regularities in their behaviour and people's reactions to them. If you can't identify such regularities you probably won't know that you have a problem that might benefit from counselling. This suggests that most 'identity' problems are going to relate to the urge for consistency across settings, the urge for consistency with roles, and the desire for a socially acceptable self.

Consistency

Consistency is a problem because there are so many settings and domains across which one has to be consistent. To consider themselves confident, clients have to act confidently in a range of settings, such as within the family, at work, in education and when dealing with professionals like doctors and lawyers. If clients find themselves acting confidently in one setting but not in others, then they will find it difficult to label themselves as confident and will have a problem in deciding what they are. It is unlikely that you will ever be able to help clients become fully consistent across settings so it is sensible to work towards the more modest goal of enabling clients to think about themselves in a more complex way that accommodates inconsistency. For example, someone who is confident around their family but deferential to authority figures might come to see that behaviour depends on setting and role as well as the individual and see that their behaviour towards professionals does not reflect a personal lack of confidence but a sensitivity to the demands of roles.

Consistency across domains means consistency between the sort of person you think yourself to be and the sort of person you think should be occupying the roles you occupy. Trainee counsellors might experience inconsistency if they considered themselves to be talkative, dominant and sympathetic while seeing the role of counsellor as requiring someone who was quiet, non-directive and empathic. Total consistency is unnecessary if they can see their professional roles as just that, roles which they can adopt when it is appropriate but which do not form the core of their identity. Counsellor skills training, for example, enables us to develop a non-directive, empathic stance in which listening is more important to us than talking when working with clients, but those skills need not be applied outside the therapeutic setting.

Consistency with social norms and values is the most difficult issue for many of our clients. When a client tells me that they don't know who they are, I often wonder whether they are really telling me that they know full well but they do not have permission to be that person. How you deal with this problem depends on the model with which you work. Long-term approaches, like client-centred and psychodynamic work, deal with it through offering the client a secure relationship in which they can express their 'real' selves without criticism so that they acquire permission to be themselves through their experience of the relationship. Many of us are constrained to work on a much shorter time scale and cannot allow the counselling relationship alone to do the work. In brief therapies, the issue of permission to be oneself has to be tackled directly using techniques based on verbal self-direction.

One of the big changes in counselling practice in the past decade is an awareness of the political dimension of people's actions so that we no longer view all actions in the same dispassionate, non-critical way. When a client indicates an identity that is built around activities like paedophilia or beating up their partner, then you are not expected to help them acquire permission to be that person. Counsellors can censure clients, but they must do so from within an effective therapeutic relationship that enables the client to attend to the criticism and respond to it.

Gender issues

Gender issues are becoming increasingly important in counselling and there are two trends of which we should all be aware. The first is a move to remove all traces of sexism from our practice and the second is an awareness that there are issues unique to female clients as a result of their position within the political power structures. Developmental psychology can tell us less about either of these points than you might think because they are social and political, rather than psychological. Nevertheless, psychological factors are likely to constrain the ways in which gender-related issues can be tackled in counselling.

Gender matters to people; the way that very young children seek out gender-related information and attempt to regulate their actions according to their understanding of gender roles suggests that it is central to identity formation. Enabling clients to act and think in ways that are contrary to established gender roles is likely to be very difficult and require a very good therapeutic alliance. Moreover, given the importance attached in most societies to adopting specific gender roles, counsellors have to think through very carefully the social consequences for their clients of moving away from these roles without establishing a supportive social framework for the client.

However, the content of gender roles is mutable. Biology confers on us at most gender-related styles of acting and, possibly, the desire to learn one's appropriate gender role but it does not dictate the content of those roles. Should it be appropriate, there is no developmental reason why people cannot learn new interpretations of gender-related behaviour, in the same way that they learn new interpretations of other roles. A male client who has learned to be violent as part of his male role cannot appeal to biological determinism to maintain that element of his role, any more than a female client who reacts to violence with passivity can make the same appeal. Some changes in gender-related behaviour are possible, but are going to be most easily attained if the client can view them as lying within the range of acceptable behaviour for their sex.

Section summary

- **Complete consistency of action across roles and settings is unrealistic. The goal should be to foster a sufficient degree of cognitive complexity to accommodate the inconsistencies that arise.**

- As a counsellor you may experience inconsistencies between your identity and what you believe is required in the role of counsellor.

- When clients say that they don't know who they are or what they want to be, they may be expressing concern about the social acceptability of their actions and plans rather than a lack of self-knowledge.

- Some actions are socially unacceptable and the counsellor may be obliged to point this out to clients. It is unethical to enable clients to be comfortable with their identities as paedophiles or spouse-batterers.

- Gender matters in most societies. There are limits to the degree to which people can change their behaviour before they violate the socially accepted norms for their sex and encounter major social difficulties.

Chapter Summary

Psychological development takes place throughout our lives but, because they lay the foundations of our adult selves, the events that occur in infancy and childhood have a particular importance. Some counselling models give early experiences a particular prominence and define the tasks of counselling in terms of correcting developmental aberrations. Other approaches, particularly recent brief therapies (Epston and White, 1992), are less concerned with development but an understanding of developmental ideas is still relevant because they give us an idea of the tasks that one has to accomplish to become an autonomous adult, which may help us clarify the difficulties encountered by our clients and ensure that counselling matches clients' current levels of development.

There is little evidence that human development proceeds by a series of rigid stages of the sort described by Freud or Piaget, but 'stage' models are helpful in clarifying the developmental tasks that clients need to complete. Infants and children seem to be more prepared to utilize developmentally significant experiences, such as a secure relationship with a caretaker or exposure to language, at some ages than at others, but appropriate experience outside these 'sensitive' periods can go a long way to redressing the effects of early experience.

Immediately after birth, infants appear largely asocial; their emotional reactions largely reflect what the world has done to them and they do not discriminate between caretakers so long as they are fed and kept warm and clean. However, awareness of other people develops surprisingly early. Quite young infants are sensitive to the identity of the adults around them and usually become upset if they are deserted by their primary caretaker, especially when strangers are present. However, infants can become dependent on multiple caretakers so they are not wholly dependent on their mothers; what matters is the quality and continuity of the relationship rather than the biological relatedness of the caretaker. Infants can show self-conscious, social emotions like pride or shame and an awareness of others' feelings, rapidly learning to dissimulate their emotions to avoid hurting other people. By the time they can talk, children can be expected to be quite socially competent.

Intellectual development runs alongside social development. One of the most important events in human intellectual development is the acquisition of language, which provides the child with a range of problem-solving tools and acts as a stimulus for further intellectual development. Understanding of the physical world is accompanied by understanding of the much more complex social world the child inhabits.

Development of emotions, desires and abilities is accompanied by an emergence of a sense of self, of being a unique individual located in a social framework with particular competencies, rights and obligations. Along with a sense of self comes the learning of the rules of the social roles the individual will occupy as an adult, such as occupational and family roles. Of particular importance is the development of an individual's gender role and there is evidence that children actively seek out information to define their own gender roles.

8

Epilogue

Writing is as much a voyage of discovery as reading is, so I thought I would use this final chapter to tell you about some of the things that I have learned while preparing this book. They fall under three headings:

1) most counselling practice makes psychological sense;
2) we often don't know the things that we think we know; and
3) life places incredible psychological demands on people, so we should be respectful of *their* solutions to problems and modest about our own.

Counselling Practice Makes Psychological Sense

Counselling practice makes psychological sense at a number of levels. Although contemporary psychology seems to be out of sympathy with the broadly cast theories with which counsellors work, it actually makes sense to work with such models. Within any model, psychology makes sense of the particular practices promoted by the model.

As I pointed out in the introduction, one of the paradoxes of our modern approach to counsellor training is its emphasis on the application of models coupled with immense tolerance of one's choice of model. Discussion is about how well one has used a model, rather than whether a particular model is 'right' or 'wrong'. From the traditional academic perspective this is bizarre, but placing the *practices* of counsellors in a psychological framework has helped me make sense of it. Models do a number of things that benefit both counsellors and clients. From the counsellor's point of view they greatly simplify interactions with clients; they also constrain the actions of the counsellor, to eliminate counter-therapeutic practices. From the client's point of view, they ensure that the interaction with the counsellor is coherent.

As the chapters on social behaviour and decision-making revealed, our world is too complex for us to be able to make fully 'rational' decisions all of the time. Even if we had the intellectual capacity to handle all of the information necessary to make rational decisions, we would make them so slowly that opportunities would have passed us by before we had reached our decision. Instead of making rational decisions we rely on short-cuts, known as *heuristics*, which are rules of thumb that are not fully rational but tend, on average, to produce the right decision. We use heuristics continuously when making decisions about what to say and do next in social situations and the fluency of our social interactions often depends on people sharing heuristics with us.

Counselling models provide us with the heuristics for running counselling sessions. They may not be completely rational but they simplify the situation so that we can cope with it, which is why the application of a particular model is so important early on in training. These heuristics take the form of rules for interpreting the interaction with the client that guide us in our decisions about what to say or do next. The psychodynamic approach encourages you to interpret your clients' reactions to *your* behaviour as a therapist as if they are reacting to some other significant person in their life, and your reactions to your client as if you are reacting to someone significant in your own life; transference and counter-transference. It then encourages you to comment on the 'transference'. The person-centred approach encourages you to treat your clients' statements as distortions of reality brought about by their burden of conditions of worth and to react to all statements in a way that consistently and unconditionally values the client, no matter what they have said.

By providing frameworks for interpreting and responding to your clients, models significantly inhibit your choices. The main counselling models forbid you to argue with your clients and they leave them as the final arbiters of the truth of anything that you, the counsellor, have said. They also ban social chit-chat with clients, or any other conversational ploys that make the counselling conversation like a 'normal' social interaction for the client. You are not supposed to reassure your clients or comfort them when they are upset. Counselling gains its impact because counsellors consistently breach the rules of normal conversation that have helped maintain the problem with which they are working. It is remarkably difficult for most of us to act in this way without the structure of a model to guide us.

We see ourselves as members of the 'helping professions', giving time and effort to our clients so that they may lead better lives. Consequently, there is a danger of forgetting what we ask of our clients in return, particularly the degree of trust we expect of them when we ask them to divulge intimate details of their lives and submit themselves to the rigours of our interventions. Part of that trust is institutionalized, being linked to the *role* of counsellor in much the same way as it used to be linked to the role of priest in more religious times. The rest of that trust has to be earned while working with the client and that depends on appearing to know what you are doing. Since few clients are experts in therapy, they cannot judge the fine points of your technique so they will look for other cues, such as the consistency of your actions. Inconsistency will probably come across as lack of confidence or skill. If your inconsistency is influenced by your clients' behaviour, then you will undermine their confidence further because they will not feel that you have the strength to withstand their emotions. For example, if you change approach after your client has become angry then that is telling your client that you are unable to cope with anger. Sticking to a single model stops you being inconsistent and thus provides a basis of trust.

Although counselling models seem very diverse, they have a lot in common that makes good psychological sense. Much of what we do involves helping our clients change their attitudes towards themselves and other people. Research on attitude change has consistently shown that people are more likely to change their attitudes if they are given freedom of choice and least likely to change if they are coerced. Presenting one-sided arguments is less effective than enabling someone to see both sides. Most counselling models incorporate these principles.

Counselling skills training addresses the memory demands of counselling. We have to listen to our clients, often for minutes at a time, before commenting on what they have said. Typically this involves handling a stream of information that exceeds the immediate capacity of our memory. We have to learn strategies of active listening that apply what we know about the most effective ways of reducing demands on our short-term memories, such as the use of 'chunking', and facilitating transfer to our long-term memories, such as thinking about the meaning of our clients' words.

A developmental perspective can help make sense of the range of counselling models available to me. Developmental psychology tells us that people have to solve problems in an appropriate sequence in order to develop into competent adults. Socially, we have to learn whether we can trust other people before we can rely upon them and a lot of the events in infancy and early childhood revolve around the child developing a sense of being able to rely on other people. Children who have not developed this sense often experience serious difficulties in a range of social situations and these difficulties may extend into adulthood. Since many of the methods of *technique*-based therapy, such as cognitive behaviour interventions, require a considerable degree of trust on the part of the client, such approaches are unlikely to be helpful with clients who have not established the ability to trust others. In the cognitive sphere, we have to master some of the rules of grammar before we can speak or understand other people's speech, so a client who lacks basic verbal skills is unlikely to benefit from approaches based on complex verbal feedback. When I meet a client, I now ask myself 'What cognitive, social or emotional accomplishments does this person need for therapy to be effective?'. If those accomplishments are those we normally associate with the early years of development, I might choose to work in the relationship, using basic counselling skills to establish the therapeutic alliance. If those accomplishments are associated with later levels of development I might feel comfortable in moving straight into a more directive technique that relies on the understanding and co-operation of my client.

We Know Less Than We Think

One of the problems with working with models is that they encourage us to believe that we know more than we do. So long as we treat this as a heuristic to enable us to practise, this is not a problem, but it can get in the way of good counselling if we become dogmatic about our knowledge. There are many areas of mental life that are fundamental to counselling practice about which we know surprisingly little, and many of the things that we commonly think are true turn out not to be so simple on closer inspection.

Behavioural (including cognitive behavioural) approaches are particularly prone to underestimating the complexity of emotion. They do so in two ways. The first is that they artificially separate emotional experience into independent components, such as thinking, feeling and acting, even though the research literature suggests that these components cannot be separated in this way. The second is that they assume that our emotional reactions to situations can be explained in terms of simple processes such as associative learning or the application of logical rules of inference.

As we saw in the chapter on feelings, it is difficult to separate emotions into independent components because people use aspects of emotional experience to attribute other components to them-selves. We use knowledge of what we were thinking about in a particular situation to attribute feelings to ourselves, and knowl-edge of how we were feeling to attribute thoughts. Attempts to provide logical accounts of the sorts of emotional problems encoun-tered by our clients enjoy limited success. Associative learning accounts are completely circular unless the counsellor and client can identify the learning experiences that have generated and maintained their reaction, which is very rare. Similarly, the whole point of many of the emotional reactions experienced by our clients is that they defy the rules of logical inference and occur in situations in which those 'rules' identified in cognitive theories tell us that those reactions should not occur. Being frightened of snakes when walking in tropical countries can be explained in terms of logical reasoning. Explaining a fear of snakes that prevents someone sleeping at night in a house in London in the same terms is less convincing and demands impressive intellectual ingenuity.

However, associative learning and cognitive accounts of emotion work well in some contexts. It may be possible to trace a specific phobia, such as fear of thunderstorms or going to the dentist, back to a particular experience such as being nearly struck by lightening as a child or finding one's first visit to the dentist particularly painful. Cognitive accounts of the way in which panic attacks feed upon themselves to create agoraphobia and further panic attacks are also very convincing, although they are not very good at explaining why a particular person had an initial attack.

Many counselling models are theories of human development that explain current psychological problems in terms of inappropri-ate childhood experiences, and there is a widespread view in counselling circles that the purpose of counselling is to offset the damage done by these experiences. Many of these developmental ideas have become part of the mental furniture of counsellors and we tend to talk about developmental ideas like 'complexes', 'stages' and 'fixations' as if they are as real as buses, cars and bicycles. However, few of these ideas are based on direct observation of children. Both Freud and Rogers based most of their ideas on work with adults and attributed all sorts of psychological events to childhood to make their models work. Freud's notions of infantile sexuality were not based on observations of children, or an attempt to determine the prevalence of childhood sexual abuse, but on the narratives of his adult patients. Later psychoanalytic writers did work with children, but their observations were conditioned by the expectations raised by theory. Developmental research presents us with a much more complex, but at the same time more optimistic, view of human development that tells us of the importance of early experience but also of the value of later experience in helping people overcome poor starts in life.

Another concept that has a similar uncertain heritage is 'repression', which is widely used to explain memory failures and the sudden recovery of memory during therapy. We use the term so widely that we forget that most of the arguments for it are circular and there is little consistent experimental or other evidence to demonstrate its occurrence. In most instances there are much simpler explanations for loss and 'recovery' of memory than repression. For one thing, memory is remarkably fallible under the best of conditions, so it is not surprising if adults have difficulty remembering events from childhood. Memory tends to be context-dependent, so recall is unlikely to occur until circumstances comparable to those obtaining at the time of the initial event are recreated. Finally, memory is an act of construction rather than retrieval, so we can never be sure that anyone has 'recovered' a memory unless we have independent evidence of the original event.

One of the biggest social changes in the half century I have been alive has been in our attitudes towards variations in sexual orientation. When I was a child (and counselling was in its infancy as well), the only acceptable form of adult sexuality was heterosexuality. Homosexuality was illegal in males and simply not discussed in females, homosexuals were victims of assault and blackmail and admission of homosexuality was usually social and professional suicide. With the legalization of adult male homosexuality the legal risks were reduced but the social hostility persisted. Thirty more years on in the United Kingdom, and the scene has changed to the extent that homosexuals are seen as a potent political force and homosexuality is accepted, if not condoned.

We would expect counselling models to have mirrored these social and legal changes but some of them are still rooted in the ethos of earlier times that treated homosexuality as an aberration, possibly in need of treatment. There is still a widespread assumption that heterosexual attraction is 'normal' and, therefore, does not require an explanation, while homosexual attraction is seen as some sort of aberration of the developmental process. Some models view homosexuality as such a serious sign of deviant psychosexual development that it is something that needs to be 'cured' during the personal therapy that is part of the training. However, the origins of heterosexual attraction are as much a mystery as those of homosexual desire and there is currently no reason to presuppose that one is more indicative of psychological health than the other.

Models do not supply you with enough information for you to be able to work effectively, so you have to fill in the gaps with other sources of knowledge. Most of us rely on experience and draw on that vast, culturally determined repertoire of facts that we call 'common sense' to make sense of what our clients tell us and to anticipate how they will react to situations. When we are trying to be 'empathic' we have to draw on pre-existing knowledge of what someone in our client's circumstances is likely to feel like and how they are likely to be disposed to act. For example, if a client says, 'I want to kill the person who raped me', then that may be reflected back to them as 'You are very angry with the person who violated you', but you can only do this because you have a common sense view of the world that links the desire to kill someone to the emotion of anger. Another client might say, 'I become ill when I have to talk in public', to which the counsellor might say 'You are anxious about dealing with strangers'. In this case you have moved from a description of a specific experience to a generalization about the personality of the client, that they are prone to anxiety. Again, you can only do this because you have a common sense model of specific actions being linked to general tendencies to act in particular ways across a variety of settings.

Common sense may be common but it is often anything but sense. Time and again, systematic observation of people has demonstrated that the things that we take for granted are not generally true. Fat people are not universally jolly, and thin people are not exceptionally well-endowed intellectually. People who are brave in one setting can be incredibly anxious in others, like a student I taught a few years ago who had spent a year out living in villages in Thailand but panicked when asked to give a tutorial presentation.

We also know why we are so bad at working out which characteristics go together, which is that psychological attributes are only likely to go together probabilistically, and psychological research has consistently shown how poor we are at working out rules that are based on probabilities. The problem would not be so bad if we simply failed to arrive at generalizations and said 'I do not know which human characteristics go together,' but we do not do that. What we are prone to doing is misinterpreting our experience and coming up with quite dogmatic, absolute rules, that are not supported by systematic observation. If you are going to make generalizations about people on the basis of limited samples of their behaviour, which we often do in counselling practice, it makes sense to base them on research into personality rather than your personal prejudices.

The same points can be made about the lessons we learn from our experiences of counselling practice. Our personal investment in being good counsellors is likely to encourage the self-serving bias to creep into interpreting good and bad outcomes: if the client benefits it is because of something we did but if the client doesn't benefit, it is because of extraneous factors, such as the client's attitude to counselling. Beneficial interventions are likely to be effective with some clients but not others, so our effectiveness is at best probabilistic. The well-established difficulty people have with probabilities means that we are likely to misattribute our successes. Our capacity for misinterpreting experience means that we should be cautious about making claims about therapeutic effectiveness and we should be cautious about accepting other people's claims as well.

One of the best ways of checking on claims is to seek independent corroboration. No source of corroboration is without its errors and biases, but different approaches have different biases and it is unlikely that two approaches to a problem will give the same answer unless the answer has some merit in it. Experience is one source of evidence that a particular practice is valuable but the story will be more convincing if you can show that your insights are supported by systematic study, such as well-controlled outcome research, and are compatible with what we already know about psychology. I would find a claim for a therapeutic practice more convincing if a number of therapists independently showed that more of their clients benefited from it than from other practices they favoured and the practice could be justified in terms of what we know of the communication of feelings through body language than if the claim was from a single therapist, there was no evidence for the intervention being any more effective than any other and the practice only made sense if I assumed that clients could read my mind directly. Psychology demands that we are as modest about our claims to know things that are based on experience as we are about claims based on research. Ideally, we only make and accept claims that are corroborated by a number of independent sources of evidence.

Not knowing does not mean not acting. What it does mean is being respectful of other points of view. After writing this book I came to realize that the appropriate question for a counsellor to ask about an idea is 'Under what circumstances is this likely to be true?', not 'Is it true?', and to recognize that the truth of one view does not always imply the error of another. The fact that psychodynamic accounts of emotion are very effective in some contexts, such as explaining the often fleeting but very powerful emotions that sweep over us and our clients in contexts in which those emotions would not be expected, does not mean that behavioural accounts are not more appropriate in other settings.

Not knowing also means being respectful of your clients' knowledge and opinions. If clients tell you that they are afraid of thunderstorms but never experienced a particularly traumatic storm when younger then you should believe them rather than insisting on prior trauma because it is demanded by your model. If clients have problems with eating but insist that they had a perfectly normal and happy childhood then you should think about revising your model of eating disorders rather than seeking to rewrite the clients' histories to make them compatible with your idea that they stem from family dysfunction.

Be Modest About Your Own Accomplishments and Respectful of Others'

Traditional models present counselling as a relationship between a 'high functioning' individual, the counsellor, and a lower functioning person, the client. The client benefits from being in a relationship with someone whose actions and perceptions of the world are not distorted by excessive conditions of worth or unresolved complexes. The danger with this approach is that the novice counsellor does not read the small print which tells them the level of psychological functioning is relative, rather than absolute, and that all of us, clients and counsellors alike, are subject to intellectual and emotional distortions. A proper reading of psychology reinforces the small print.

As we have seen in a number of chapters in this book, the psychological limitations that affect our clients also apply to us. Personal psychological counselling may help you resolve some of the emotional biases that can influence your work with clients but it will not eliminate them completely and it will not help you deal with the intellectual biases. Few people make decisions that can be justified on fully rational grounds, which is not surprising given the complexity of decision-making, so it is unwise for counsellors to set themselves up as paragons of rationality or logic.

When you make decisions you will ignore relevant sources of information, under- and over-estimate the probabilities of significant events, and probably fail to carry out a complete analysis of the utilities of different choices. You will probably have failed to consider all of the choices in the first place. 'Utility' itself is not as rational as decision theorists might have us believe because, at its heart, the concept requires us to decide how much we value something and that is an emotional rather than an intellectual issue. The very fact that you are working as a counsellor means that you have made an irrational leap of faith, in believing that you will get value from working in this way.

Your cognitive and emotional biases will be particularly prominent when working with clients because the time pressures will force you to rely on simple heuristics rather than think through the situation completely. One of the advantages of supervision is that you can review your decision-making in a more leisurely setting and revise your heuristics to help you make better decisions.

When a client seems to be making bad decisions or behaving 'irrationally' it is wise to remember the limits of your own rationality. It is also useful to remember that most of us survive socially by thinking irrationally and applying a range of distorting attributional biases, such as the self-serving bias, which encourages us to attribute our own successes to our abilities and our failures to external circumstances beyond our control. As an exercise in modesty, you could try reviewing a major decision in your own life in the light of utility theory. This will help you with being empathic and it will also help you avoid blaming clients for their own problems.

Our practice will be limited by other cognitive imperfections, such as memory failures. When we finish a session most of us think that we have a complete understanding of what happened and happily write up our notes as if they are a complete and accurate record of events. Memory research warns us of all of the distortions that are likely to creep in. Primacy and regency effects will give undue prominence to the beginnings and ends of sessions, unusual events will stand out and our account of events will be distorted to fit the story we are constructing about our client. If we have worked a lot with a particular type of problem in the past, we will find it very difficult to remember the circumstances of a specific client and will probably remember generalities in place of specific details. For example, if clients are depressed we may find ourselves filling in gaps in their stories with our general knowledge of depression rather than remembering the specific events narrated by them.

Summary

I find that knowledge of psychology helps me as a counsellor in three ways. The first is that it helps me make sense of what I am doing with clients and reassures me that I am doing something sensible. The second is that it reminds me of the limits of my understanding and stops me presuming things about my clients. The third is that it reminds me of my own limits. What strikes me as I finish this book is that psychology helps me, but it does not dictate to me. It informs my thinking about my practice but it doesn't tell me that there is a single best way to conduct it. I can use a knowledge of psychology like an architect uses a knowledge of mechanics. Mechanics tells architects whether the buildings they want to construct are likely to stay up, but it doesn't tell them how to design a building to satisfy a particular client and it doesn't tell them whether the client will like the building once it has been built. Psychology tells me whether my practices as a counsellor are likely to engage meaningfully with the psychological capacities of my client, but it doesn't tell me what is best for a particular client nor whether they are going to feel good about the direction their life is taking after therapy.

If you have followed me to this point, then I hope that you have benefited in some of these ways and that some of the ideas I have discussed in this book have whetted your appetite for further learning about psychology.

References

Alexander, B.K. and Hadaway, P.F. (1982). Opiate addiction: the case for an adaptive orientation. *Psychological Bulletin, 92,* 367–381.

Allais, M. (1953). Le comportement de l'homme rationnel devant le risque: critique des postulats et axioms de l'ecole americaine. *Econometrica, 21,* 503–546.

Alloy, L.B., Abramson, L.Y. and Dykman, B.M. (1990). Depressive realities and nondepressive optimistic illusions: the role of the self. In R.E. Ingram (Ed.) *Contemporary Psychological Approaches to Depression: Treatment, research and theory.* New York: Plenum.

Asch, S.E. (1955). Opinions and social pressure. *Scientific American, 193 (5),* 31–55.

Baddeley, A. (1983). *Your Memory: A user's guide.* Harmondsworth: Penguin.

Baddeley, A. (1990). *Human Memory: Theory and practice.* Hove and London: Lawrence Erlbaum Associates.

Baker, J.E., Sedney, M.A. and Gross, E. (1992). Psychological tasks for bereaved children. *American Journal of Orthopsychiatry, 62,* 105–116.

Bandura, A. (1986). *Social Foundations of Thought and Action: A social cognitive theory.* Englewood Cliffs, NJ: Prentice-Hall.

Bannister, D. and Fransella, F. (1971). *Inquiring Man: The theory of personal constructs.* Harmondsworth: Penguin.

Baron, J. (1994). *Thinking and Deciding.* Cambridge: Cambridge University Press.

Baron, R.A. and Byrne, D. (1997). *Social Psychology, 8th edn.* Boston: Allyn and Bacon.

Bartlett, F.C. (1932). *Remembering.* Cambridge: Cambridge University Press.

Bateson, G. (1973). *Steps to an Ecology of Mind.* London: Granada Publishing.

Batson, C.D. and Weeks, J.L. (1996). Mood effects of unsuccessful helping – another test of the empathy–altruism hypothesis. *Personality and Social Psychology Bulletin, 22,* 148–157.

Bekerian, D.A. and Goodrich, S.J. (1995). Telling the truth in the recovered memory debate. *Consciousness and Cognition, 4,* 120–124.

Bermond, B., Fasotti, L., Nieuwenhuyse, B. and Schuerman, J. (1991). Spinal cord lesions, peripheral feedback and intensities of emotional feelings. *Cognition and Emotion, 5,* 201–220.

Berry, D.C. and Broadbent, D.E. (1984). On the relationship between task performance and verbalisable knowledge. *Quarterly Journal of Experimental Psychology, 36,* 209–231.

Blaxton, T.A. (1989). Investigating dissociations among memory measures: support for a transfer-appropriate framework. *Journal of Experimental Psychology, 15,* 657–668.

Bless, H., Schwarz, N., Clore, G.L., Golisano, V. and Rabe, C. (1996). Mood and the use of scripts – does a happy mood really lead to mindlessness? *Journal of Personality and Social Psychology, 71,* 665–679.

Booth, D.A., Gibson, E.L., Toase, A-M. and Freeman, R.P.J. (1994). Small objects of desire: the recognition of appropriate foods and drinks and its neural mechanisms. In C.R. Legg and D.A. Booth (Eds) *Appetites: Neural and behavioural bases*. Oxford: Oxford University Press.

Bowlby, J. (1969). *Attachment*. Harmondsworth: Penguin.

Brown, J.A.C. (1964). *Freud and the Post-Freudians*. Harmondsworth: Penguin.

Brown, R. and McNeill, D. (1966). The 'tip of the tongue' phenomenon. *Journal of Verbal Learning and Verbal Behaviour, 5*, 325–337.

Bruner, J. (1986). *Actual Minds, Possible Worlds*. Cambridge, Mass.: Harvard University Press.

Bruner, J.S., Goodnow, J.J. and Austin, G. (1956). *A Study of Thinking*. New York: Wiley.

Campfield, L.A. and Smith, F.J. (1990). Systemic factors in the control of food intake. In E.M. Stricker (Ed.) *Handbook of Behavioural Neurobiology, Vol. 10: Neurobiology of food and fluid intake*. New York: Plenum.

Carroll, D. and Huxley, J.A.A. (1994). Young people and fruit-machine gambling. In C.R. Legg and D.A. Booth (Eds) *Appetites: Neural and behavioural bases*. Oxford: Oxford University Press.

Cattell, R.B. (1965). *The Scientific Analysis of Personality*. Baltimore: Penguin.

Chomsky, N. (1959). Review of Skinner's Verbal Behaviour. *Language, 35*, 26–58.

Chomsky, N. (1968). *Language and Mind*. San Diego: Harcourt Brace Jovanovich.

Clark, D.M. and Teasdale, J.D. (1981). Diurnal variation in clinical depression and accessibility of positive and negative emotions. *Journal of Abnormal Psychology, 91*, 87–95.

Clore, G.C. (1994a). Why emotions are felt. In P. Ekman and R.J. Davidson (Eds) *The Nature of Emotion: Fundamental questions*. New York: Oxford University Press.

Clore, G.L. (1994b). Why emotions require cognition. In P. Ekman and R.J. Davidson (Eds) *The Nature of Emotion: Fundamental questions*. New York: Oxford University Press.

Coccaro, E.F. (1992). Impulsive aggression and central serotonergic system function in humans – an example of a dimensional brain–behavior relationship. *International Clinical Psychopharmacology, 7*, 3–12.

Cohen, G. (1989). *Memory in the Real World*. Hove and London: Lawrence Erlbaum Associates.

Coombs, C.H., Dawes, R.M. and Tversky, A. (1970). *Mathematical Psychology: An elementary introduction*. Englewood Cliffs, NJ: Prentice-Hall.

Culley, S. (1991). *Integrative Counselling Skills in Action*. London: Sage.

Darley, J.M. and Latane, B. (1968). Bystander intervention in emergencies: diffusion of responsibility. *Journal of Personality and Social Psychology, 8*, 377–383.

Davey, G.C.L. (1989). Dental phobias and anxieties: evidence for conditioning processes in the acquisition and modulation of a learned fear. *Behavioural Research and Therapy, 27*, 51–58.

Destun, L.M. and Kuiper, N.A. (1996). Autobiographical memory and recovered memory therapy integrating cognitive, clinical, and individual difference perspectives. *Clinical Psychology Review, 16*, 421–450.

Dimberg, U. (1988). Facial expressions and emotional reactions: a psycho-biological analysis of human social behaviour. In H.L. Wagner (Ed.) *Social Psychophysiology and Emotion: Theory and clinical applications*. Chichester: Wiley.

Edwards, D. and Potter, J. (1995). Remembering. In R. Harre and P. Stearns (Eds) *Discursive Psychology in Practice*. London: Sage.

Egan, G. (1994). *The Skilled Helper: A problem-management approach to helping*. Pacific Grove: Brooks/Cole.

Elkin, R. and Leippe, M. (1986). Physiological arousal, dissonance, and attitude change: evidence for a dissonance-arousal link and 'don't remind me' effect. *Journal of Personality and Social Psychology, 51*, 55–65.

Elliot, A.J. and Devine, P.G. (1994). On the motivational nature of cognitive dissonance: dissonance as psychological discomfort. *Journal of Personality and Social Psychology, 67*, 382–394.

Ellsberg, D. (1961). Risk, ambiguity, and the Savage axioms. *Quarterly Journal of Economics, 75*, 643–699.

Ellsworth, P.C. (1994). Levels of thought and levels of emotion. In P. Ekman and R.J. Davidson (Eds) *The Nature of Emotion: Fundamental questions*. New York: Oxford University Press.

Epston, D. and White, M. (1992). *Experience, Contradiction, Narrative and Imagination: Selected papers of David Epston and Michael White 1989–1991*. Adeleide: Dulwich Centre Publications.

Eysenck, H.J. (1973). *Eysenck on Extraversion*. London: Crosby Lockwood Staples.

Fazio, R.H. and Roskos-Ewoldsen, D.R. (1994). Acting as we feel: When and how attitudes guide behaviour. In S. Shavitt and T.C. Brock (Eds) *Persuasion*. Boston: Allyn and Bacon.

Festinger, L. (1957). *A Theory of Cognitive Dissonance*. Evanston, ILL: Row, Peterson.

Flavell, J.H. (1963). *The Developmental Psychology of Jean Piaget*. New York: Van Nostrand Reinhold.

Freud, S. (1943). *A General Introduction to Psychoanalysis*. Garden City, N.Y.: Garden City Publishing Co.

Frijda, N. and Jahoda, G. (1966). On the scope and methods of cross-cultural research. *International Journal of Psychology, 1*, 110–127.

Frijda, N.H. (1986). *The Emotions*. Cambridge: Cambridge University Press.

Frijda, N.H. (1994). Emotions are functional, most of the time. In P. Ekman and R.J. Davidson (Eds) *The Nature of Emotion: Fundamental questions*. New York: Oxford University Press.

Gardiner, J.M. (1996). On consciousness in relation to memory and learning. In M. Velmans (Ed.) *The Science of Consciousness: Psychological, neuropsychological and clinical reviews*. London: Routledge.

Goertzel, B. (1995). Belief Systems as Attractors. In R. Robertson and A. Combs (Eds) *Chaos Theory in Psychology and the Life Sciences*. Mahwah, New Jersey: Lawrence Erlbaum Associates.

184

Goffman, E. (1959). *The Presentation of Self in Everyday Life*. Garden City, NJ: Doubleday Archer.

Gottschalk, A., Bauer, M.S. and Whybrow, P.C. (1995). Evidence of chaotic mood variation in bipolar disorder. *Archives of General Psychiatry, 52,* 947–959.

Gray, J.A. (1975). *Elements of a Two-Process Theory of Learning*. London: Academic Press.

Green, M.W., Rogers, P.J. and HedderleY, D. (1996). The time-course of mood-induced decrements in color-naming of threat-related words. *Current Psychology, 14,* 350–358.

Green, P.J. and Suls, J. (1996). The effects of caffeine on ambulatory blood-pressure, heart-rate, and mood in coffee drinkers. *Journal of Behavioural Medicine, 19,* 111–128.

Haaken, J. (1995). The debate over recovered memory of sexual abuse a feminist-psychoanalytic perspective. *Psychiatry Interpersonal and Biological Processes, 58,* 189–198.

Haney, C., Banks, C. and Zimbardo, P. (1973). Interpersonal dynamics in a simulated prison. *International Journal of Criminology and Penology, 1,* 69–97.

Harre, R. (1995). Discursive psychology. In J.A. Smith, R. Harre and L. Van Langenhove (Eds) *Rethinking Psychology*. London: Sage.

Harre, R. and Secord, P.F. (1972). *The Explanation of Social Behaviour*. Oxford: Blackwell.

Hoffman, L. (1989). The family life cycle and discontinuous change. In B. Carter and M. McGoldrick (Eds) *The Changing Family Life Cycle: A framework for family therapy, 2nd edn*. Boston: Allyn and Bacon.

Hohmann, G.W. (1966). Some effects of spinal cord lesions on experienced emotional feelings. *Psychophysiology, 3,* 143–156.

Hull, C.L. (1952). *A Behavior System*. New Haven: Yale University Press.

Hutchins, E. (1996). *Cognition in the Wild*. London: The MIT Press.

Izard, C.E. (1994). Cognition is one of four types of emotion-activating systems. In P. Ekman and R.J. Davidson (Eds) *The Nature of Emotion: Fundamental questions*. New York: Oxford University Press.

James, W. (1884). What is an emotion? *Mind, 9,* 188–205.

Johnson, B.A., Oldman, D., Goodall, E.M., Chen, Y.R. and Cowen, P.J. (1996). Effects of GR–68755 on d-amphetamine-induced changes in mood, cognitive performance, appetite, food preference, and caloric and macronutrient intake in humans. *Behavioural Pharmacology, 7,* 216–227.

Johnson-Laird, P.N., Legrenzi, P. and Legrenzi, M.S. (1972). Reasoning and a sense of reality. *British Journal of Psychology, 63,* 395–400.

Jones, E.E. and Davis, K.E. (1965). From acts to disposition: the attribution process in person perception. In L. Berkowitz (Ed.) *Advances in Experimental Social Psychology, Vol. 2*. New York: Academic Press.

Kavoussi, R.J. , Liu, J. and Coccaro, E.F. (1994). An open trial of sertraline in personality disordered patients with impulsive aggression. *Journal of Clinical Psychiatry, 55,* 137–141.

Kelly, G. (1955). *The Psychology of Personal Constructs*. New York: Norton.

Kelly, H.H. (1972). Attribution in Social Interaction. In E.E. Jones (Ed) *Attribution: Perceiving the Causes of Behaviour*. Morristown, NJ: General Learning Press.

Kidd, J.M. (1996). Career development work with individuals. In R. Woolfe and W. Dryden (Eds) *Handbook of Counselling Psychology*. London: Sage.

Klein, M. (1986). *The Selected Melanie Klein*. Harmondsworth: Penguin.

Kline, P. (1991). *Intelligence: The psychometric view*. London: Routledge.

Kogan, N. and Wallach, M.A. (1964). *Risk Taking: A study in cognition and Personality*. New York: Holt.

Kyes, R.C. , Botchin, M.B. , Kaplan, J.R. , Manuck, S.B. and Mann, J.J. (1995). Aggression and brain serotonergic responsivity – response to slides in male macaques. *Physiology and Behavior, 57*, 205–208.

Lachman, J.L., Lachman, R. and Thronesberry, C. (1979). Metamemory through the adult life span. *Developmental Psychology, 15*, 543–551.

LaPiere, R.T. (1934). Attitude and actions. *Social Forces, 13*, 230–237.

Lazarus, R. (1994). Appraisal: the long and the short of it. In P. Ekman and R.J. Davidson (Eds) *The Nature of Emotion: Fundamental questions*. New York: Oxford University Press.

Legg, C.R. (1994). Appetite – a psychological concept. In C.R. Legg and D.A. Booth (Eds) *Appetites: Neural and behavioural bases*. Oxford: Oxford University Press.

Legg, C.R. (1997). Science and family therapy. *Journal of Family Therapy, 19*, 401–415.

Levenson, R.W. (1994). Emotional control: variation and consequences. In P. Ekman and R.J. Davidson (Eds) *The Nature of Emotion: Fundamental questions*. New York: Oxford University Press.

Levenson, R.W., Ekman, P. and Friesen, W.V. (1990). Voluntary facial action generates emotion-specific autonomic nervous system activity. *Psychophysiology, 27*, 363–384.

Levin, R.J. (1994). Human male sexuality: appetite and arousal, desire and drive. In C.R. Legg and D.A. Booth (Eds) *Appetites: Neural and behavioural bases*. Oxford: Oxford University Press.

Levinger, G. and Clark, J. (1961). Emotional factors in the forgetting of word associations. *Journal of Abnormal and Social Psychology, 62*, 99–105.

Ley, P. (1978). Memory for medical information. In M.M. Gruneberg, P.E. Morris and R.N.Sykes (Eds) *Practical Aspects of Memory*. London: Academic Press.

Lichtenstein, S., Slovic, P., Fischhoff, B., Layman, M. and Coombs, B. (1978). Judged frequency of lethal events. *Journal of Experimental Psychology: Human Learning and Memory, 4*, 551–578.

Lieberman, S. (1965). The effects of changes of roles on the attitudes of role occupants. In H. Proshansky and B. Seidenberg (Eds) *Basic Studies in Social Psychology*. New York: Holt, Rinehart and Winston.

Linton, M. (1978). Real world memory after six years: an in vivo study of very long-term memory. In M.M. Gruneberg, P.E. Morris and R.N.Sykes (Eds) *Practical Aspects of Memory*. London: Academic Press.

Lloyd, H.M., Rogers, P.J., Hedderley, D.I. and Walker, A.F. (1996). Acute effects on mood and cognitive performance of breakfasts differing in fat and carbohydrate content. *Appetite, 27,* 151–164.

Loftus, E.F. and Palmer, J.C. (1974). Reconstruction of automobile destruction: an example of the interaction between language and memory. *Journal of Verbal Learning Verbal Behaviour, 13,* 585–589.

Lorenz, K. (1937). The companion in the birds' world. *Auk, 54,* 245–273.

Madigan, S.P. (1992). The application of Michel Foucault's philosophy in the problem externalizing discourse of Michael White. *Journal of Family Therapy, 14,* 265–279.

Mancuso, J.C. (1986). The acquisition and use of narrative grammar structure. In T.R. Sarbin (Ed.) *Narrative Psychology: The storied nature of human conduct.* New York: Praeger.

Manki, H., Kanba, S., Muramatsu, T., Higuchi, S., Suzuki, E., Matsushita, S., Ono, Y., Chiba, H., Shintani, F., Nakamura, M., Yagi, G. and Asai, M. (1996). Dopamine d2, d3 and d4 receptor and transporter gene polymorphisms and mood disorders. *Journal of Affective Disorders, 40,* 7–13.

Manstead, A.S.R. (1988). The role of facial movement in emotion. In H.L. Wagner (Ed.) *Social Psychophysiology and Emotion: Theory and clinical applications.* Chichester: Wiley.

Maranon, G. (1924). Contribution a l'etude de l'action emotive de l'adrenaline. *Revue Francaise d'Endocrinologie, 2,* 301–325.

Matsushita, S., Ono, Y., Chiba, H., Shintani, F., Nakamura, M., Yagi, G. and Asai, M. (1996). Dopamine D2, D3 and D4 receptor and transporter gene polymorphisms and mood disorders. *Journal of Affective Disorders, 40,* 7–13.

McElroy, S.L. and Keck, P.E. (1995). Recovered memory therapy false memory syndrome and other complications. *Psychiatric Annals, 25,* 731–735.

Michelini, S. , Cassano G.B. , Frare, F. and Perugi, G. (1996). Long-term use of benzodiazepines – tolerance, dependence and clinical problems in anxiety and mood disorders. *Pharmacopsychiatry, 29,* 127–134.

Milgram, S. (1974). *Obedience to Authority.* New York: Harper.

Miller, G.A. (1956). The magical number seven, plus or minus two: Some limits on our capacity for processing information. *Psychological Revue, 63,* 81–97.

Mischel, W. (1993). *Introduction to Personality, 5th edn.* Fort Worth: Harcourt Brace.

Mitchell, P. (1997). *Introduction to the Theory of Mind: Children, autism and apes.* London: Arnold.

Much, N. (1995). Cultural Psychology. In J.A. Smith, R. Harre, and L. Van Langenhove (Eds) *Rethinking Psychology.* London: Sage.

Murray, K.D. (1995). Narratology. In J.A. Smith, R. Harre and L. Van Langenhove (Eds) *Rethinking Psychology.* London: Sage.

Nakamura, G.V., Graesser, A.C., Zimmerman, J.A. and Riha, J. (1985). Script processing in a natural situation. *Memory and Cognition, 13,* 140–144.

Oaksford, M., Morris, F., Grainger, B. and Williams, J.M.G. (1996). Mood, reasoning, and central executive processes. *Journal of Experimental Psychology – Learning Memory and Cognition, 22*, 476–492.

Oatley, K. (1992). *Best Laid Schemes: The psychology of emotions.* Cambridge: Cambridge University Press.

Paré, D.A. (1995). Of families and other cultures – the shifting paradigm of family therapy. *Family Process, 34*, 1–19.

Parkin, A.J. (1987). *Memory and Amnesia: An introduction.* Oxford: Blackwell.

Parkinson, B. (1988). Arousal as a cause of emotion. In H.L. Wagner (Ed.) *Social Psychophysiology and Emotion: Theory and clinical applications.* Chichester: Wiley.

Pavlov, I.P. (1927). *Conditioned Reflexes.* London: Oxford University Press.

Petty, R.E., Cacioppo, J.T., Strathman, A.J. and Priester, J.R. (1994). To think or not to think: exploring two routes to persuasion. In S. Shavitt and T.C. Brock (Eds) *Persuasion.* Boston: Allyn and Bacon.

Potter, J. (1996). *Representing Reality: Discourse, rhetoric and social construction.* London: Sage.

Queller, S., Mackie, D.M. and Stroessner, S.J. (1996). Ameliorating some negative effects of positive mood – encouraging happy people to perceive intragroup variability. *Journal of Experimental Social Psychology, 32*, 361–386.

Robinson, J.O., Rosen, M., Revill, S.I., David, H. and Rus, G.A.D. (1980). Self-administered intravenous and intramuscular pethidine. *Anaesthesia, 35*, 763–770.

Rogers, C.R. (1961). *On Becoming a Person: A therapist's view of psychotherapy.* Boston: Houghton Mifflin.

Rogers, C.R., Dymond, R.F. (Eds) (1954). *Psychotherapy and personality change: Co-ordinated studies in the client-centered approach.* Chicago: University of Chicago Press.

Rosenthal, R. (1966). *Experimenter Effects in Behavioural Research.* New York: Appleton-Century-Crofts.

Rotter, J.B. (1966). Generalized expectancies for internal versus external control of reinforcement. *Psychological Monographs, 80*, Whole No. 609.

Rust, J. and Golombok, S. (1989). *Modern Psychometrics: the science of psychological assessment.* London: Routledge.

Schacter, D.L., Chiu, C-Y.P. and Oochsner, K.N. (1993). Implicit memory: a selective review. *Annual Revue of Neuroscience, 16*, 159–182.

Schachter, S. and Singer, J.E. (1962). Cognitive, social and physiological determinants of emotional state. *Psychological Review, 69*, 379–399.

Scherer, K. (1994a). Toward a concept of 'Modal Emotions'. In P.Ekman and R.J. Davidson (Eds) *The Nature of Emotion: Fundamental questions.* New York: Oxford University Press.

Scherer, K.R. (1994b). Emotion serves to decouple stimulus and response. In P.Ekman and R.J. Davidson (Eds) *The Nature of Emotion: Fundamental questions.* New York: Oxford University.

Scott, M.J. and Dryden, W. (1996). The cognitive-behavioural paradigm. In R.Woolfe and W. Dryden (Eds) *Handbook of Counselling Psychology.* London: Sage.

Segall, M.H., Campbell, D.T. and Herskovits, M.J. (1963). Cultural differences in the perception of geometric illusions. *Science, 139,* 769–771.

Seligman, M.E.P. (1971). Phobias and preparedness. *Behaviour Therapy, 2,* 307–320.

Shaffer, D.R. (1996). *Developmental Psychology: Childhood and Adolescence, 4th edn.* Pacific Grove: Brooks/Cole.

Shatz, C. (1993). The Developing Brain. In *Mind and Brain: Readings from Scientific American.* New York: W.H. Freeman.

Sheingold, K. and Tenney, Y.J. (1982). Memory for a salient childhood event. In U. Neisser (Ed.) *Memory Observed: Remembering in natural contexts.* San Francisco: W.H. Freeman.

Skinner, B.F. (1957). *Verbal Behaviour.* New York: Appleton-Century-Crofts.

Smith, J.A. (1995). Repertory Grids: An Interactive Case-Study Perspective. In J.A. Smith, R. Harre, and L. Van Langenhove (Eds) *Rethinking Methods in Psychology.* London: Sage.

Smith, J.A., Harre, R., and Van Langenhove, L. (1995). Introduction. In J.A. Smith, R. Harre and L. Van Langenhove (Eds) *Rethinking Psychology.* London: Sage.

Smith, P.B. and Bond, M.H. (1993). *Social Psychology Across Cultures.* Boston: Allyn and Bacon.

Spielberger, C.D., Gorsuch, R. and Lushene, R.E. (1987). *The State–Trait Anxiety Inventory.* Windsor, UK: NFER-Nelson.

Stainton-Rogers, R. (1995). Q Methodology. In J.A. Smith, R. Harre, and L. Van Langenhove (Eds) *Rethinking Methods in Psychology.* London: Sage.

Strongman, K.T. (1978). *The Psychology of Emotion: Theories of emotion in perspective, 2nd edn.* Chichester: Wiley.

Strongman, K.T. (1996). *The Psychology of Emotion: Theories of emotion in perspective, 4th edn.* Chichester: Wiley.

Toulmin, S.E. (1958). *The Uses of Argument.* Cambridge: Cambridge University Press.

Trevarthen, C. (1979). Instincts for human understanding and for cultural co-operation: their development in infancy. In M. von Cranach, K. Foppa, W. Lepenies and D. Ploog (Eds) *Human Ethology: Claims and limits of a new discipline.* Cambridge: Cambridge University Press.

Tversky, A. and Kahnemann, D. (1982). Evidential impact of base rates. In D. Kahnemann, P. Slovic and A. Tversky (Eds) *Judgement Under Uncertainty: Heuristics and biases.* Cambridge: Cambridge University Press.

Van Deurzen-Smith, E. (1988). *Existential Counselling in Practice.* London: Sage.

Van Langenhove, L. (1995). The theoretical foundations of experimental psychology and its alternatives. In J.A. Smith, R. Harre and L. Van Langenhove (Eds) *Rethinking Psychology.* London: Sage.

Vygotsky, L.S. (1962). *Thought and Language.* Cambridge, Mass: The M.I.T. Press.

Wagner, H.L. and Calam, R.M. (1988). Interpersonal psychophysiology and the study of the family. In H.L. Wagner (Ed.) *Social Psychophysiology and Emotion: Theory and Clinical Applications.* Chichester: Wiley.

Wason, P.C. (1968). Reasoning about a rule. *Quarterly Journal of Experimental Psychology, 20*, 273–281.

Watkins, P.C., Vache, K., Verney, S.P., Muller, S. and Mathews, A. (1996). Unconscious mood-congruent memory bias in depression. *Journal of Abnormal Psychology, 105*, 34–41.

Watson, J.B. (1925). *Behaviourism*. New York: Norton.

Watson, J.B. and Rayner, R. (1920). Conditioned emotional reactions. *Journal of Experimental Psychology, 3*, 1–14.

Wefelmeyer, T. and Kuhs, H. (1996). Diurnal mood variation in melancholic patients and healthy controls. *Psychopathology, 29*, 184–192.

Wells, A.S. and Read, N.W. (1996). Influences of fat, energy, and time of day on mood and performance. *Physiology and Behaviour, 59*, 1069–1076.

Westermann, R., Spies, K., Stahl, G. and Hesse, F.W. (1996). Relative effectiveness and validity of mood induction procedures – a metaanalysis. *European Journal of Social Psychology, 26*, 557–580.

Wise, R.A. (1994). A brief history of the anhedonia hypothesis. In C.R. Legg and D.A. Booth (Eds) *Appetites: Neural and behavioural bases*. Oxford: Oxford University Press.

Wittgenstein, L. (1968). *Philosophical Investigations*. Oxford: Blackwell.

Woolfe, R. (1996). The Nature of Counselling Psychology. In R. Woolfe and W. Dryden (Eds) *Handbook of Counselling Psychology*. London: Sage.

Zajonc, R.B., Murphy, S.T. and Inglehart, M. (1989). Feeling and facial efference: implications of the vascular theory of emotion. *Psychological Review, 96*, 395–416.

Index

Addiction 52
adolescence 152
  identity and 165
amnesia
  anterograde 115
  retrograde 115
antecedent, affirming the 65, 66
anxiety 12
aptitude 127, 128
  tests of 132–133
Asch, S.E. 23–24, 25, 28, 29
attachment 144, 150
  avoidant 151
  secure 151
  strange situation 151
attitude 124
  behaviour and 124, 126
  change 125
  change in counselling 128
  and cognitive dissonance 125
  reactance 126
  and trivialization 126
attribution 19, 20, 25, 26–27
  biases 27, 180
  fundamental error 20, 26, 27
  goals 58
  self-serving bias 21, 26, 27, 177
autonomic nervous system 34, 123

Behaviour, and genetic
  determination 145–146
behaviourism 123
beliefs 11
British Psychological Society,
  The 6, 136

Case studies
  George 10–11
  Alan 31–32
  Peter 57
  Jennifer 84–85
  John 119
  Mary 139
cognition
  and development 158
  language and 156
  social 157
  understanding in children 158
cognitive models 43–44
conditioning 39–40, 3–4, 175
  operant 4
consequent, infirming the 65, 66
counselling
  as craft 5, 7
  attitude change in 173
  core relationship 154
  decision-making 81
  and experience,
    misinterpretation of 177
  goal-setting 61–64
  memory demands 173
  practice of 171–173, 175–179
  and psychology, 6–8
    differences between 6–7
  roles in 173
  theories of 1, 4
  thinking about practice 71
critical periods 143
culture 11, 12, 16, 30
  expectations 12, 17
  norms 17
  and roles 14

Decision-making 57–83
  discounting the future 78, 80
  establishing goals in 58–59
  in groups 25
  Multiattribute Utility Theory
    74, 80
  preference for certainty 76
  scaling values 73
  and sub-goals 59–60
  sunk-cost effect 78, 80
  transition points in life, and
    61
  utility of 72–73, 75
dementia
  Alzheimer's disease 116
  multi-infarct 115
desire 32, 41–43, 51–54, 150
  avoidance strategies 54
  development of 150–153
  and drugs 52
  elicitation by cues 53
  exposure to objects of desire
    54
  role of bodily state 52
  sexual 53
development
  of abilities 155–158
  cognitive 156
  critical periods in 143–145
  of desires 150–153
  of dispositions 148–153
  of feelings 148–150
  stages 40–43, 146–148
    methods of investigating
      142
    methods of study 175
    psychological or logical
      143
    as sub-goals in counselling
      147
  zone of proximal
    development 156, 159

Eclecticism 6, 27, 46, 147
ego 3

emotion 1, 5, 32, 33, 45, 174
  'Little Albert' experiment 39
  adrenaline 35
  attribution from bodily
    reactions 34
  basis in desire 41
  behaviour 33, 36
  behavioural analysis 45
  blocking 37, 45
  bodily reactions 33, 34, 25,
    45
  cognition 38
  cognitive models 43
  communication of 37, 45,
    149
  consciousness in 33, 38
  definition of 33
  development of 148
  expression of 35, 37
  and familiarity 40
  models 38
    behavioural 39
    psychodynamic 41
  occurrence of 38–39
  preparedness 40
  role of meaning 43
  self-conscious 149
  self-control 149, 153
  self-control by counsellor 154
  sensitivity to others 149
  social cues 33
  social function of 36
  stonewalling of 38, 45
  symbolic representation of
    meaning 44
  symbolic transformation of
    desire 41
empathy 127, 177, 180
existential approach 61
expectations 11

Feelings, development of
    148–150
Freud, S. 3, 43, 122, 141

Gender
  identity 164–165
  issues 168
genetics 145, 147
  constraint 146
goals
  final 59
  generating options 61
  implicit in therapy 63
  lack of information 62
  long-term 58
  motivation to achieve 62
  short-term 59
  socially approved 62
  sub-goals 59
  working back from final goal
      61, 62

Heuristics 22, 23, 28, 59
  representativeness 23
  counselling models as 172
homosexuality 13, 17, 176

Id 3
identity
  consistency in 160, 161, 166
  development of 159–166
  gender 164–165, 168
  roles and 163
  self-description 160
  self-recognition 160
  sexual 163
  sexual orientation 165
  social 162
  social approval 162, 167
imprinting 143
individual differences
  assessment of 129–137
  and capacity 126–127
  and disposition 120–124
  and values 124–126
integrative practice 6, 147
intelligence 127
interpretation 5

Janet, Pierre 112

Language 13–14, 25
learning
  experiential 1, 7
lived experience 16, 25, 90

Memory 1, 5
  absent-mindedness 93
  accuracy 88
  and amnesia 115–116
  assessment of 104–107
  chunks 87
  clients' recall of instructions
      100
  clients' rehearsal of stories
      93
  confidence in 88
  context dependency 108, 109,
      110, 111
  explicit vs. implicit 106, 107
  and eye-witness testimony
      98, 101
  flashbulb 98
  for painful events 112
  generation effect 103, 104
  idealized forms of 89
  knowing vs. remembering
      105, 108
  level of processing 102, 103
  long-term 87–90
  motivation for rehearsal 93
  narrative structure 90
  and neurological disorders
      115–117
  Post-Traumatic Stress Disorder
      (PTSD) 101
  primacy effect 94, 100, 180
    in counselling practice 100
  recall of past events 85–86
  recency effect 94, 96, 180
    in counselling practice 100
  recovered 101, 114
  rehearsal of 89, 91–93, 94
  remembering as act 91

salience of events 94, 97
scripts 99, 102, 180
short-term 86, 90
state dependency 109
tip-of-the-tongue 104, 108
Milgram, S. 24, 25, 29
Minnesota Multiphasic
Personality Inventory
(MMPI) 135
modernism 3
mood 32, 46, 51, 124
cheerfulness 26
counsellor's 50
depression 26, 51
eliciting conditions 47
effect of drugs on 47, 49
psychological factors 47,
50
stories 49, 50
persistence 48
and thinking, effects on 48
Multiattribute Utility Theory
74

Narrative theory
stories 13, 49, 50

Pavlov, I. 3, 53
person centred approach 1, 61,
147
conditions of worth 5
positive regard
conditional 3
unconditional 1, 3, 5
personal psychological
counselling 179
personality 120, 121
fundamental dimensions of
121
idiographic approach to 129
nomothetic approach to 129,
130
projective tests 131
tests 130
theories of 122

phenomenology 26
Piaget, J. 141
Post-Traumatic Stress Disorder
(PTSD) 10
probability, estimations of
69–70
prototypes 22, 27
psychic energy 3
psychodynamic theory 1, 5, 42,
61, 108, 111, 123, 141, 142,
147, 153, 172
death instinct 42
depressive position 42
dream analysis 108
free association 108
life instinct 42
psychology, research-based
2–7

Reflex, conditioned 3
reliability 131
repression 111, 176
basis in desire 113
laboratory study 112
symbolic transformation of
forgotten event 113
Rogers, C. 1–3, 5
role 14, 15, 17
client 17
conflict 16, 17
theory 15

Schemata
role 21
scripts 21, 22, 27
social 21
self 3, 15
sensitive periods 145
sexual abuse 85, 101, 103
sexuality 152, 154
orientation 176
homosexual 13, 17, 176
social skills and 153
skilled helper 61, 147
social construction 12

social influence 28
  and bystander apathy 24
  conformity 23
  obedience 24
  rationality 25
  risk taking 25
social psychology 5, 18
social relationships
  regulation by language 14
social skills 154
socialization 17
State/Trait Anxiety Inventory 132
stories 13–14
strange situation 151–152
superego 3
supervision 50, 81, 154, 180

Temperament 123
tests
  appropriateness of for client
    136
  aptitude 132
  assessment, use in 134
  clinically significant change
    137
  consent to use 136
  cultural fairness 134

ethical use of 136
  idiographic 133
  Q-sort 133
  reliability and validity of
    131–134
  repertory grid 133
  state vs. trait 132
  training for use 136
thinking
  descriptive accounts 65
  deterministic rules 68
  generating possibilities 67, 70
  logic 65, 66
  normative 65
  prescriptive 65
  probabilities 68, 69, 70, 71
  rationality 70
  search-inference approach 67
  testing assumptions 70
transference 1, 6, 27, 42, 153,
  172
  counter-transference 42
trust 147, 155, 173, 174

Validity 131

Watson, J.B. 3